BASEBALLL IN MONTGOMERY

Front Cover: The multitalented Roy "Goat" Walker was once a symbol of baseball in Montgomery, having twice been given a Roy Walker Day by the team and fans. Today, he has been almost forgotten by current fans. (Courtesy of Alan T. "Tommy" Horn.)

Cover Background: The 2014 Montgomery Biscuits mark baseball's renaissance in Montgomery. The team is no longer the smaller sibling to the other Southern baseball clubs, but is equal in every way. (Courtesy of the Montgomery Biscuits.)

Back Cover: In 2004, Montgomery did not just build a ballpark, it incorporated several features that bring together the history of the location, the river, the old railroad, and the future of baseball. Riverwalk has done what it was created to do—serve as a catalyst to revive the downtown area. (Author's collection.)

BASEBALL IN MONTGOMERY

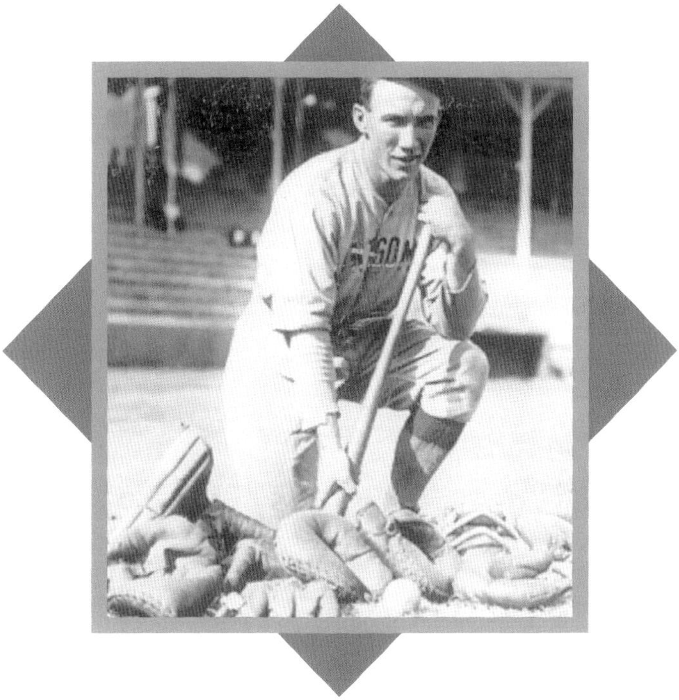

Clarence Watkins

ARCADIA PUBLISHING

ISBN 978-1-4671-2483-6

Published by Arcadia Publishing
Charleston, South Carolina

Printed in the United States of America

Library of Congress Control Number: 2016956726

For all general information, please contact Arcadia Publishing:
Telephone 843-853-2070
Fax 843-853-0044
E-mail sales@arcadiapublishing.com
For customer service and orders:
Toll-Free 1-888-313-2665

Visit us on the Internet at www.arcadiapublishing.com

This book is dedicated to the baseball fans of Montgomery, Alabama. It is my hope that this book will rekindle your love for the history of our great game in a wonderful city. This book is not the complete story, but the beginning of the story that will encourage you to ask questions and search for the complete history of baseball in Montgomery.

CONTENTS

ACKNOWLEDGMENTS

Baseball in Montgomery was a new experience for me. I have never lived in Montgomery; my time there has been related to business going back to the 1970s. I decided to take on this project due to my closeness to Montgomery and my fascination with the player Roy "Goat" Walker. After several years of thinking about writing this book, I happened upon Alan Horn, the great-nephew of Walker. From then on, the book had to be done! Besides Horn's appearance, there was a select group of baseball researchers who have always been there for me. This includes Skip Nipper, Chuck Stewart, Bill Plott, Layton Revell, and Shane Ernest. Former Montgomery Rebel Ted Brazell gave me insight into the dynasty era of the 1970s.

Staci Wilkenson, marketing director of the Montgomery Biscuits, provided me with media guides and access to the ballpark.

Many thanks go to the staff of the Alabama Department Archives and History for their help over a four-year period.

Lastly, to my wife, Carol, for help with the keyboard and being my "grammar police."

INTRODUCTION

Montgomery, Alabama, has several meaningful nicknames that tell us a lot about its past, like "the Cradle of the Confederacy," "the Birthplace of the Civil Rights Movement," and even "the Sports Capital of the South." However, you really do not think of Montgomery as a baseball town. Only if you dig deep into a forgotten history will you discover a city that always loved and supported the game of baseball.

Montgomery got a jump on most of the other Southern cities after the Civil War when a former Confederate army surgeon named Aleck T. Pearsall settled here. Before the war, Pearsall had been the first baseman for the Brooklyn Excelsiors, one of the dominant teams in the New York area where the game evolved. By 1868, the Montgomery newspaper reported that the Montgomery team left by train one morning for a series of games with the Dramatics, a team in Mobile, Alabama.

A history divided among several different leagues and many years without a franchise made it difficult to have a consistent story to be handed down from generation to generation. The people of Montgomery loved their baseball teams; there just were not always enough of them.

By 1900, other regional cities were passing Montgomery in population. This made it very difficult for Montgomery to compete with other large Southern cities such as Memphis, Birmingham, and Atlanta. Retelling that story makes it difficult to compare the histories of the Southern League to the Southeastern League, or the South Atlantic League.

As late as 1979, a group of sports writers from the *Montgomery Advertiser* published a series of articles on the history of professional baseball in the city. In particular, Bob Mayes wrote an article that detailed the sport from the 1920s through the 1940s. Mayes focused on the career of a player named Roy "Goat" Walker, a player whose career exemplified the same traits as Montgomery's struggling history. For Baseball in Montgomery, Walker is the Buck O'Neil of this story. Walker had that "never say quit" attitude; if you are released you go down to a lower-level league, work your way back. This is what Walker and Montgomery did, sometimes together. Today, we see the results of that determination as we enjoy the success of the Biscuits.

Montgomery endured a 24-year absence of professional baseball after producing a dominating dynasty from 1972 to 1977. Such a long-term period of winning back-to-back championships is extremely difficult in Minor League Baseball, due to the continued call-up to the parent club of any player who performs at a high level.

Finally, in 1980, the league and local ownership realized Montgomery could not support a team at the attendance level other cities, like Memphis and Nashville, were showing, and a winning team was not enough. The league would have to make a move, and baseball fans would suffer for a long time. When the opportunity came back, the city and fans made it happen. Today, baseball is alive and well in Montgomery, helping the downtown area grow and prosper.

1

Baseball Beginnings in Montgomery

Baseball in Montgomery began in New York City long before the Civil War started. This connection gives Montgomery a history much more interesting than most Southern cities could conceive.

Before the war, Aleck Pearsall was a member of the Brooklyn Excelsior Baseball Club, remembered for their 1860 tour around large cities in the New York area and credited with the introduction of the modern-style baseball cap with a long visor.

Pearsall was a doctor by profession, and when the Civil War broke out, he joined the Confederate army as a surgeon. After the war, he settled in Montgomery, bringing the New York style of play to the Deep South.

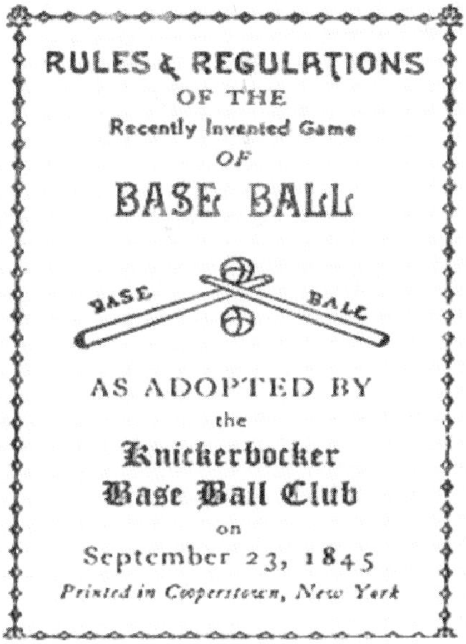
RULES & REGULATIONS
OF THE
Recently Invented Game
OF
BASE BALL

BASE BALL

AS ADOPTED BY
the
Knickerbocker
Base Ball Club
on
September 23, 1845
Printed in Cooperstown, New York

To understand the early history of baseball in Montgomery, one must travel back to New York City in 1847, when the New York Knickerbockers, headed by Alexander Cartwright, spelled out the rules to govern the game of baseball in writing. Within a few years, New York had a group of 30 to 40 teams playing by the Knickerbockers' rules. One of these teams is the Brooklyn Excelsiors. This team will be credited for several baseball firsts, including its connection to baseball in Montgomery, Alabama. (Author's collection.)

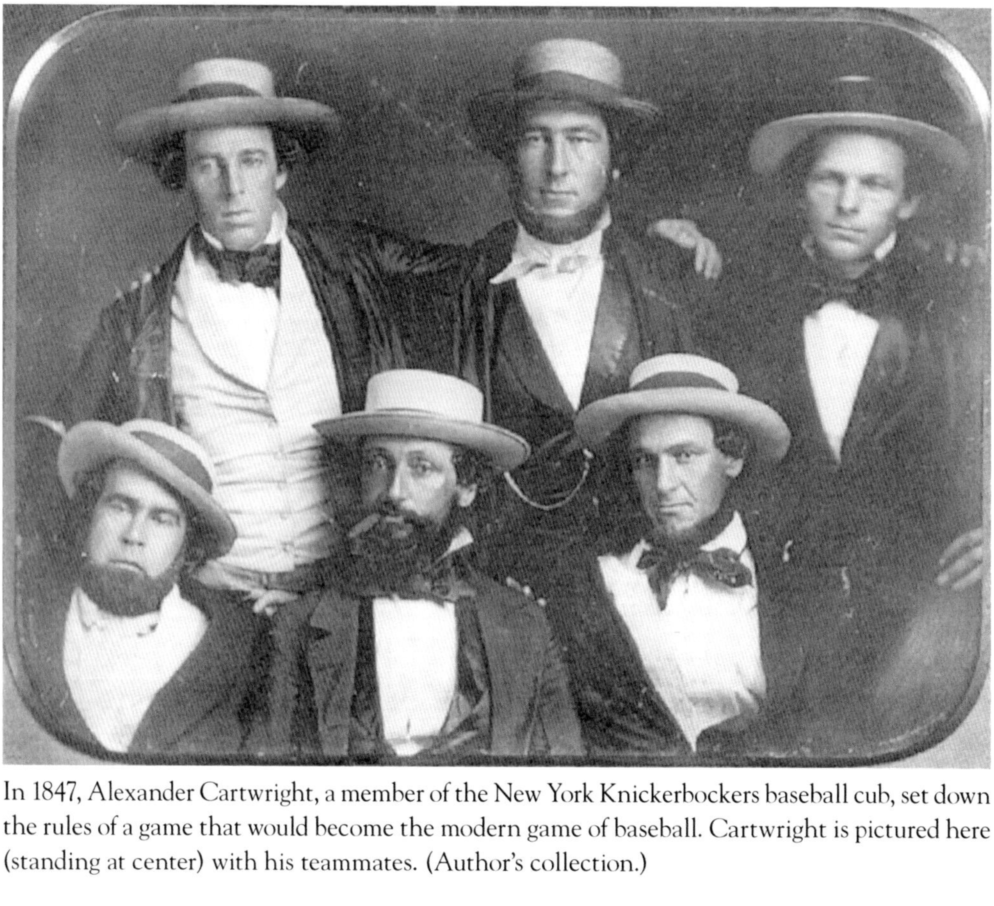

In 1847, Alexander Cartwright, a member of the New York Knickerbockers baseball cub, set down the rules of a game that would become the modern game of baseball. Cartwright is pictured here (standing at center) with his teammates. (Author's collection.)

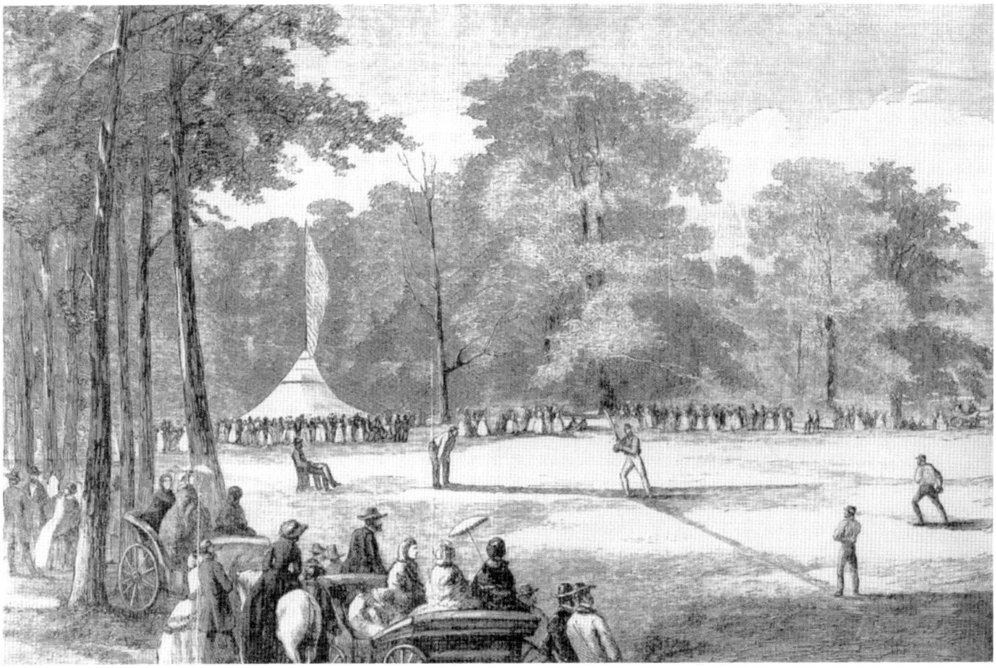

The preferred place for baseball games in New York was an idyllic meadow across the river from New York City named the Elysian Field. It was named after the final resting place of Greek gods. Suitable fields for a baseball game had become scarce within the city. (Author's collection.)

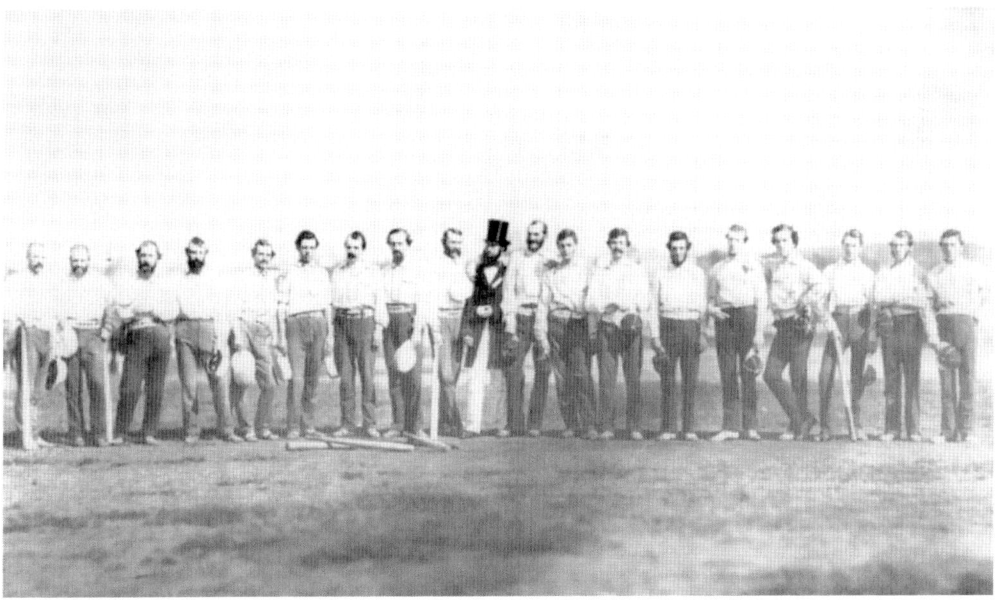

This rare photograph was taken at a game between the Knickerbockers and the Brooklyn Excelsiors. This meeting took place in 1858 at the now famous Elysian Field in New Jersey. (Author's collection.)

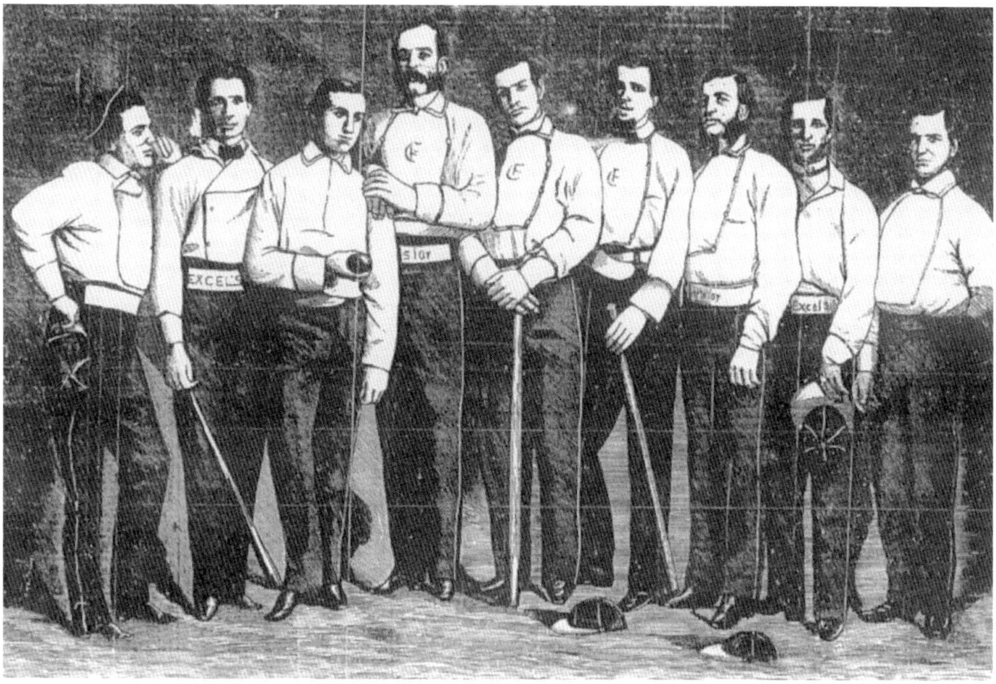

Before the Civil War, Aleck T. Pearsall was a member of the Brooklyn Excelsiors, one of the early teams that helped establish baseball as America's Game. They are remembered for their 1860 tour around large cities in the New York area. The Excelsiors are credited with introducing the modern-style baseball cap with a visor. Though a baseball player, Aleck Pearsall was a doctor by profession. When the war broke out, Pearsall joined the Confederate army as a surgeon. After the war, he settled in Montgomery, bringing with him the New York style of play to the Deep South. Pearsall is pictured at center. (Author's collection.)

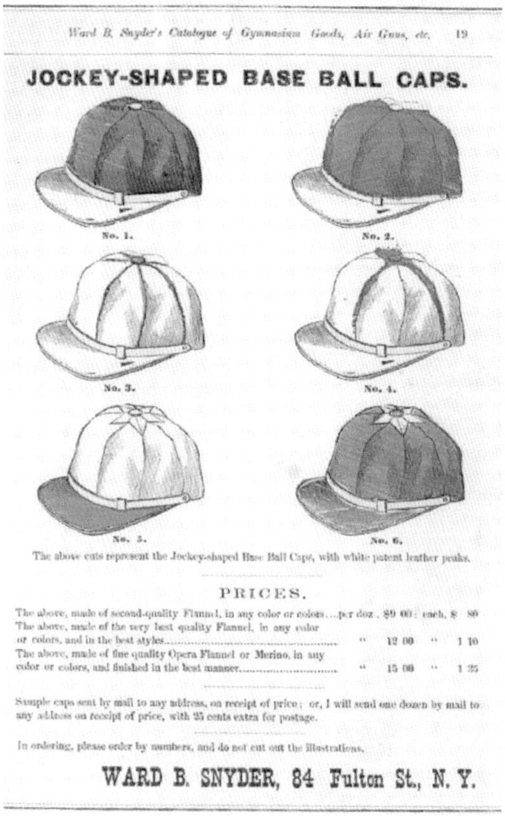

Ward B. Snyder's Catalogue of Gymnasium Goods, Air Guns, etc. 19

JOCKEY-SHAPED BASE BALL CAPS.

No. 1. No. 2.

No. 3. No. 4.

No. 5. No. 6.

The above cuts represent the Jockey-shaped Base Ball Caps, with white patent leather peaks.

PRICES.

The above, made of second-quality Flannel, in any color or colors....per doz., $9 00; each, $ 80
The above, made of the very best quality Flannel, in any color or colors, and in the best styles.......... " 12 00 " 1 10
The above, made of fine quality Opera Flannel or Merino, in any color or colors, and finished in the best manner.......... " 15 00 " 1 25

Sample caps sent by mail to any address, on receipt of price; or, I will send one dozen by mail to any address on receipt of price, with 25 cents extra for postage.

In ordering, please order by numbers, and do not cut out the illustrations.

WARD B. SNYDER, 84 Fulton St., N. Y.

Wearing a hat or cap while playing baseball was not unusual, but in 1860, the Brooklyn Excelsiors began wearing what is known today as a baseball cap. It was a short-brim cap, and all team members wore the same style and color. (Author's collection.)

Another first of the Excelsiors was the road trip. In 1862, they traveled to several cities in upstate New York, spreading the new baseball rules. With the new rules, baseball got the nickname the "New York Game." (Author's collection.)

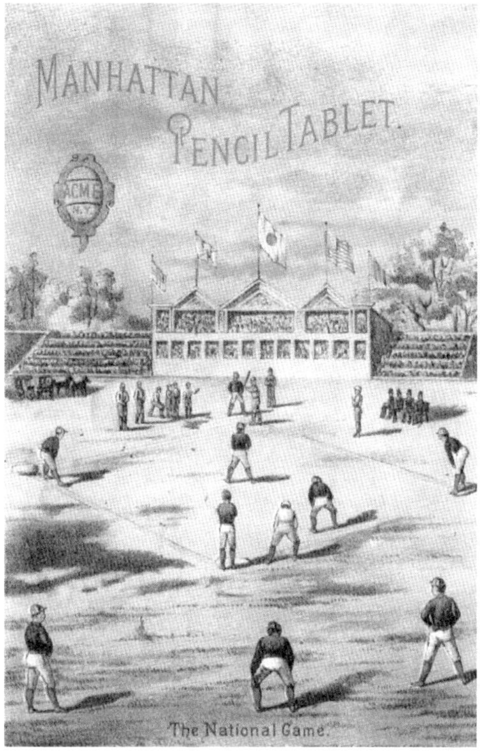

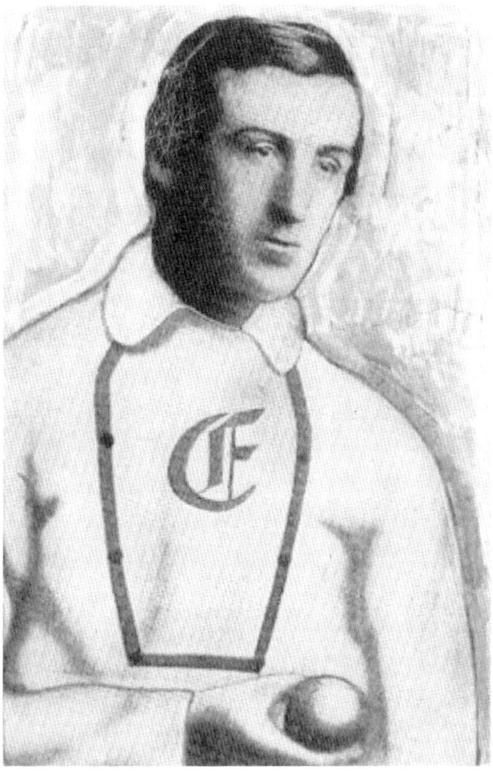

The Brooklyn Excelsiors also produced the first superstar of baseball, pitcher Jim Creighton. He was known for his pitching technique that allowed him to throw the ball with speed without bending his wrist or elbow. He changed the focus of the game from the fielders to the pitcher-and-batter confrontation. (Author's collection.)

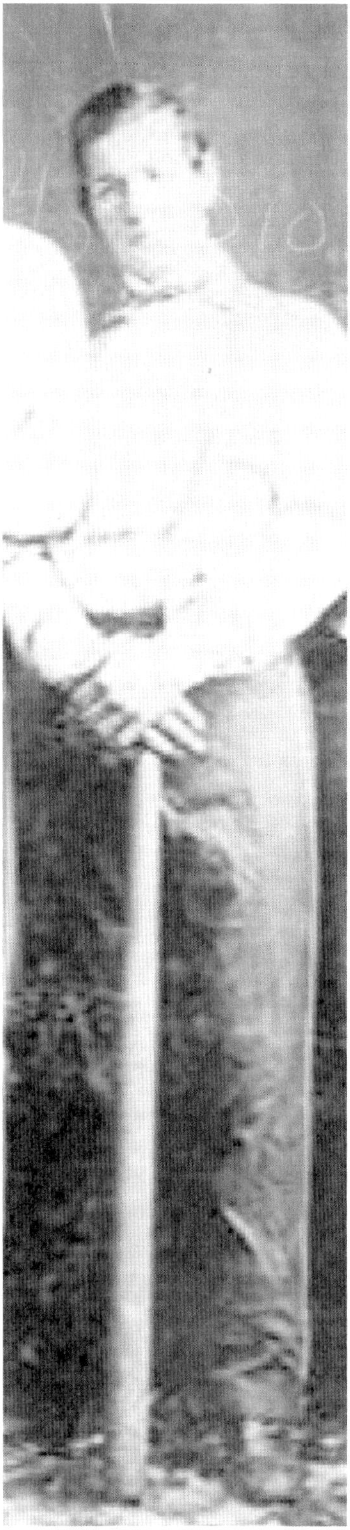

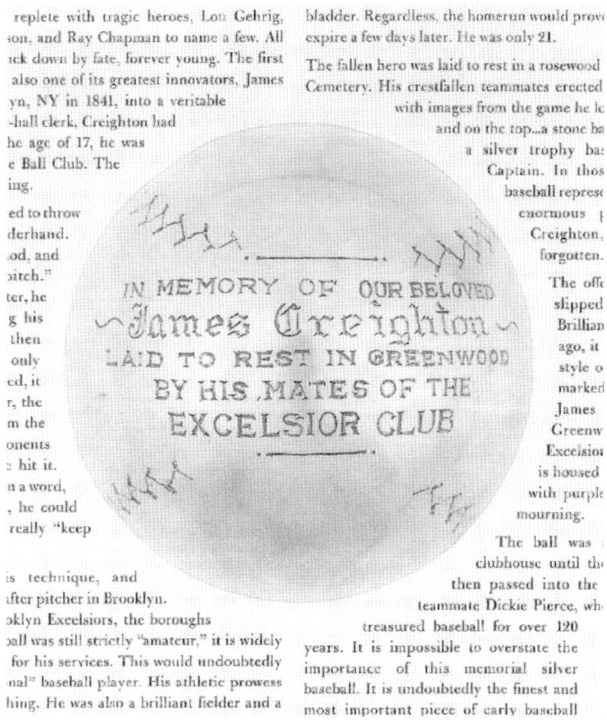

Jim Creighton's death in 1862 from an abdominal rupture caused by a violent swing at a ball made him a beloved figure. For over 20 years, his picture on Excelsior scorecards was draped in black. Years later, fans would rate a new pitcher by commenting, "He's no Creighton!" Pictured is a memorial baseball. (Author's collection.)

Montgomery's baseball connection, Aleck Pearsall, played first baseman for the Excelsiors prior to the Civil War. When the war broke out, Pearsall went south, joining the Confederate army as a surgeon. When word of his position in the Confederate army reached the Excelsiors, the team banned Pearsall from baseball. (Author's collection.)

This early box score from a game in 1868 shows Pearsall playing first base for a Montgomery team. That is the same position he played for Brooklyn. The newspaper this box score appeared in also mentioned the Montgomery team going on a road trip to Mobile to play the Dramatics. (Author's collection.)

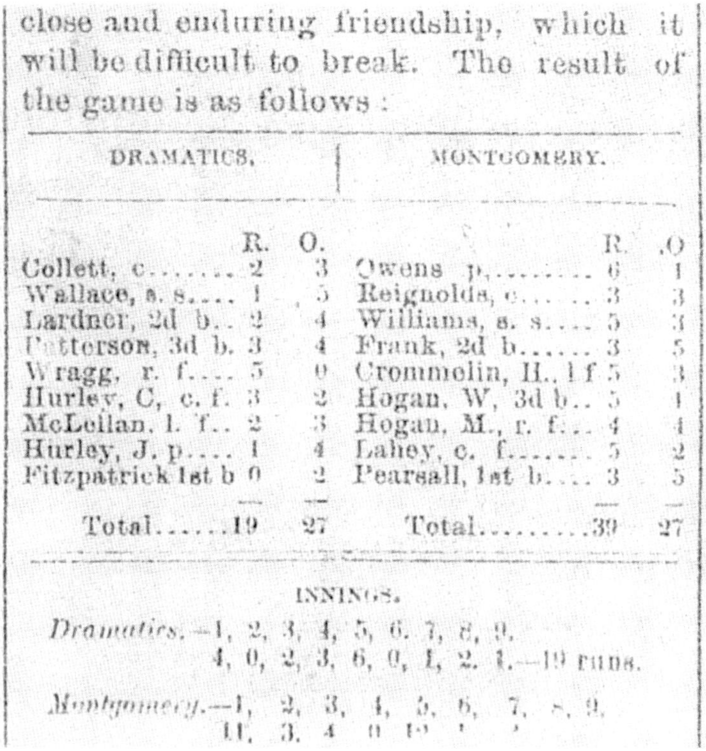

close and enduring friendship, which it will be difficult to break. The result of the game is as follows:

DRAMATICS.	R.	O.	MONTGOMERY.	R.	O.
Collett, c.......	2	3	Owens p.........	6	1
Wallace, s. s....	1	5	Reignolds, c......	3	3
Lardner, 2d b..	2	4	Williams, s. s....	5	3
Patterson, 3d b.	3	4	Frank, 2d b.......	3	5
Wragg, r. f....	5	0	Crommelin, H., l f	5	3
Hurley, C, c. f.	3	2	Hogan, W, 3d b..	5	1
McLellan, l. f..	2	3	Hogan, M., r. f...	4	4
Hurley, J. p....	1	4	Lahey, c. f.......	5	2
Fitzpatrick 1st b	0	2	Pearsall, 1st b....	3	5
Total......19		27	Total.........39		27

INNINGS.

Dramatics.—1, 2, 3, 4, 5, 6, 7, 8, 9.
4, 0, 2, 3, 6, 0, 1, 2, 1.—19 runs.

Montgomery.—1, 2, 3, 4, 5, 6, 7, 8, 9.
11, 3, 4

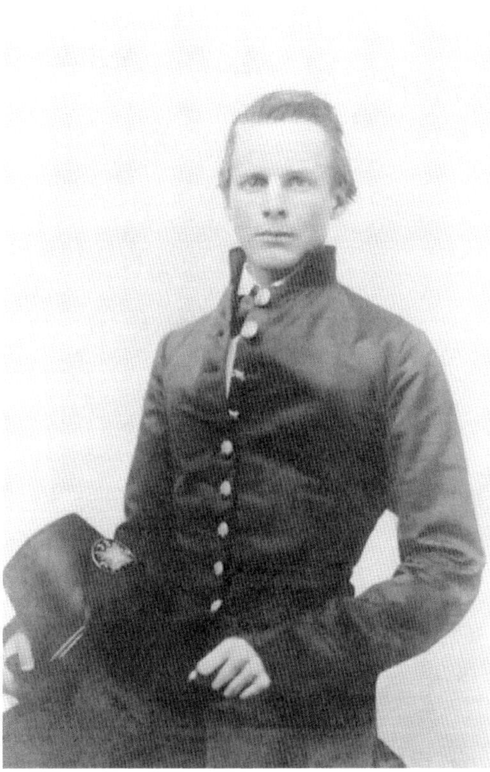

The Montgomery team was nicknamed the "Pelhams" in honor of Col. John Pelham of Alabama. Pelham was cited by Gen. Robert E. Lee for his bravery and skills as an artillery officer. His death leading a cavalry charge made him a hero throughout the South. (Author's collection.)

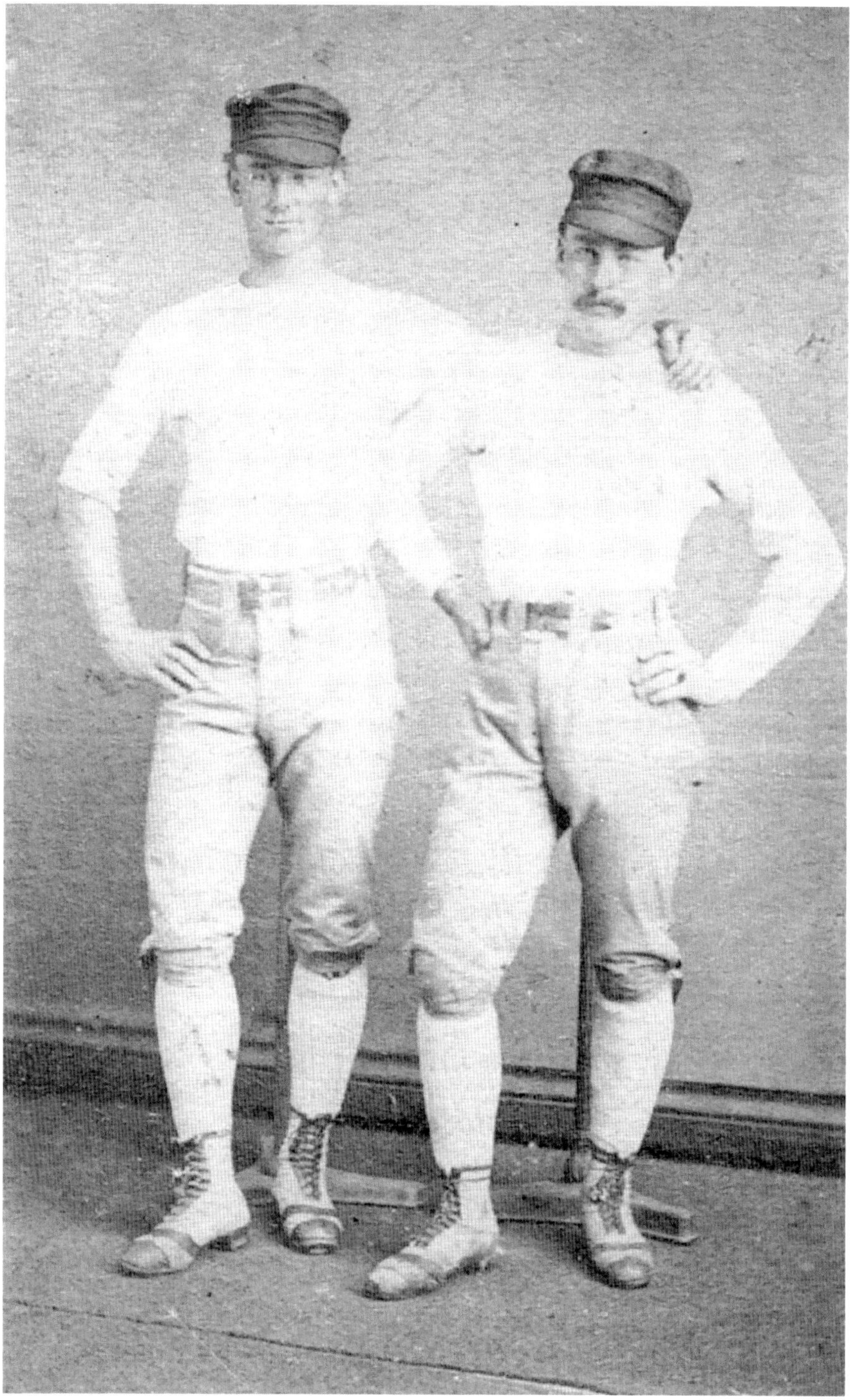

This early photograph of two unidentified baseball players was taken at a Montgomery studio. It reveals the styles of uniforms and caps of the day. There is no doubt that Dr. Pearsall had a great influence on the game and how it was played in Montgomery. (Author's collection.)

This banquet program reveals the formality baseball brought to the lives of the young men who played the game. They felt a kinship not only to their teammates but also to the players on the other team. Their out-of-town guests were treated with respect and shown a good time in a gentlemanly fashion. (Author's collection.)

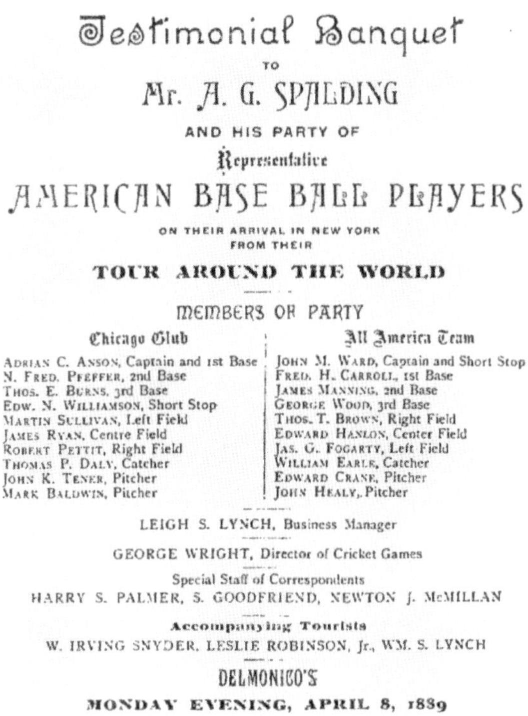

Testimonial Banquet

TO

Mr. A. G. SPALDING

AND HIS PARTY OF

Representative

AMERICAN BASE BALL PLAYERS

ON THEIR ARRIVAL IN NEW YORK

FROM THEIR

TOUR AROUND THE WORLD

MEMBERS OF PARTY

Chicago Club	All America Team
Adrian C. Anson, Captain and 1st Base	John M. Ward, Captain and Short Stop
N. Fred. Pfeffer, 2nd Base	Fred. H. Carroll, 1st Base
Thos. E. Burns, 3rd Base	James Manning, 2nd Base
Edw. N. Williamson, Short Stop	George Wood, 3rd Base
Martin Sullivan, Left Field	Thos. T. Brown, Right Field
James Ryan, Centre Field	Edward Hanlon, Center Field
Robert Pettit, Right Field	Jas. G. Fogarty, Left Field
Thomas P. Daly, Catcher	William Earle, Catcher
John K. Tener, Pitcher	Edward Crane, Pitcher
Mark Baldwin, Pitcher	John Healy, Pitcher

LEIGH S. LYNCH, Business Manager

GEORGE WRIGHT, Director of Cricket Games

Special Staff of Correspondents

HARRY S. PALMER, S. GOODFRIEND, NEWTON J. McMILLAN

Accompanying Tourists

W. IRVING SNYDER, LESLIE ROBINSON, Jr., WM. S. LYNCH

DELMONICO'S

MONDAY EVENING, APRIL 8, 1889

Aleck Pearsall would bring more than just the new rules for the game of baseball. Note that, at this early date, the word baseball was written as two words. He also introduced a new lifestyle for the young men who played the game. This image of a banquet at Delmonico's in New York is an example of the type of dinner that would be served to members of both teams as they came together in the evenings to celebrate their game. (Author's collection.)

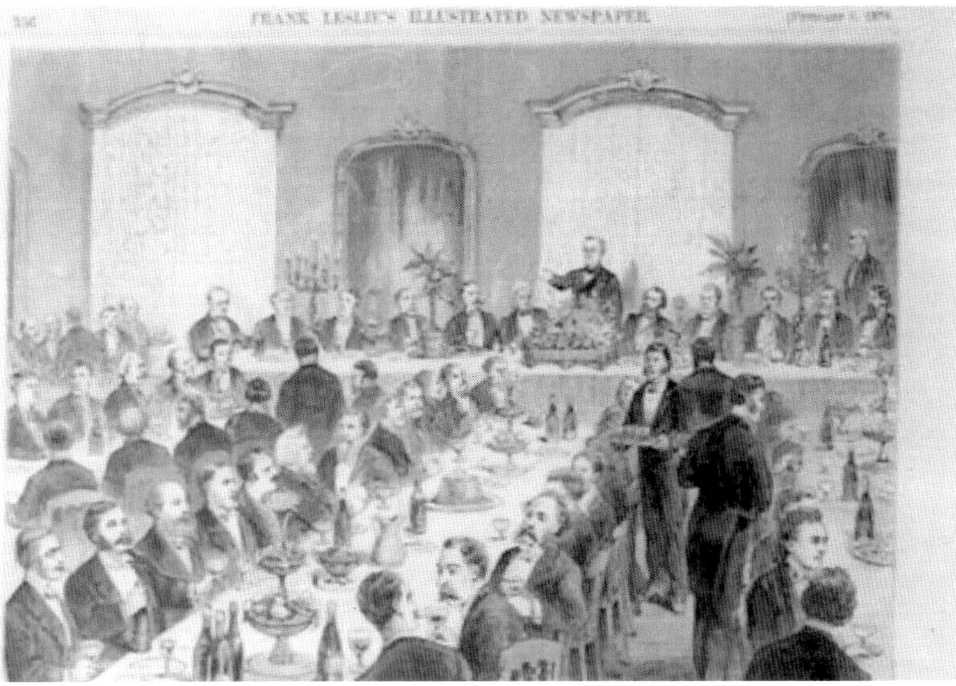

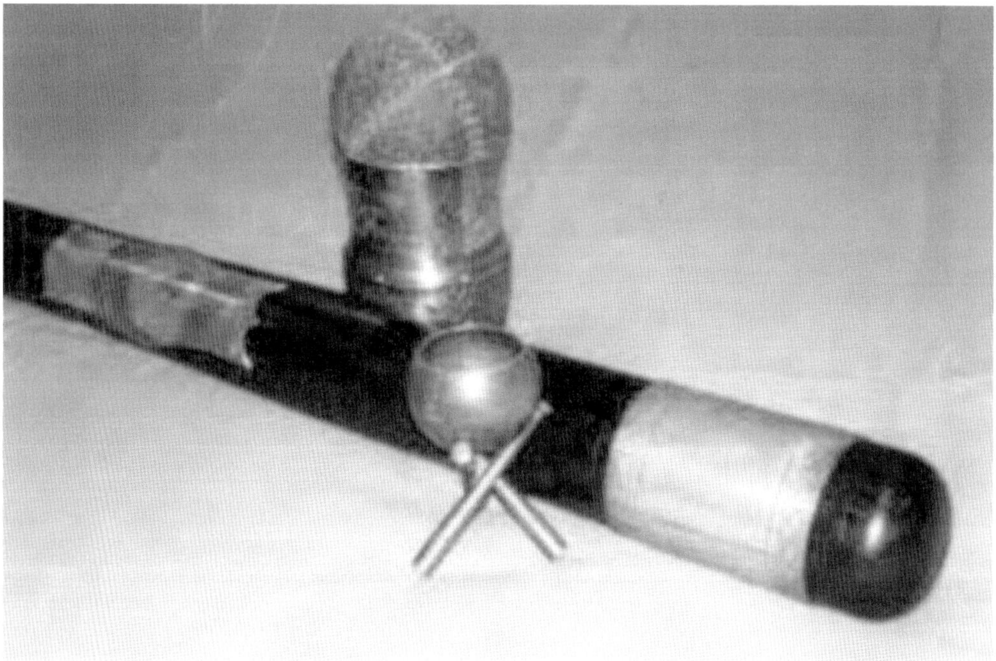

Part of the evening festivities would be the presentations of trophy baseballs and bats. These special baseballs and bats were decorated to remember the results of the special series of games. Balls and bats were painted and engraved with the scores, teams, and dates as mementos of their time together. This would have been especially true when an out-of-town team, such as the Mobile Dramatics, came to play in Montgomery. (Both, author's collection.)

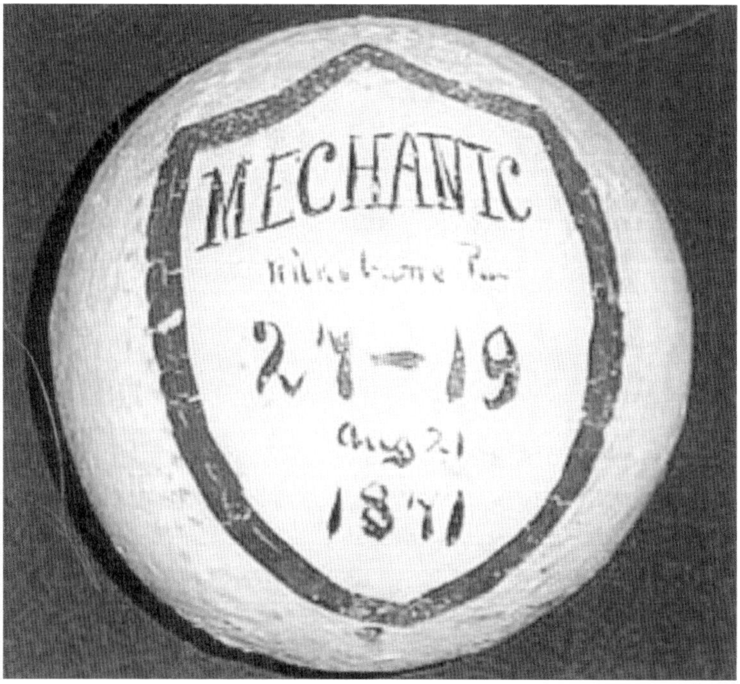

2

There Used to Be a Ballpark

Baseball fans have distinct memories of the parks they frequented during their childhoods. The smells, the green grass, the crack of the bat, and the chatter of the players and fans are what baseball is all about. Montgomery had many different ballparks, but unfortunately, no images have survived of the early-19th-century ballparks.

Some elderly fans have given some names and locations to work with. Several ballparks were part of entertainment complexes purposely located at the end of streetcar lines. These ballparks were just far enough out of town so that fans would take the streetcar to the games. Old-timers tell of ballparks such as Pelican Park, Pickens Springs, and Electric Park.

There is no doubt there are still a few fans who remember a baseball game at the Cramton Bowl. In a time when so many old baseball parks have been demolished to make way for progress, it is fortunate that Patterson Field is still in good condition and is used for high school and college baseball.

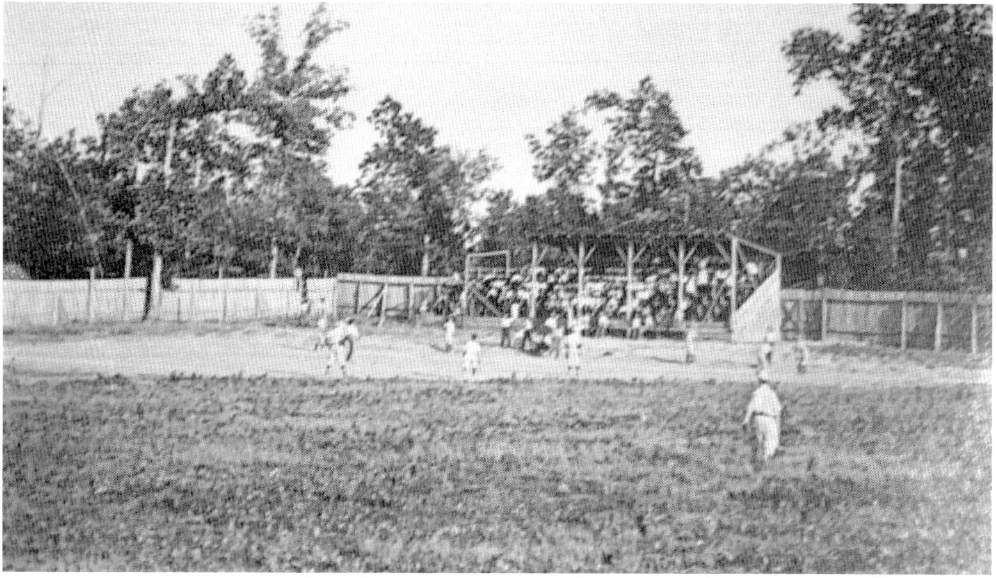

In the 19th century, baseball parks were made of wood and could be built in a month. There were several early ballparks in Montgomery such as Pelican, Pickett Springs, and Capital Grounds; however, no known images of them exist. This is an unidentified baseball field in Alabama. It gives a good example of what early ballparks looked like. (Author's collection.)

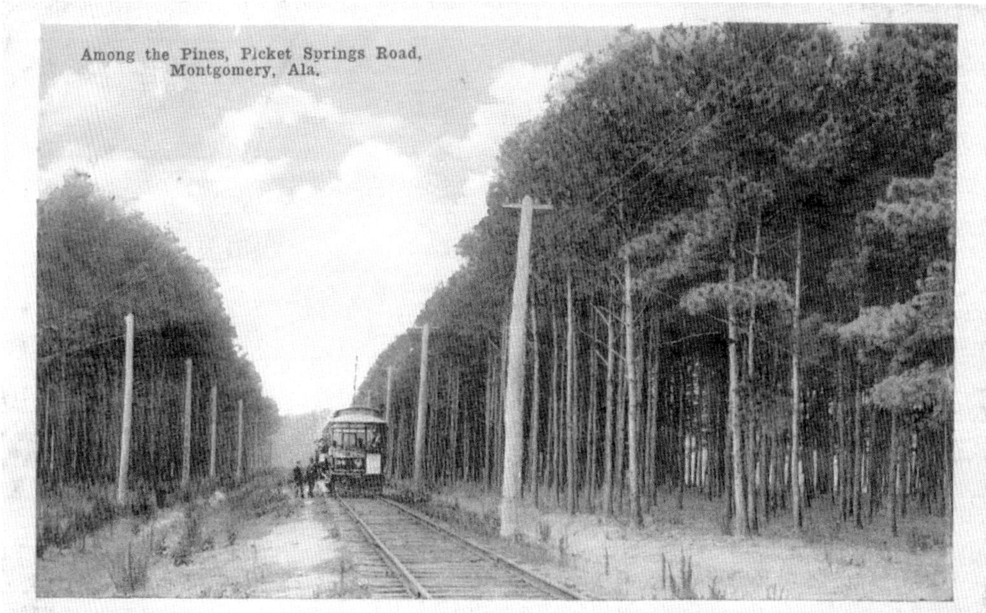

The Pickett Springs Amusement Park and baseball grounds were built on the site of the William Harris plantation. Harris's daughter Sarah married A.J. Pickett, and later, Picket Springs was part of the Chisholm community. In the 1880s, the Western Railway Company of Alabama opened the Pickett Springs Amusement Park. During World War I, the park became Camp Sheridan for Army training. (Author's collection.)

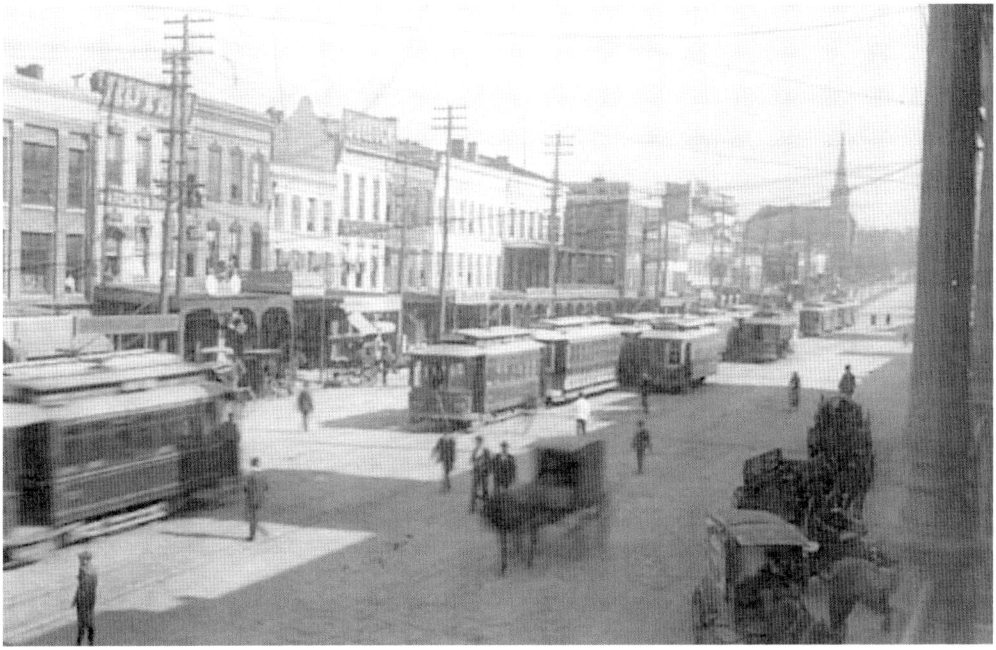

In March 1906, it was announced that the Street Railway Company had bought 10 acres for new baseball grounds at Electric Park. The new grounds would be ready for the start of the 1906 season in April. (Author's collection.)

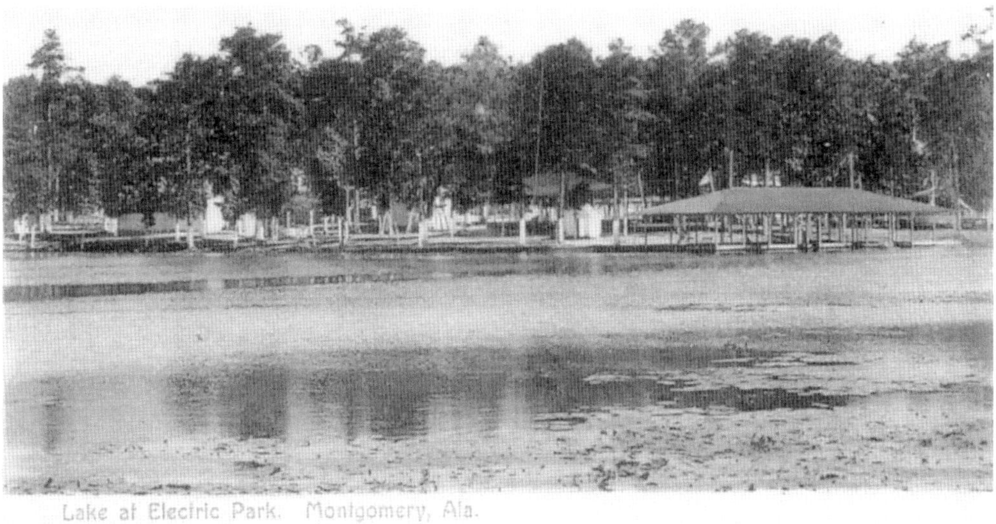

After a Southern League baseball game on May 29, 1908, a crowded electric streetcar was returning from the game. With over 100 passengers on board, the streetcar got away from the motorman coming down a steep incline east of Madison Avenue. When the motorman shouted for the streetcars ahead to pull off and give him room, passengers began jumping off. In a few brief moments, the railway was lined with injured persons. Fortunately, the streetcar was stopped at the foot of the hill without a collision. Only the passengers who jumped off were injured, none fatally. (Author's collection.)

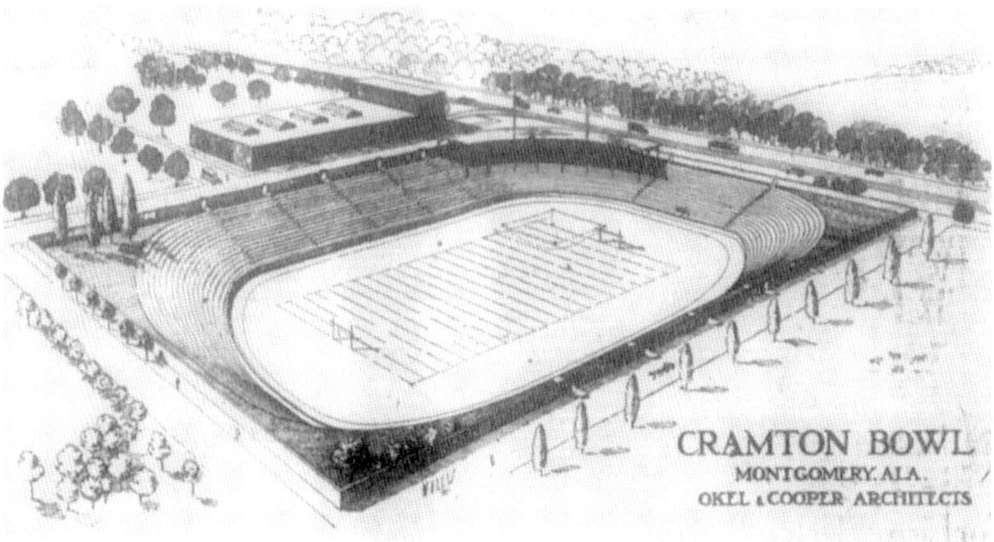

In the 1920s, the popularity of college football was booming across the nation. In Montgomery, the decision was made to build a multipurpose stadium to accommodate both football and baseball. The new stadium was named after F.J. Cramton, who headed up the fundraising drive to get the stadium built. On May 1, 1922, the first baseball game was played at the Cramton Bowl, between Auburn University and Vanderbilt. (Alabama Department of Archives and History.)

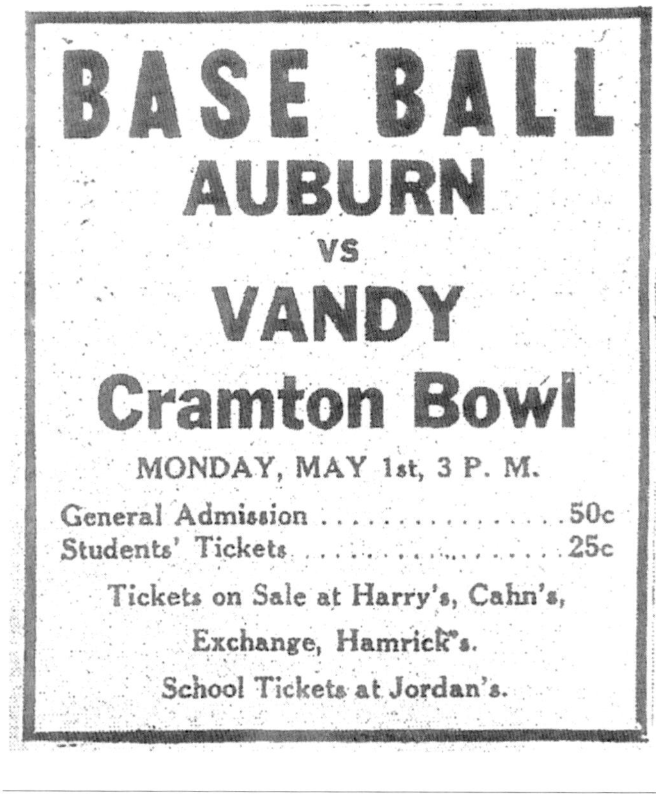
BASE BALL
AUBURN
VS
VANDY
Cramton Bowl
MONDAY, MAY 1st, 3 P. M.
General Admission 50c
Students' Tickets 25c
Tickets on Sale at Harry's, Cahn's, Exchange, Hamrick's.
School Tickets at Jordan's.

A special train brought the Auburn team, the band, and students to Montgomery. A parade included the Auburn band performing the famous "Snake Dance" when they got to Dexter Street. Fred Cramton threw out the first pitch, and Auburn won the game. (Author's collection.)

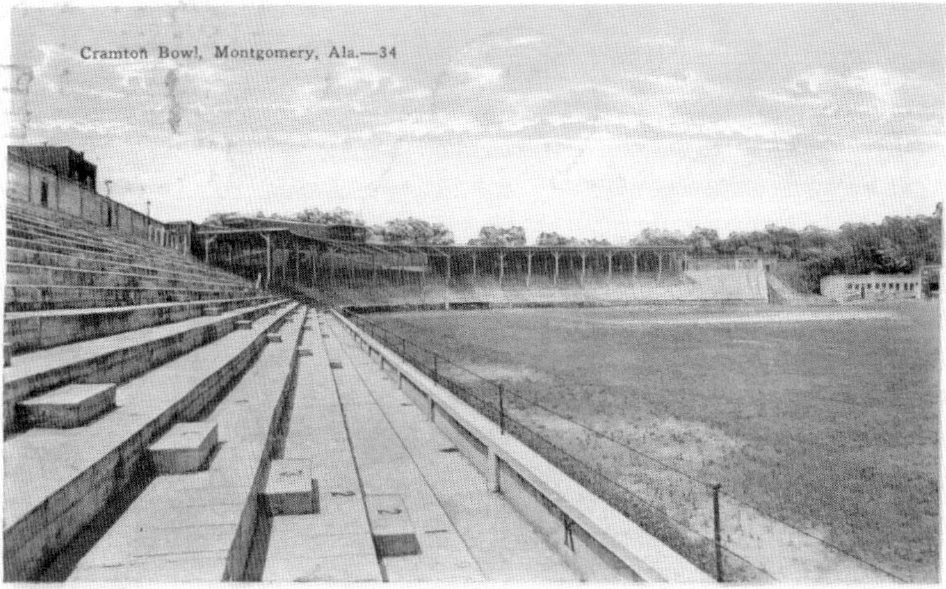

This postcard from 1930 shows the Cramton Bowl looking from the first base side toward home plate. The stands ended down the left field line, with no permanent seating on the east side of the bowl. The Cramton Bowl was a multipurpose stadium, accommodating baseball, football, and track events. (Author's collection.)

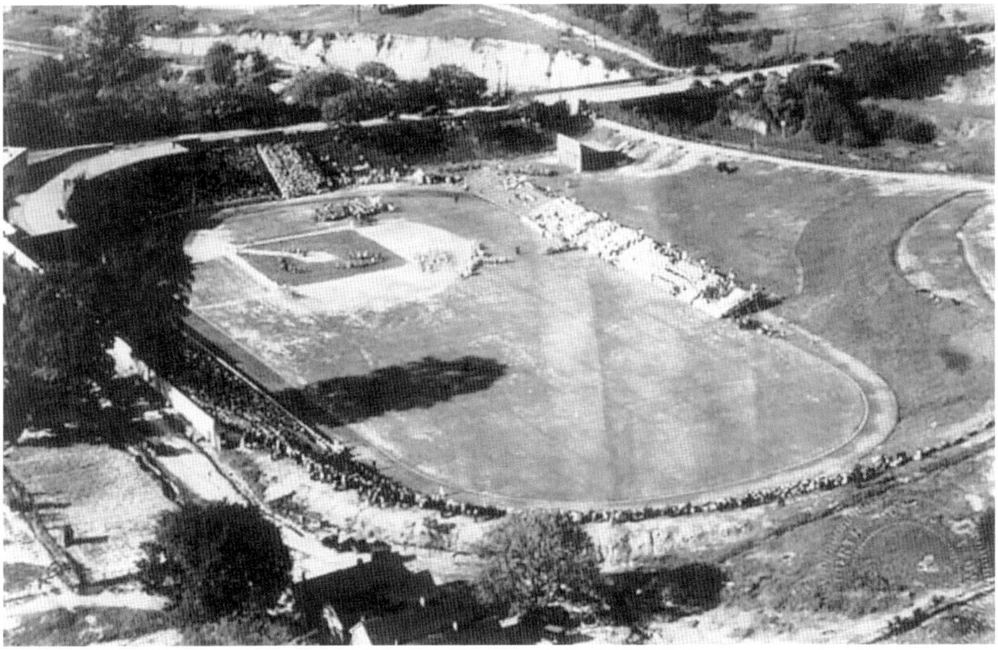

This aerial view of the Cramton Bowl from around 1930 shows pregame festivities taking place. The was most likely an opening-day game. The area at upper right is where Patterson Field would be built. (Alabama Department of Archives and History.)

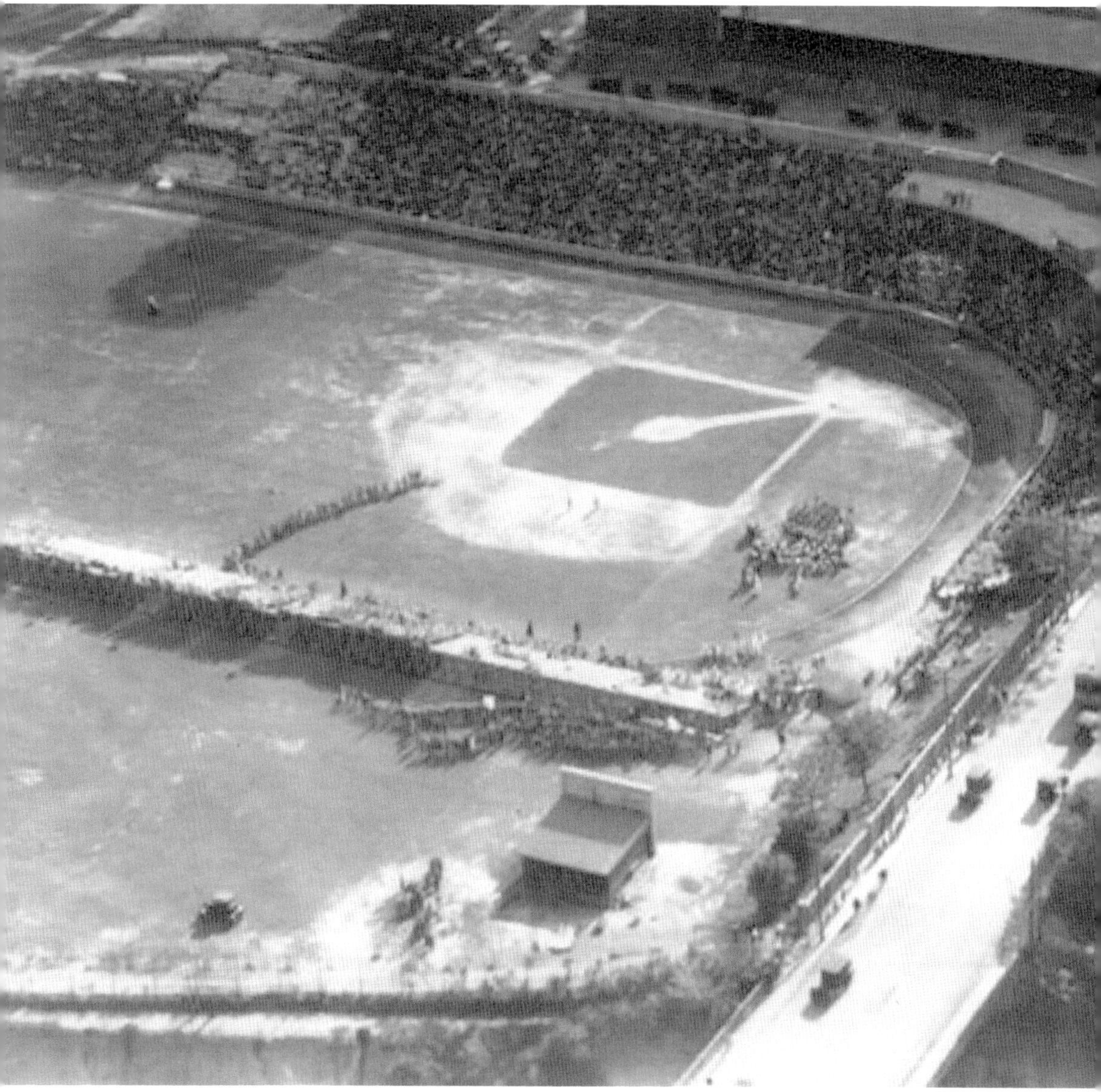

This aerial view of the Cramton Bowl taken from the northeast reveals a packed stadium for a very important game. Streetcars are lined up to drop off fans, and the field is covered with dignitaries and bands to begin the festivities. (Alabama Department of Archives and History.)

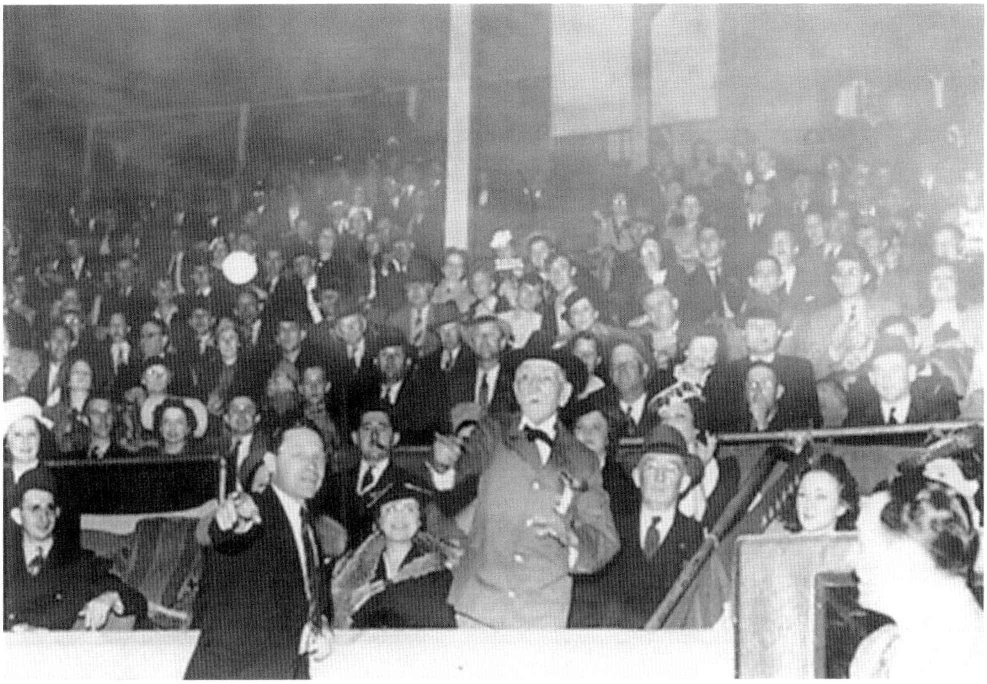

By the 1930s, Civil War veterans were becoming scarce. When one's baseball team was named the Rebels, it only made sense to have one of the few remaining veterans to have the honor of throwing out the first pitch on opening day. Former Confederate soldier Paul Sanquinetti was given the honor during a game in 1937. Unfortunately, Sanquinetti died soon after this game, by 1940. He is pictured at right in his military uniform as a young officer in Company K, 19th Virginia Infantry. (Both, Alabama Department of Archives and History.)

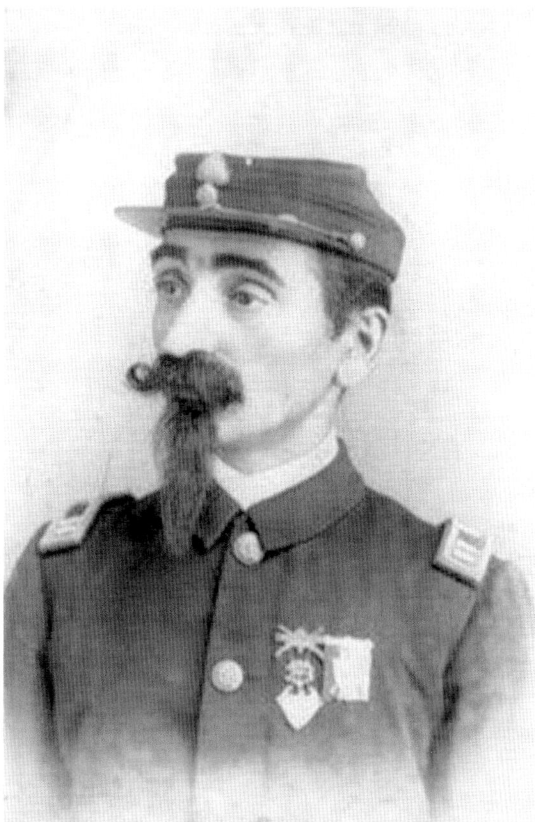

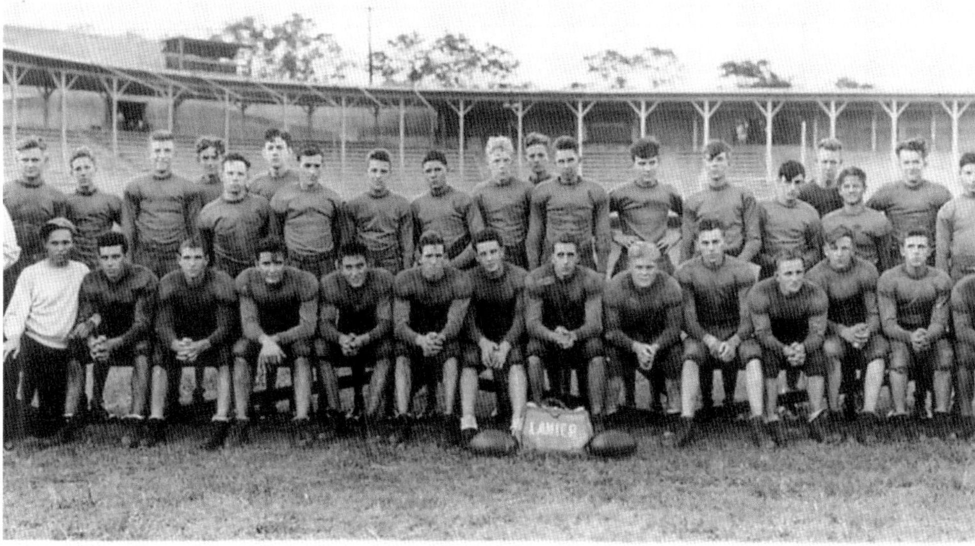

SIDNEY LANIER FOOTBALL SQUAD 1926

Line Coach; Clayton Hudson, Head Coach; Vic Price, Manager; James Wood, T; John Cain, FB; Tillie Walker, QB; George Egge, E; Clifford Carroll, HB; Winston HB; Bob Turner, E; Louie Hanks, T; Louis McRee, E; Billy Coats, Asst. Manager; Back Row, Left to Right, Merrill Jenkins, FB; Chattie Davidson, FB; Paul Duncan, T; Tom Shackleford, HB; Brooks Selcer, E; Alfred Oliver, G; Charles Crommelin, T; Merrill, E; Potice Avant, T; Bob Cone, E; Jack Trost, E; Walter Kendrick, HB; Hice, T; Bob Gafford, HB; Coach Thompson, Asst. Coach.

The Cramton Bowl was designed to be a multisport arena, but many knew football would be its main sport. This picture shows the 1926 Sidney Lanier High School football team in front of the covered baseball stands. The press box is visible over the top of the stands. (Alabama Department of Archives and History.)

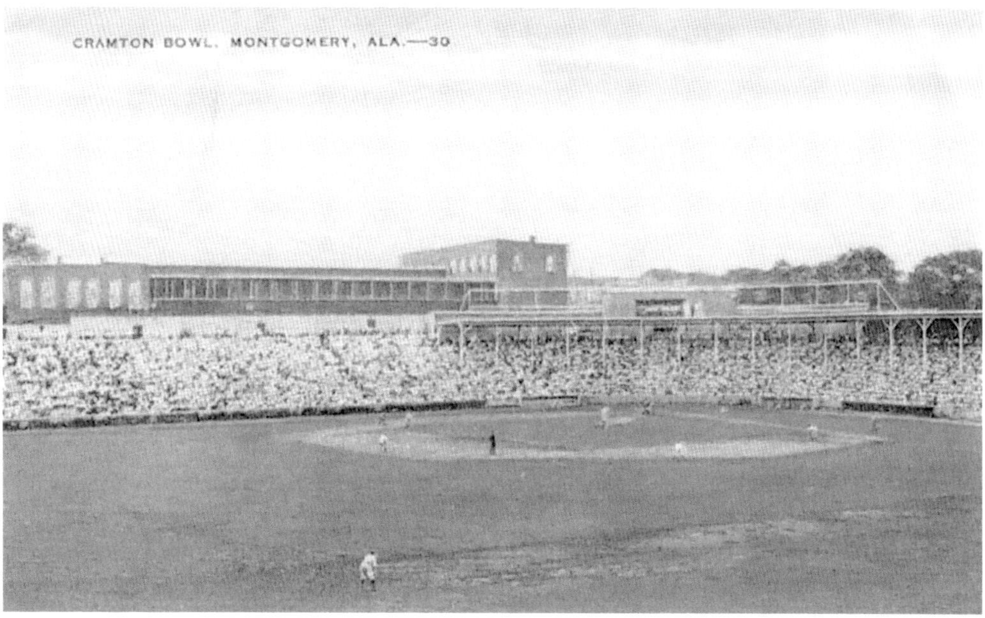

Looking in from center field, a packed house enjoys an afternoon of baseball. When the stadium was remodeled to be football-only, the cover over the seating behind home plate was removed. (Author's collection.)

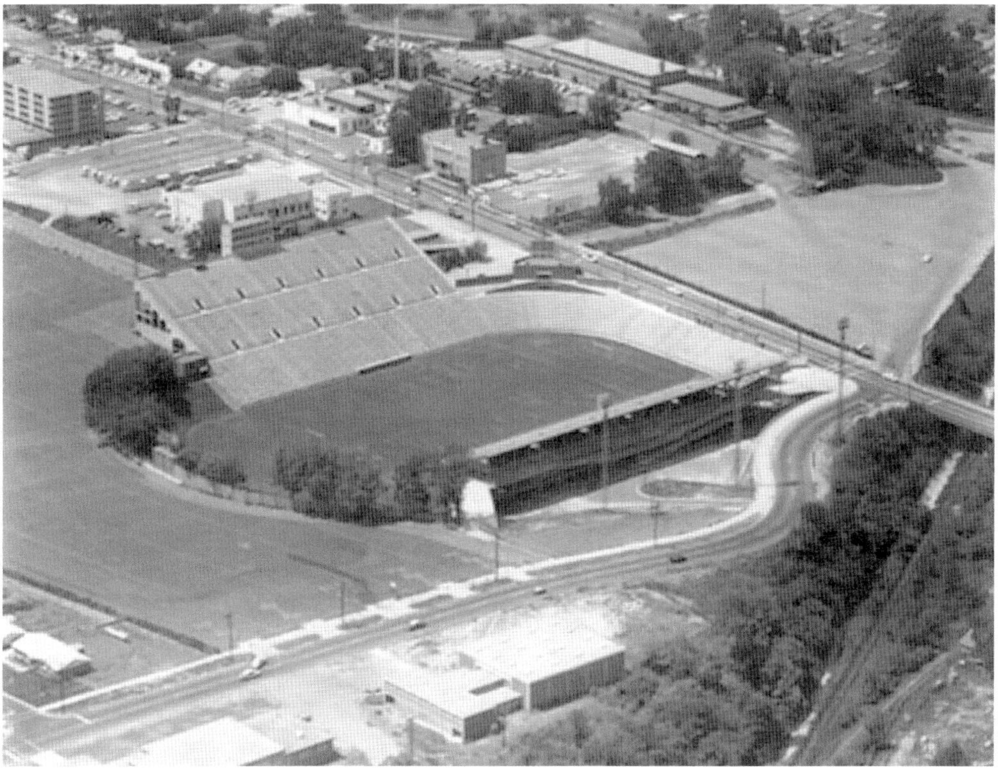

This 1964 aerial view shows the Cramton Bowl after major renovations made the stadium a football arena. The completion of the east side stands made baseball impractical. The covering for the south end stands was also removed, and the west side stands were extended higher. (Alabama Department of Archives and History.)

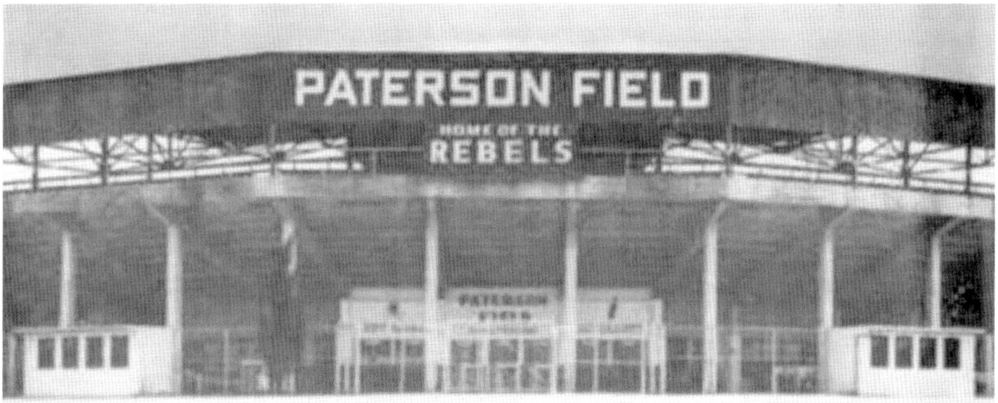

The 1946 renovations of the Cramton Bowl to increase the seating to 12,000 made the stadium less friendly for baseball. The Cramton Bowl had been slowly becoming a football-only stadium. The City of Montgomery built a new baseball stadium across the street from the Cramton Bowl. Patterson Field opened in 1949 as Montgomery became part of the South Atlantic League. Patterson Field is still in use today. (Author's collection.)

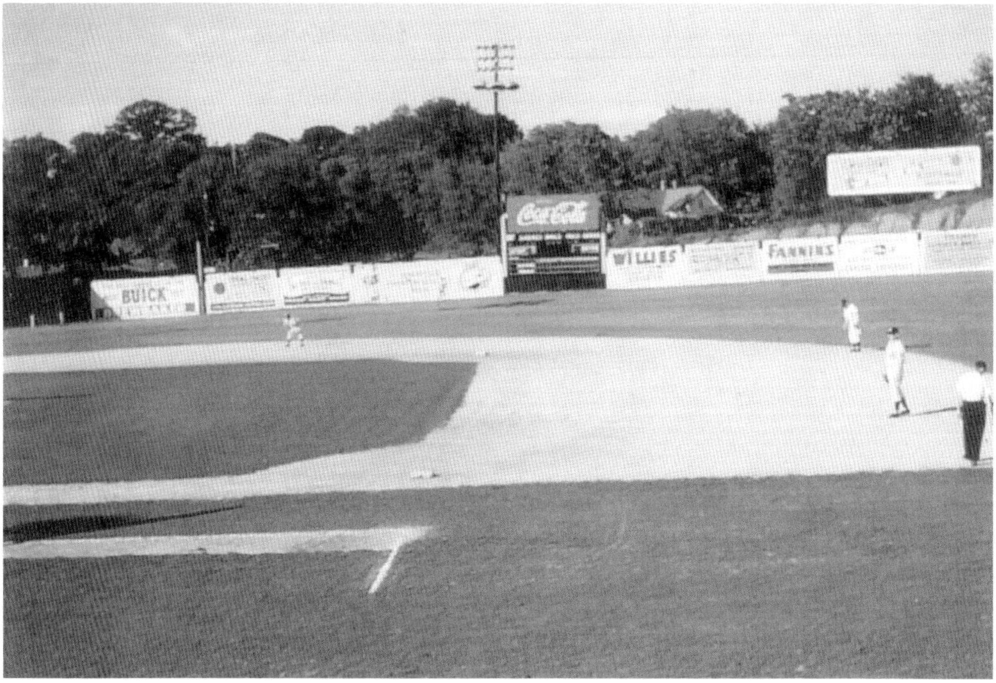

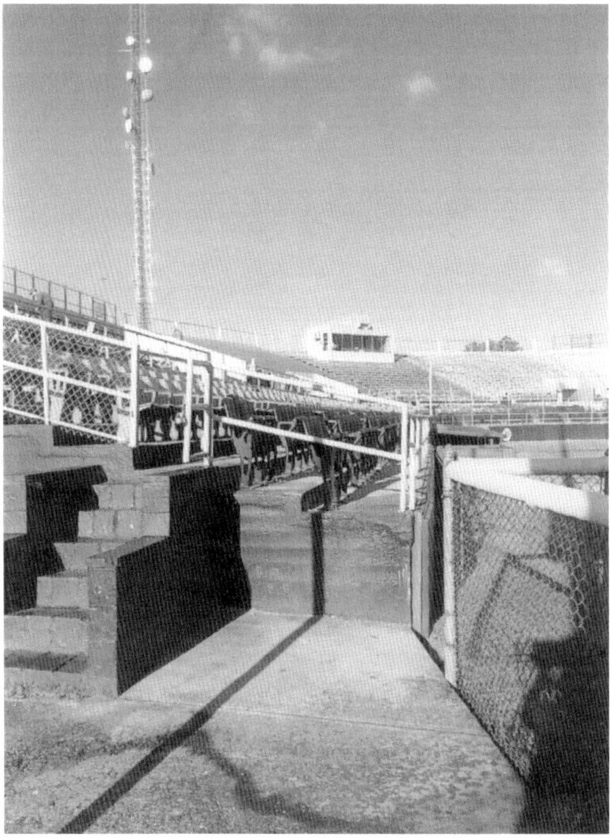

This 1955 image shows a game in progress at Patterson Field. Beyond the tree line in left field is Oakwood Cemetery, where many notable people of Montgomery are buried, including country music legend Hank Williams. (Author's collection.)

Patterson Field still stands today and is being used for baseball by city high schools and local colleges. In January 2016, the roof over the stands behind home plate was removed, apparently not to be replaced. (Author's collection.)

3

Montgomery in the Deadball Era

The Deadball Era is considered to be from 1900 to 1919. The era is noted for low-scoring games and very few home runs being hit.

Today, this style of play is called "small ball." For a team to score runs, the batters must hit-and-run and steal bases.

The players and teams described in this chapter were a product of the Deadball Era. Today's fans, for the most part, would find this style of play boring, preferring more home runs. Still, this era produced some very talented and colorful players.

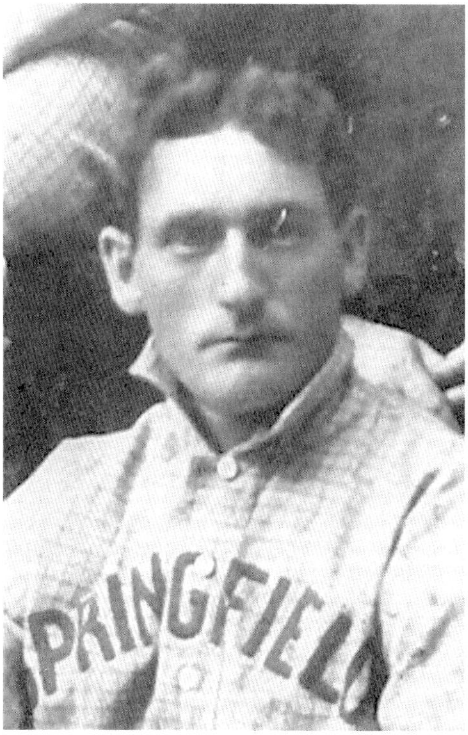

Growing up, many children idolize famous players. Talented outfielder for the 1919 Chicago White Sox Joe Jackson looked up to Montgomery player Champ Osteen (pictured). Osteen had begun his career in the textile leagues of the Carolinas. Jackson grew up in Greenville, South Carolina, and watched him play. (Author's collection.)

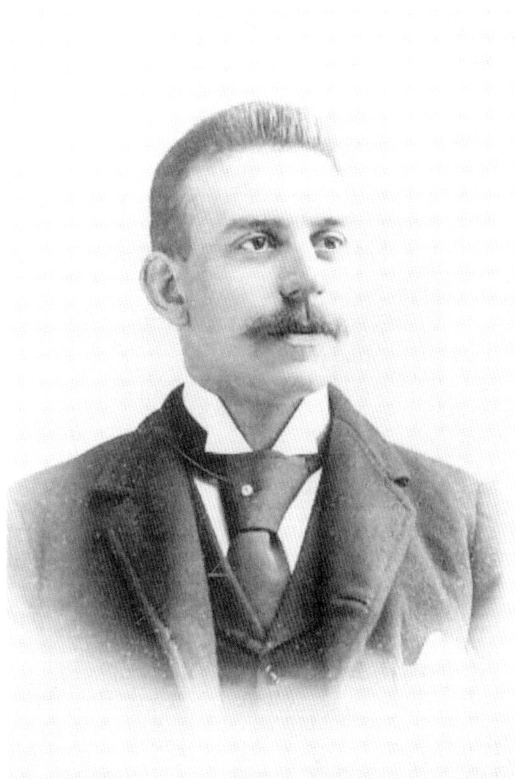

Lou Whistler played four years in the major leagues, followed by several years of playing time with Southern Association teams of Chattanooga, Mobile, and New Orleans. By 1901, Whistler was a player-manager for Chattanooga and then went on to Montgomery in 1903. As player-manager, he led the league that year with 18 home runs. The Montgomery team in 1903 was called the Black Sox, a term that would later be associated with a terrible blot on professional baseball. (Author's collection.)

Del Pratt was a star athlete at the University of Alabama. He was captain of both the football and baseball teams. After college, there were very few opportunities for football players, so Pratt chose to pursue a career in baseball. The Birmingham Barons tried very hard to sign him, but Pratt chose instead to sign with the Montgomery team. After two years in Montgomery, Pratt was sold to the St. Louis Browns. He enjoyed a 13-year career in the majors and is considered the best second baseman of the 1910s. (Author's collection.)

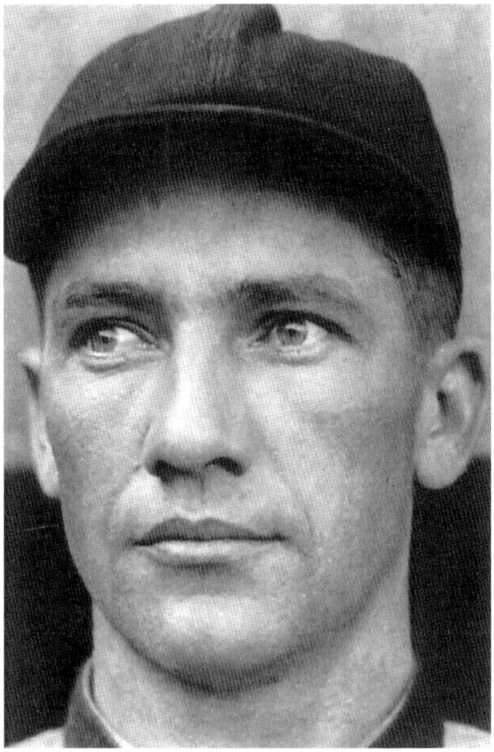

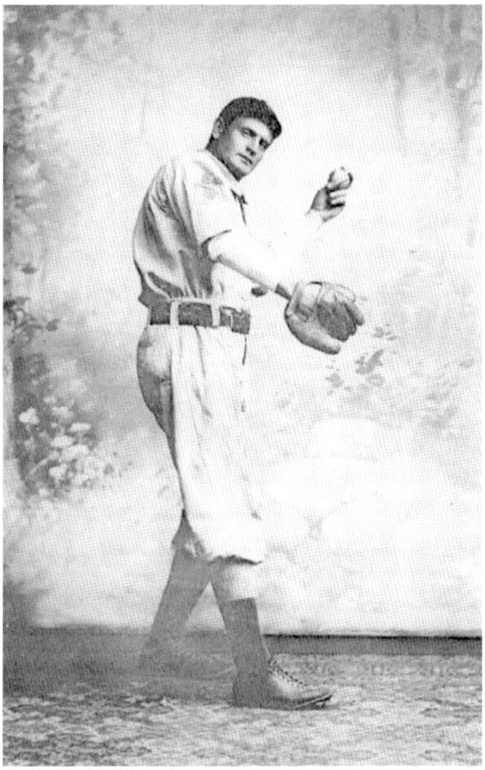

Connie Mack brought his Philadelphia Athletics to Montgomery for spring training in 1906. Mack may have hoped Montgomery would be the quiet, respectful Southern city he needed to help keep his totally unpredictable pitching star Rube Waddell (pictured) out of trouble. However, on March 12, 1906, Waddell left the hotel and was not heard from until he appeared at the police station claiming to have been "sandbagged." Then, he left the station to go missing again. Even sedate Montgomery could not help Connie Mack keep Waddell in line! (Author's collection.)

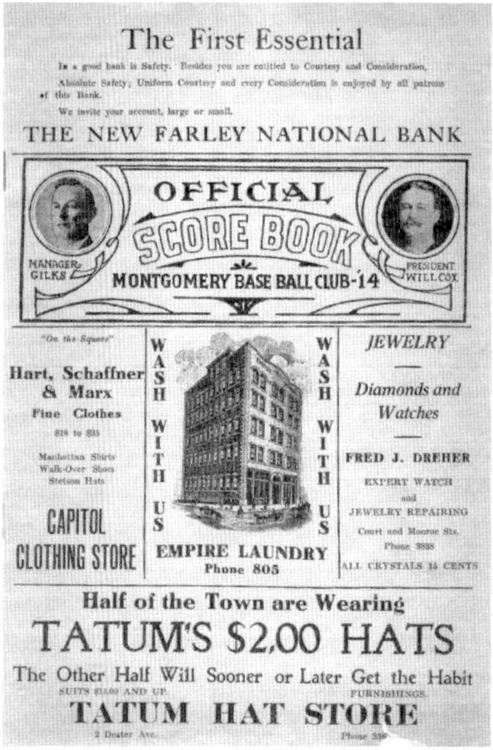

Bob Gilks played five years in the major leagues. His career began in 1884 in Hamilton, Ohio. He spent several years with a variety of Southern teams sandwiched around his major league time. Gilks closed out his baseball career managing the Montgomery Rebels-Billikens in 1914. His image appears on the cover of this 1914 program, on the left. (Author's collection.)

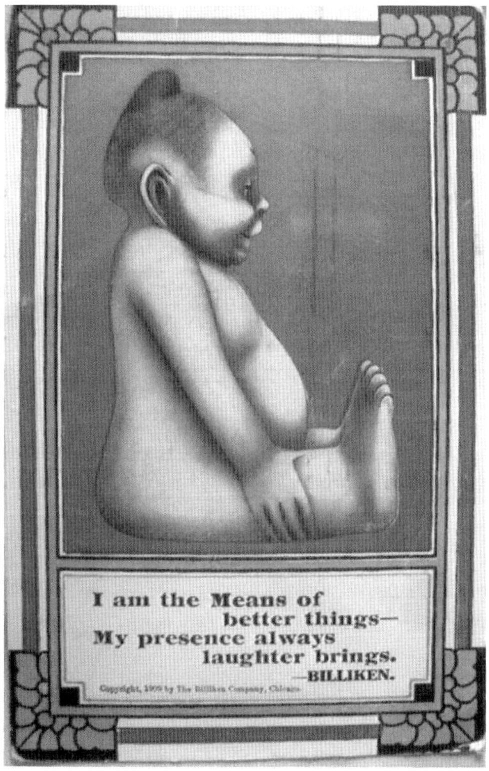

For the 1911 season, the Montgomery team was called the Billikens. In 1908, Kansas City, Missouri, art teacher Florence Pretz designed a mysterious-looking little character called Billiken. A company in Chicago started manufacturing the little statues as good luck charms. It became a very popular fad nationwide. Similar little dolls, such as Smurfs and Trolls, have ebbed and flowed in popularity over the years. Thankfully, Billikens as a mascot only lasted one year in Montgomery. (Author's collection.)

Jack Lively was an Alabama native from the Joppa community. He pitched for Montgomery on two separate occasions. In 1908–1909, he pitched a no-hitter and won 18 games. Later in life, Lively would speak of the no-hitter as his greatest baseball accomplishment. In 1911, Lively played for the Detroit Tigers, where his record was 7-5. His time with Detroit was special because he roomed with Ty Cobb. Cobb did not get along with many of his teammates, especially Northerners, but found the easygoing Lively a pleasant roommate. One of the benefits for Lively was being able to accompany Cobb on a special trip to the White House to meet President Taft. Lively returned to play for Montgomery in 1914. His son Bud also pitched for Montgomery in 1942. (Author's collection.)

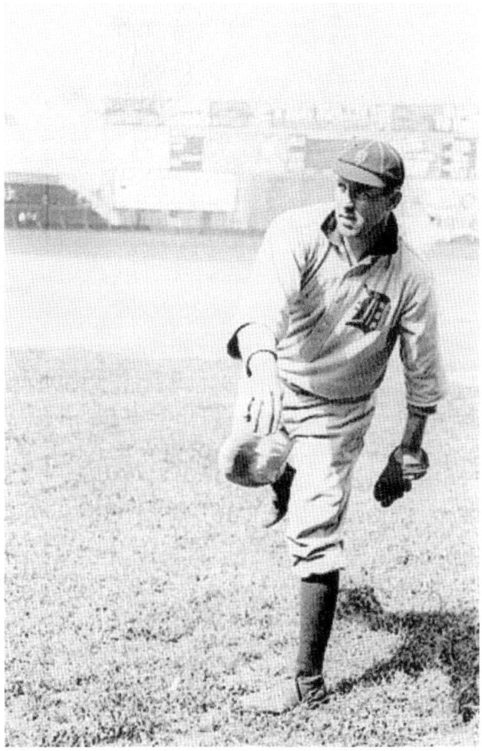

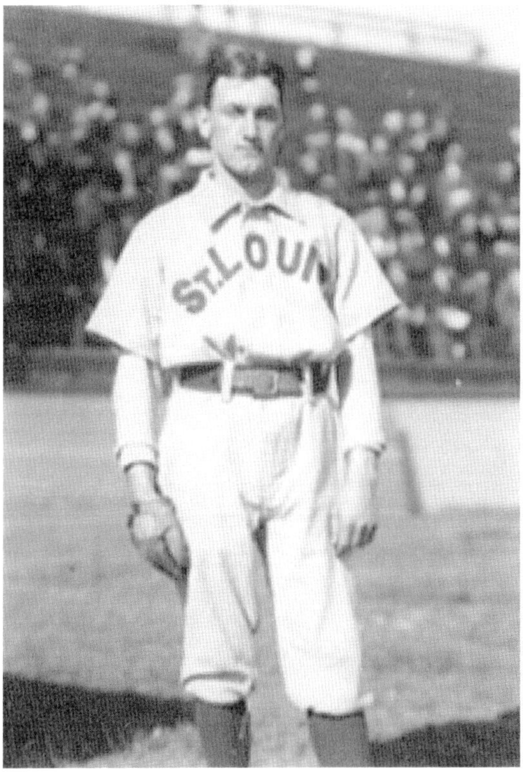

Win Kellum was the starting pitcher for the Boston Red Sox's first game in the newly formed American League in 1901, but in 1896, Kellum won 21 games for Montgomery. In 1908, Kellum pitched in the Southern Association Championship game for Nashville against New Orleans, a game for years known as the greatest game ever played in Dixie. (Author's collection.)

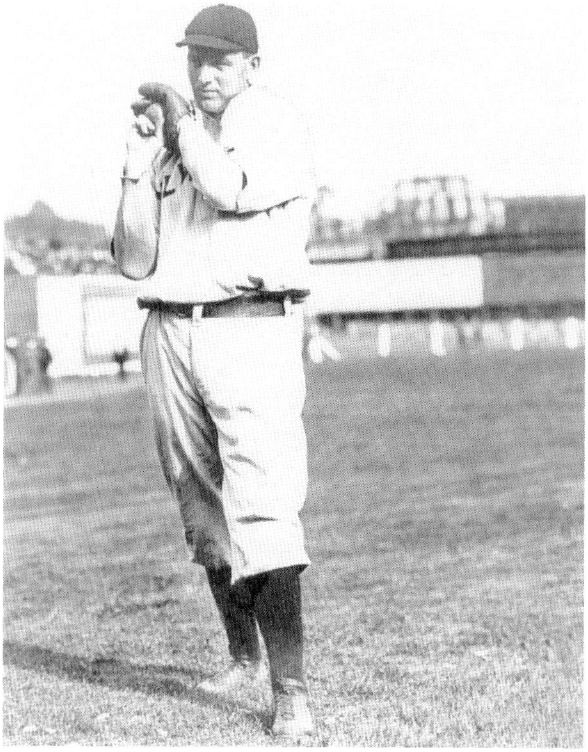

The 1893 Montgomery Colts had the distinction of having two future hall of fame players, Fred Clarke and Joe McGinnity. McGinnity began his professional career in Montgomery. His 15-20 record showed he was determined to finish what he started. He acquired the nickname "Iron Man" by pitching both games of doubleheaders. He was a 35-game winner for the world champion New York Giants of 1905. (Author's collection.)

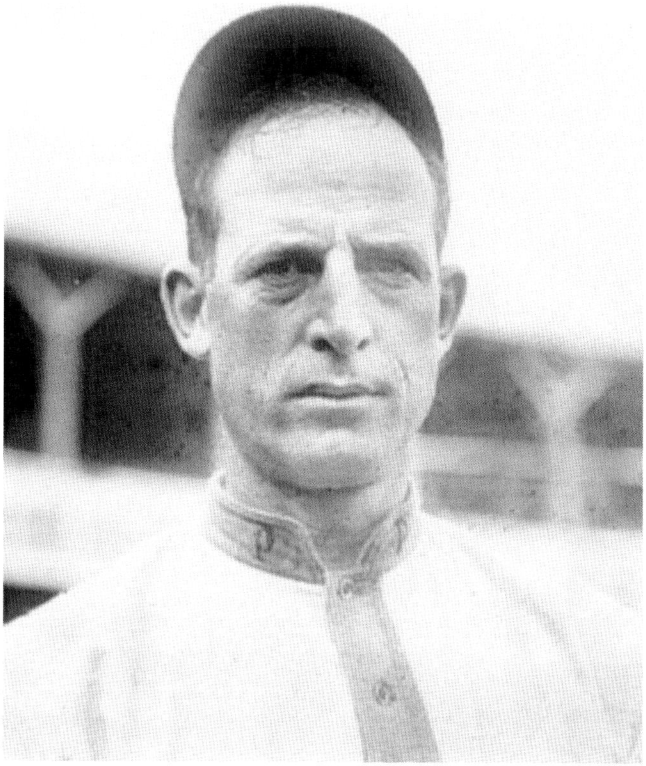

Fred Clarke played outfield for the 1893 Montgomery Colts. The next year, he made it to the major leagues. He spent most of his career as player-manager of the Pittsburgh Pirates. It was his Pirates team that played in the first World Series against the Boston Red Sox. His 1909 Pirates beat Ty Cobb and the Detroit Tigers. Clark was inducted into the hall of fame in 1945. (Author's collection.)

When the topic of who was the greatest Southern Association manager is discussed, Johnny Dobbs must be considered. Dobbs managed seven different Southern Association teams, including Montgomery, from 1911 to 1913. He managed 23 years with five championships. (Author's collection.)

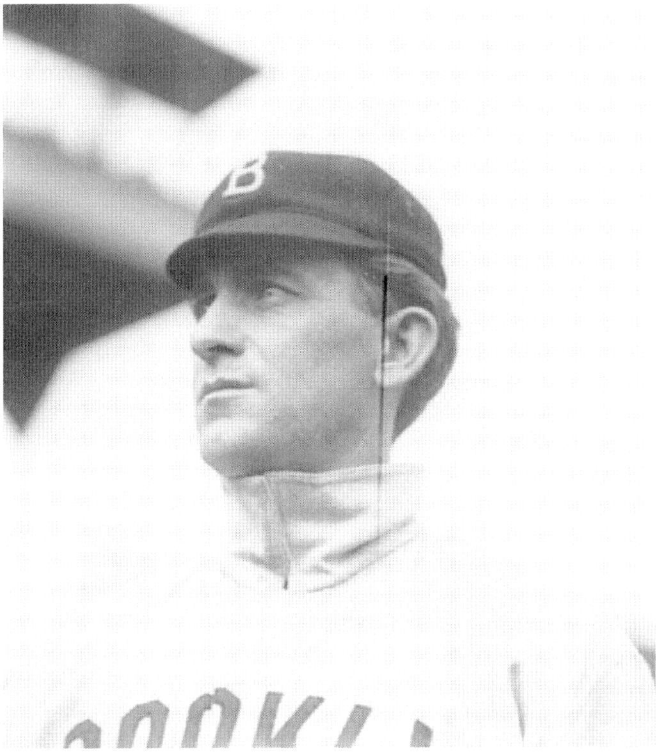

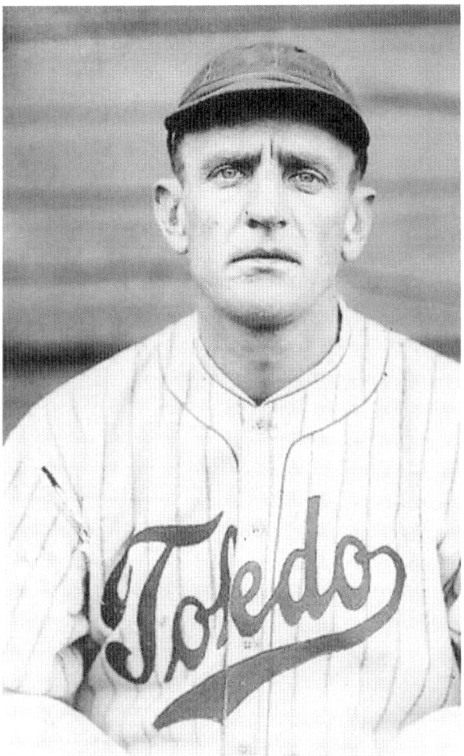

In 1912, Charles "Casey" Stengel was a young man of 22 who hit .290 for the Montgomery Club in only his third season of professional baseball. Throughout his career he was known for his tricks, which he may have learned in the minors. During a game at Pensacola, Florida, Casey was playing the outfield when he discovered a manhole cover. After close inspection, he jumped down into the hole, popping up just in time to catch a fly ball. Nicknamed "the Ole Professor," Casey later managed the Yankees. (Author's collection.)

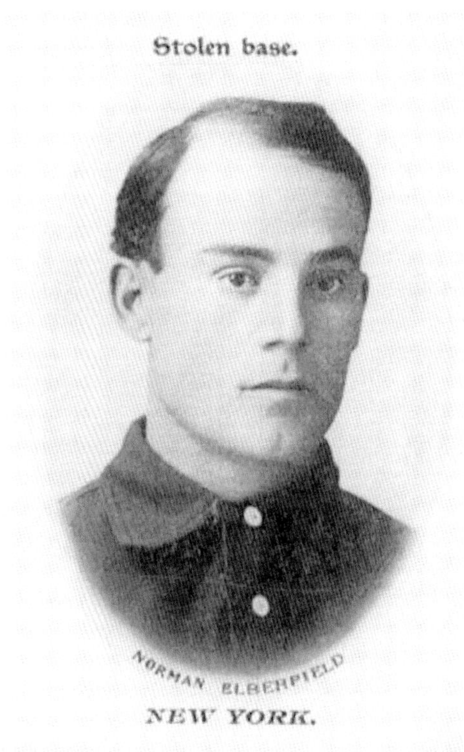

Norman "Kid" Eberfeld had a 14-year major league career. His other nickname was "the Tabasco Kid" because of his fiery temper. He gave umpires an especially hard time and was probably kicked out of more games than any player of his era. Eberfeld played for Montgomery in 1912 at the end of his major league time. After playing baseball, Eberfeld ran a baseball camp for boys in Hot Springs, Arkansas. (Author's collection.)

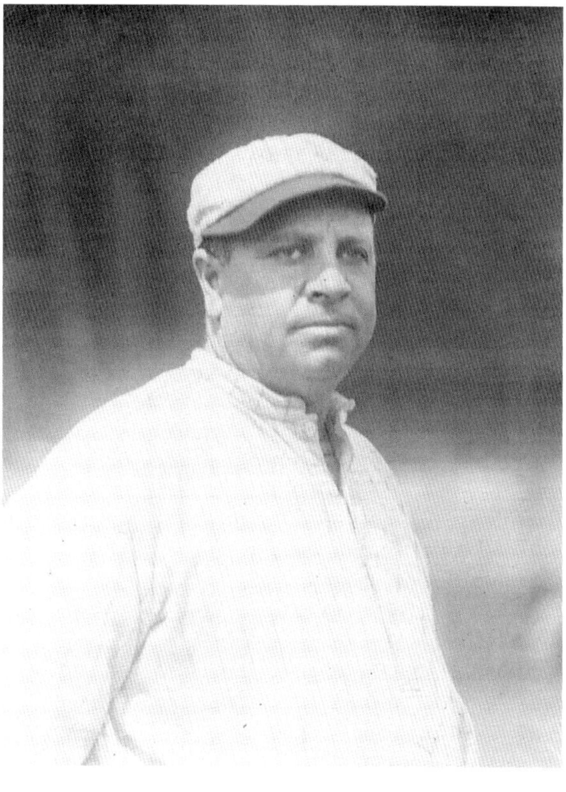

Carlton Molesworth began his baseball career with a brief attempt at pitching for the Washington Senators, which did not go well for Molesworth. The diminutive five-foot, seven-inch outfielder played three seasons for Montgomery, winning the batting title in 1905. In 1908, Molesworth moved on to Birmingham, where he would play and manage the Barons until 1922. (Author's collection.)

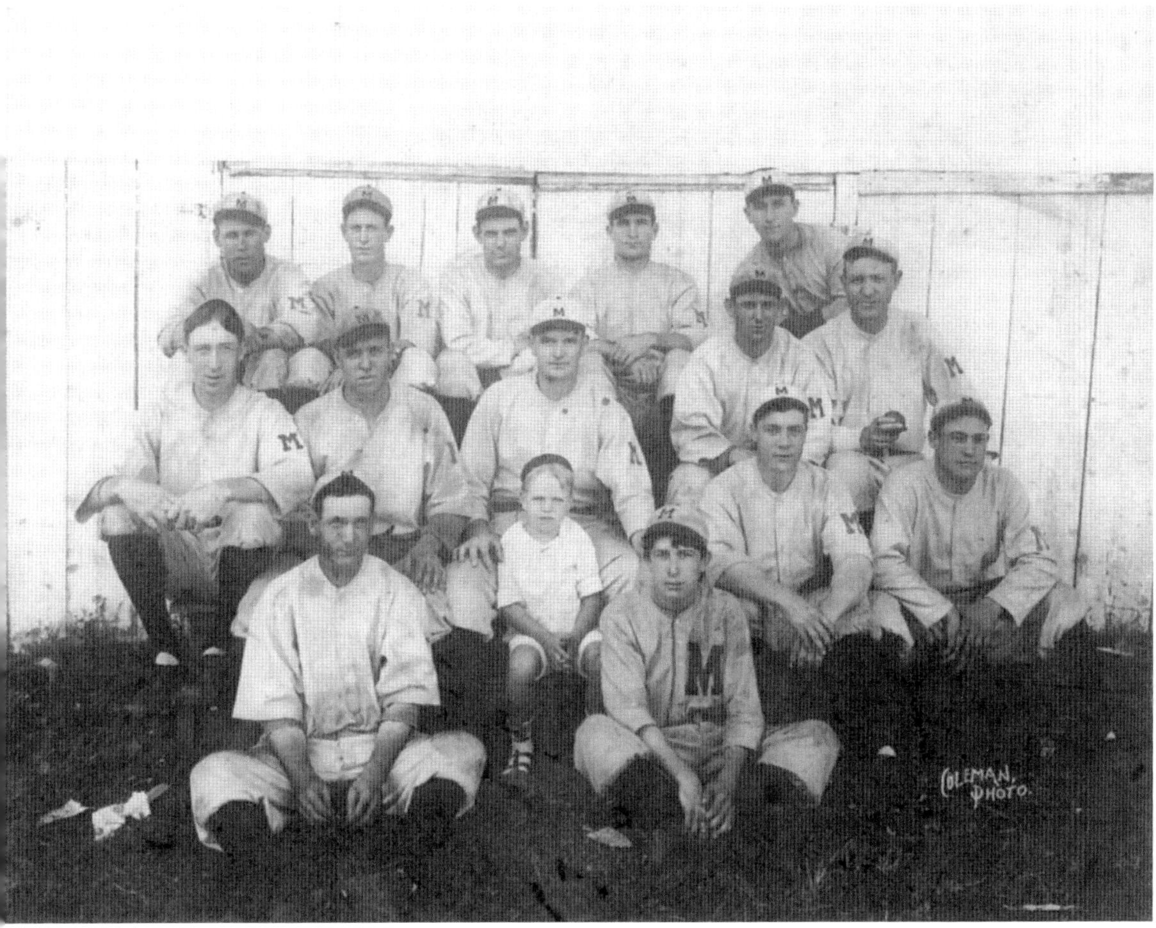

This photograph of the 1908–1909 Montgomery Senators just surfaced in the past few years. A complete list of the individual players in the picture does not exist; however, a few are easily identifiable. Player-manager Ed Grimminger is in the center of the second row with his son Ed Jr. seated below him. Also noted are Jack Lively to the left of Grimminger and Champ Osteen seated on the ground at left. This picture has brought much enjoyment for avid Montgomery baseball researchers trying to positively identify all the players. (Courtesy of John Verona.)

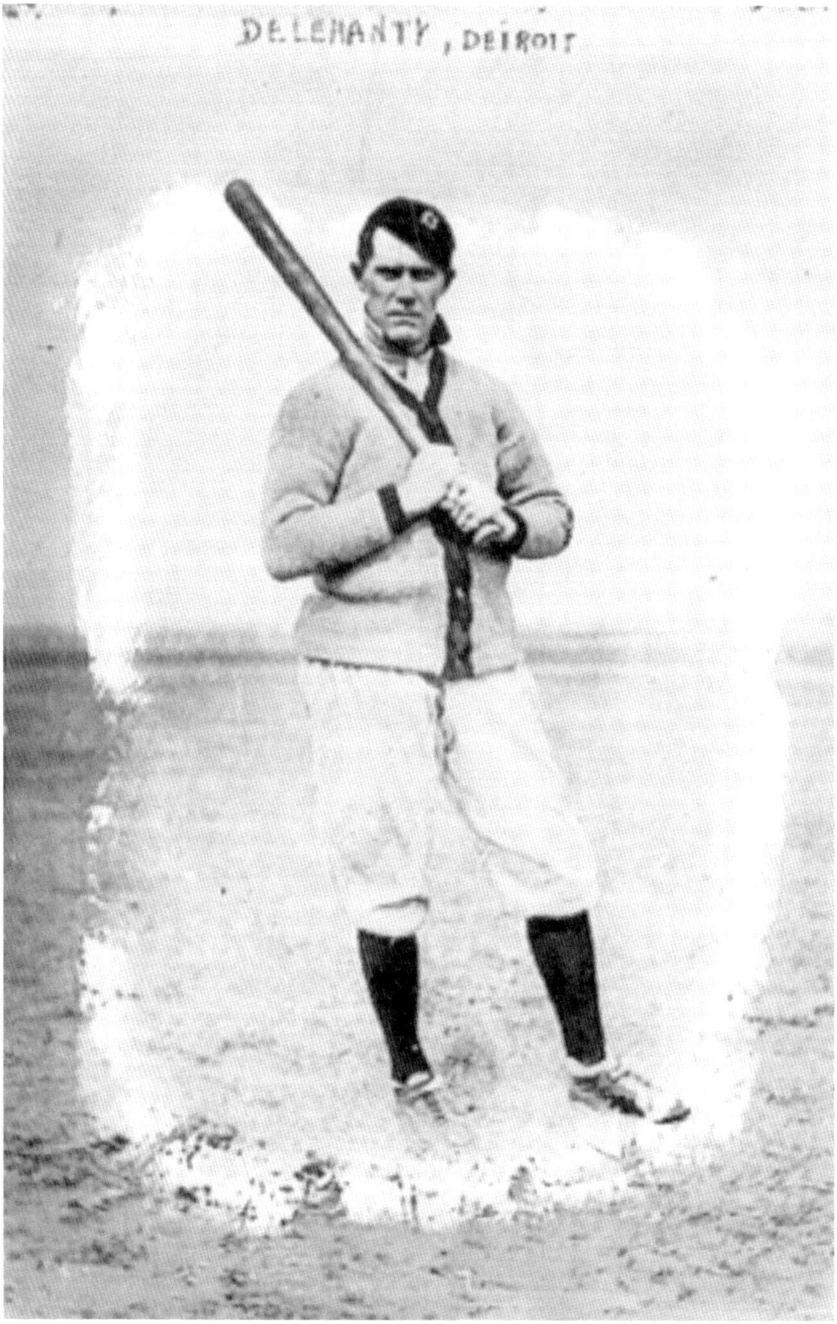

Jim Delahanty was one of five brothers who played Major League Baseball at the turn of the 20th century. Another brother, Willie, played in the minors. Jim Delahanty began his professional career with the Montgomery club in 1898. When the team folded around mid-season, he moved on to Allentown, Pennsylvania, where his brother Timmy was playing. Jim Delahanty had a 13-year career in the major leagues. After baseball, he returned to Cleveland to drive a truck for the city. (Author's collection.)

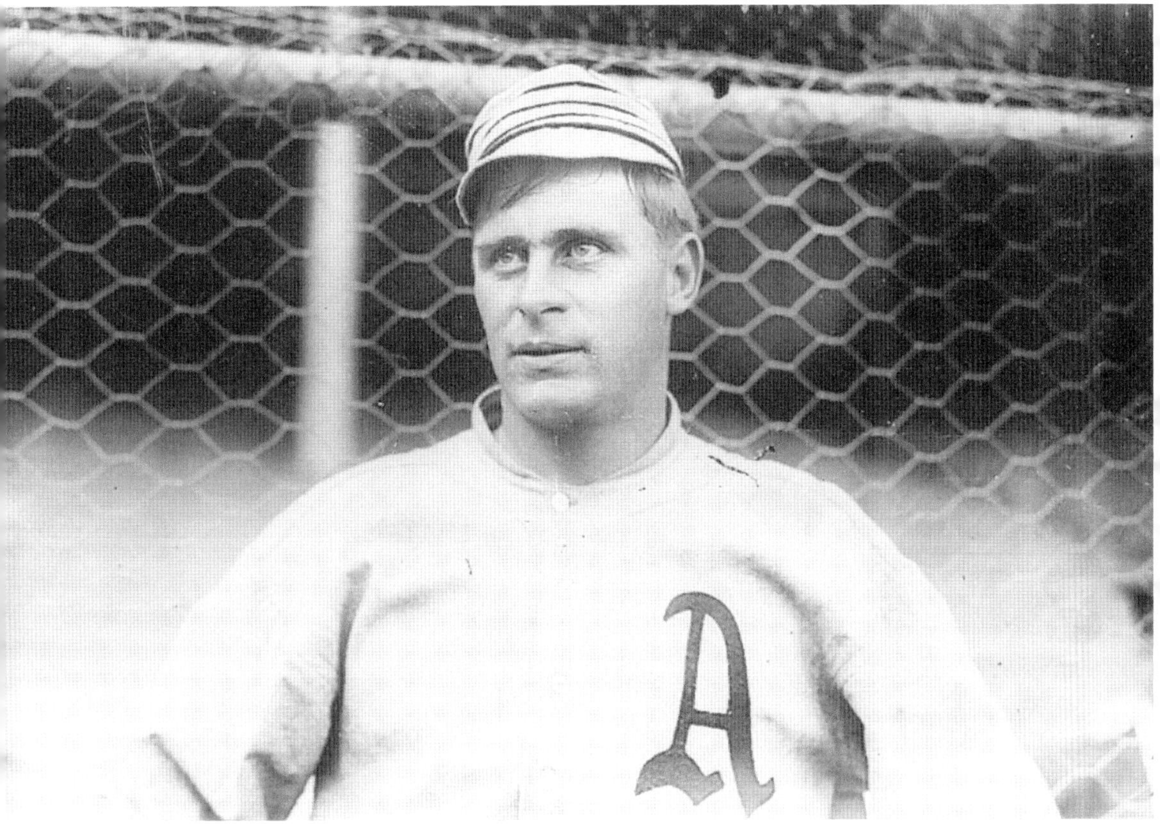

After only 67 games with Montgomery, Rube Oldring joined the New York American League club for the start of a 13-year major league career. Connie Mack soon heard of the speedy infielder and purchased his contract, turning Oldring into an outfielder. Oldring played on the Philadelphia pennant winners of 1911, 1913, and 1914. (Author's collection.)

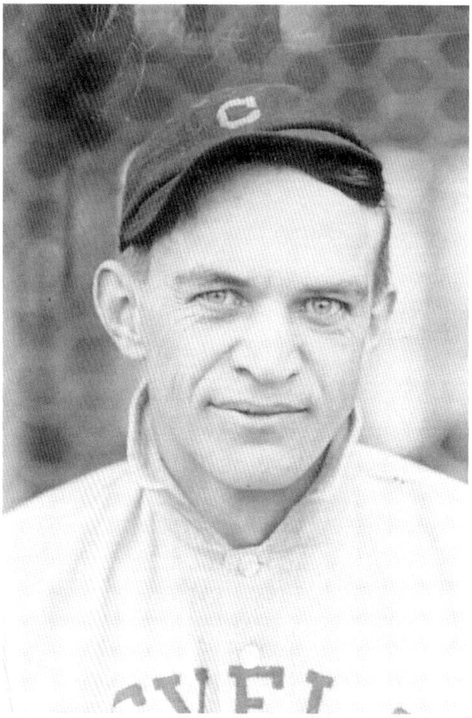

Neal Ball played shortstop for the Montgomery Senators while hitting .301 for the year of 1907. This would earn him a late season call-up to the New York Giants. The next year, he played for the Giants and stayed in the majors for six more years. Ball is most remembered for being the first player to execute an unassisted triple play while playing for Cleveland against the Boston Red Sox. (Author's collection.)

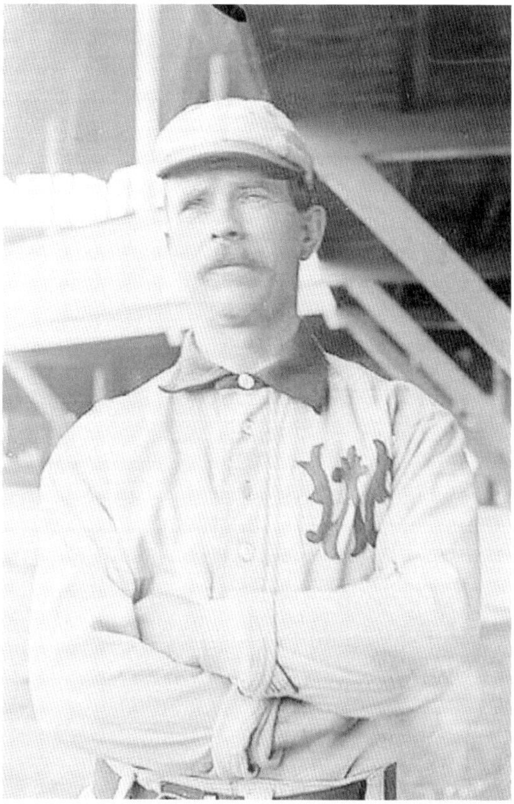

Pictured is Jimmy Ryan, longtime major league player from 1885 to 1903. He once stated that the most interesting play he ever witnessed happened in Montgomery. Ryan was the player-manager of the Senators. With men on base, the batter hit the ball to right field, but Montgomery's first baseman John "Moose" Baxter jumped as high as he could and tipped the ball with his glove. The ball sailed straight to the second baseman, who touched second, then threw back to Baxter for a double play. Baxter then had the presence of mind to turn and throw to the catcher for a triple play! (Author's collection.)

4

Goat Walker and the Lions

Montgomery had been in professional baseball since 1892 and, as of 1928, had not won a championship. This would all change in 1928. With a team full of native Alabamians and good 'ol Southern boys, the Montgomery Lions would give the city of Montgomery its first professional sports championship. One of the key players in the 1928 team was Roy "Goat" Walker. Walker would go on to be one of the most popular sports figures in Montgomery history.

The Montgomery Lions would not stop with 1928. They went on to win a second championship in 1929 with a few different players and a new manager, longtime Southern Leaguer Roy Ellam. After 1930, Walker left the team, and fans gave him the first of two Roy Walker nights. Fans loved his humble disposition and his ability to play many positions and bat well. Walker would be a fan favorite wherever he played!

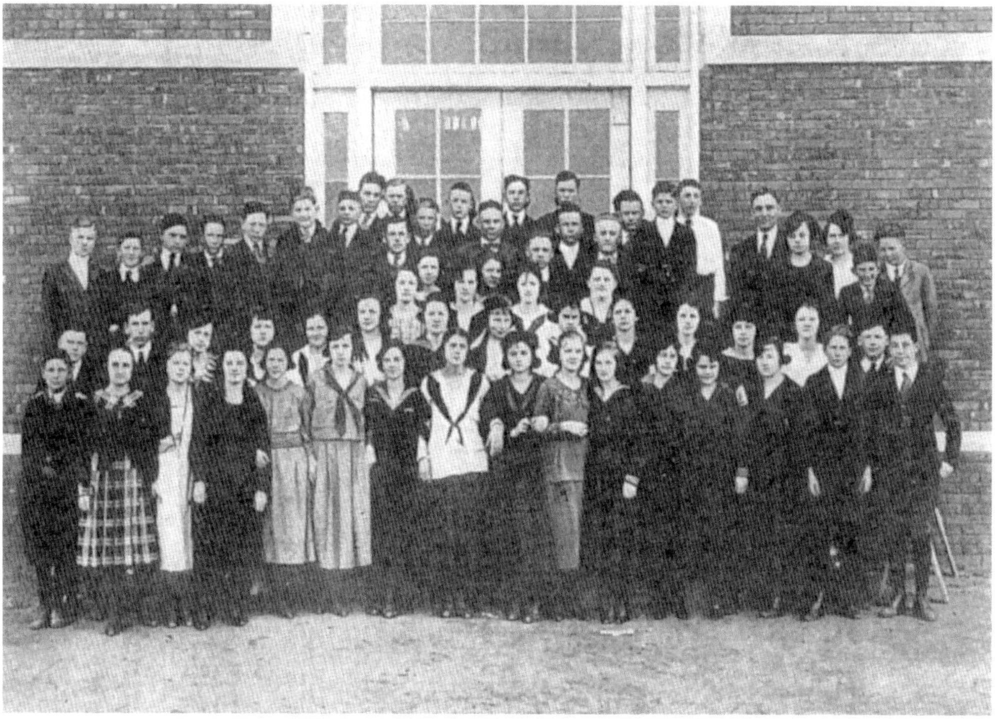

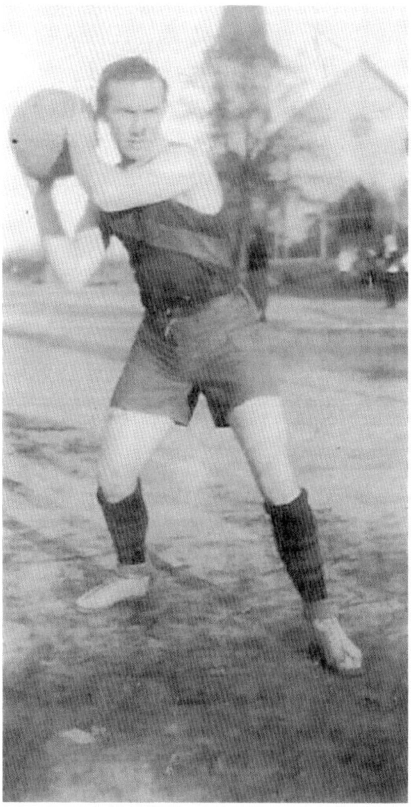

Starting in middle school, Roy Walker began to reveal his athletic abilities in all sports. He is pictured here in the third row, fourth from the left. The photograph was taken on the front steps of Troy High School in Troy, Alabama. (Courtesy of Tommy Horn.)

Roy Walker was not just an outstanding baseball player; he also excelled in several collegiate sports while attending Troy State. Basketball and boxing were also favorite sports of Walker. (Courtesy of Tommy Horn.)

Roy Walker attended Troy State Normal School, later Troy State University. According to a newspaper account, Roy got the nickname "Goat" not from any connection to baseball but from his exceptional ability to make spitballs while in school. While pitching for the Montgomery Lions in the League Championship Series against Pensacola, Walker was referred to as the "Troy Hurler." (Courtesy of Tommy Horn.)

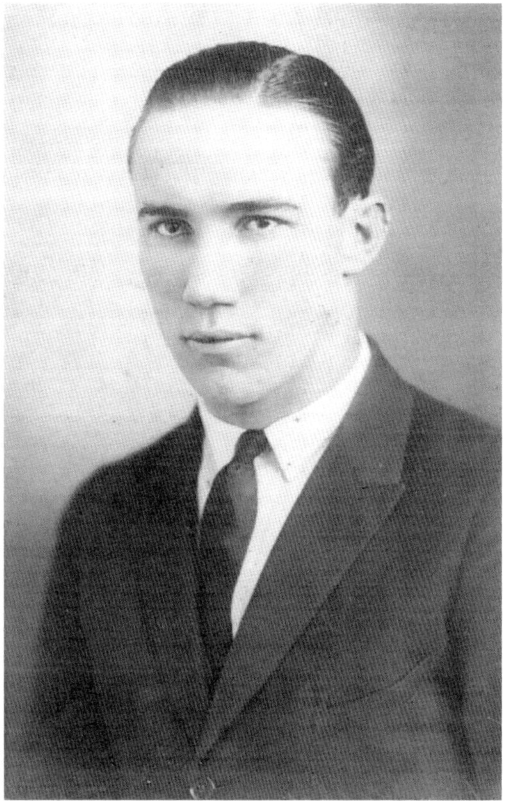

In 1923, the Troy State Normal School was undefeated and won its conference baseball championship. Their leading player was Roy Walker, shown here third from the left in the first row. By the looks on the player's faces, one would assume they finished last! (Courtesy of Tommy Horn.)

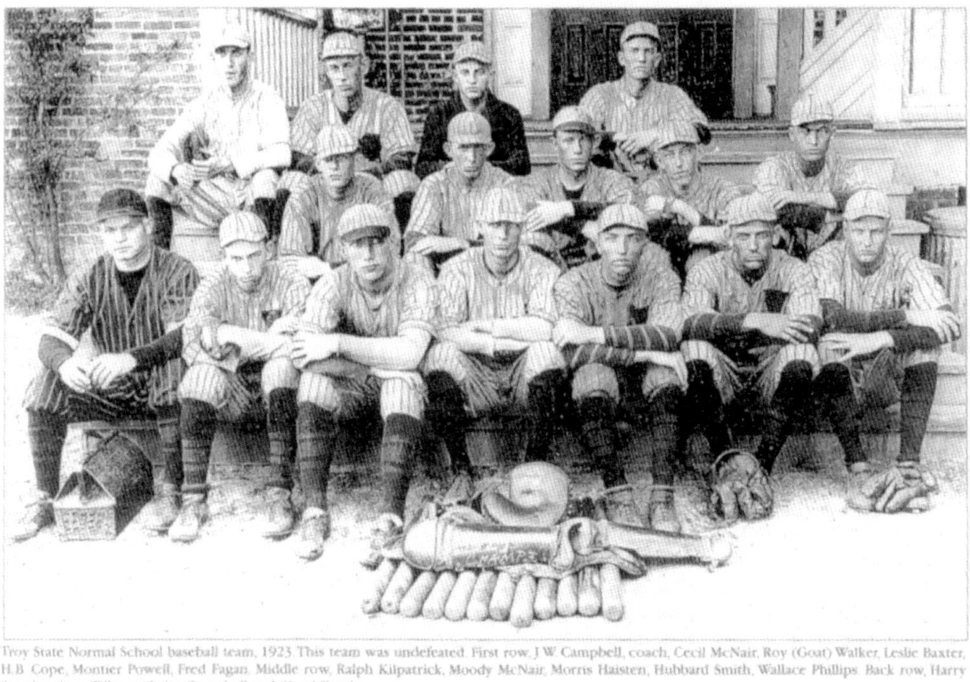

Troy State Normal School baseball team, 1923 This team was undefeated. First row, J W. Campbell, coach, Cecil McNair, Roy (Goat) Walker, Leslie Baxter, H.B Cope, Montier Powell, Fred Fagan. Middle row, Ralph Kilpatrick, Moody McNair, Morris Haisten, Hubbard Smith, Wallace Phillips. Back row, Harry Quarles, Gene Tillman. Quint Campbell and Claud Kersh.

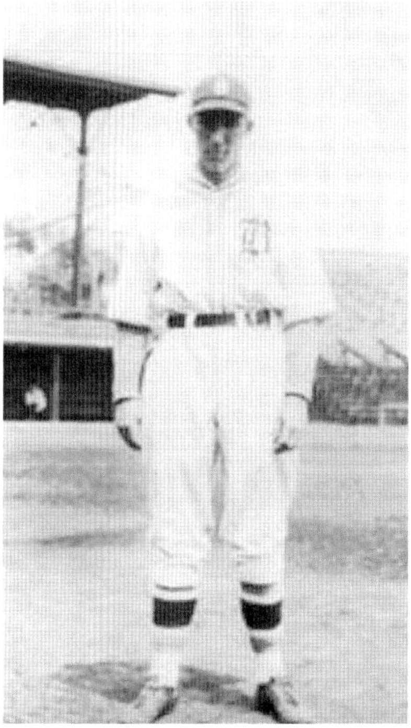

This is the only known image of rookie pitcher Roy Walker with the Birmingham Barons in 1924. Billy Smith, general manager of the Birmingham club, was responsible for bringing Walker to the Magic City. The Birmingham newspaper referred to him as "the young Mr. Walker" for his inconsistency in pitching. (Courtesy of Tommy Horn.)

This photograph of Roy Walker surrounded by every type of baseball glove and leaning on a bat tells a lot about him. Walker was primarily a pitcher, but he could hit and was capable of playing any position. At least once in his long career, he was allowed to play all nine positions in one game. The fans loved it, and they loved Roy. (Courtesy of Tommy Horn.)

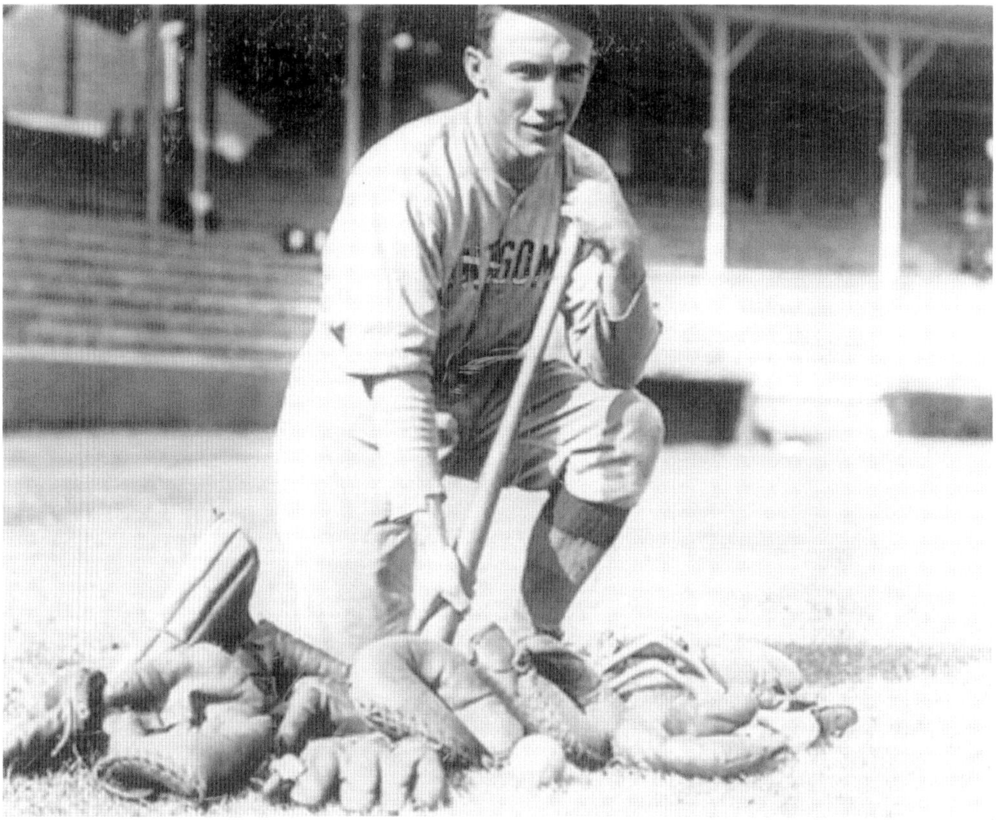

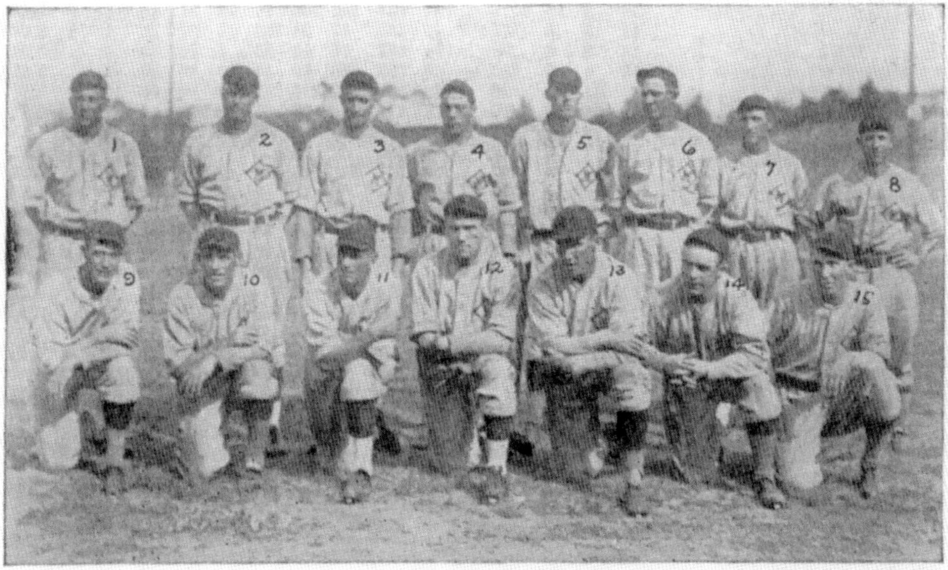

MONTGOMERY CLUB—CHAMPIONS SOUTHEASTERN LEAGUE, 1928.
1, Rodrigues; 2, Moulton; 3, Susko; 4, Palm; 5, Lauzon; 6, Harris; 7, Holt; 8, Seremba; 9, Stewart; 10, Bates; 11, W. A. Pierre, Mgr.; 12, Hutto; 13, Walker; 14, Welch; 15, Van Pelt.

The Montgomery Lions gave Montgomery its first professional sports championship, beating the Asheville Tourists in a best-of-seven series. Montgomery won the series in six games. Walker was responsible for two of the wins against Pensacola for the championship. (Author's collection.)

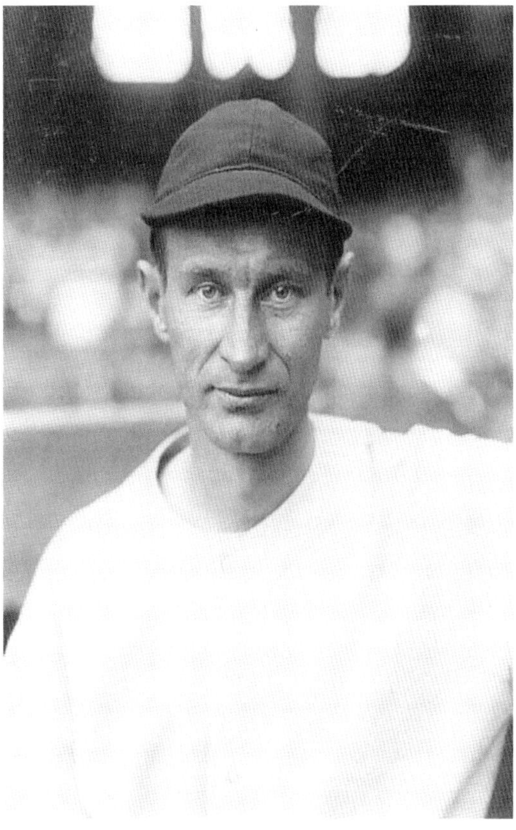

Pete Susko was a major factor in Montgomery's success in 1928. His .353 batting average led the Lions in hitting. Susko had a brief stay with the Washington Senators in 1934, but spent most of his career in the Southern Association playing outfield. (Author's collection.)

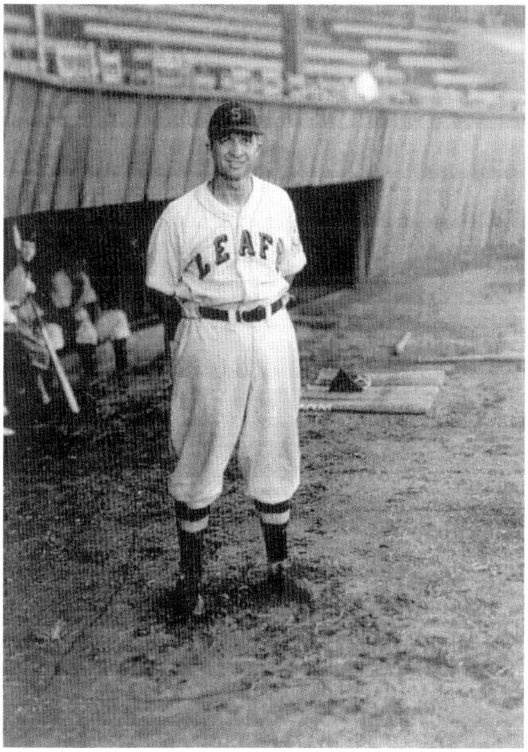

Billy Bancroft was a sports legend in Birmingham from 1924 to 1928, first at Woodlawn High School and then at Howard College. His professional baseball career began with Montgomery in 1928. Bancroft seemed to always be on the winning team. After being a part of Montgomery's first championship, he moved on to Spartanburg and to Birmingham in 1930. With the Barons, Bancroft played a key role in their much remembered and discussed 1931 Dixie Series Championship over Houston of the Texas League. (Courtesy of Chuck Stewart.)

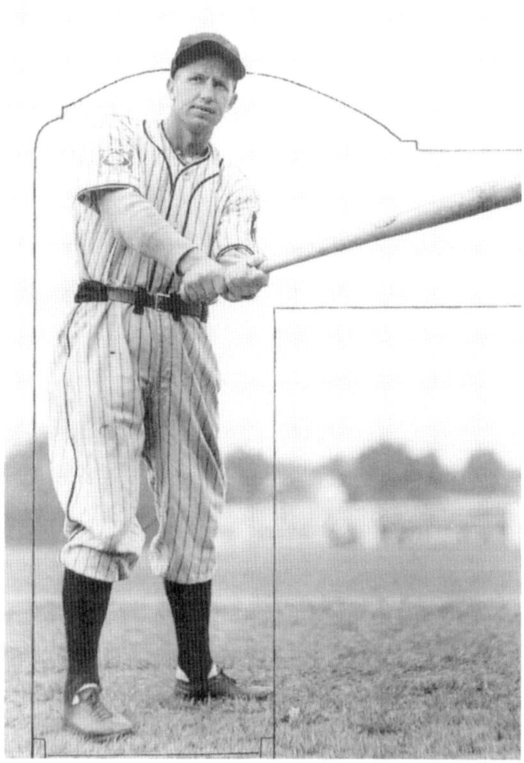

Woody Abernathy was a career minor leaguer. With a lifetime batting average of .315, one may wonder why he never got the opportunity to play in the major leagues. For the Montgomery Lions of 1929–1930, Abernathy was the hitting star of the team. Amazingly, Abernathy hit .339 both years with the Lions, which is true consistency. Abernathy grew up in Birmingham and was a star football player at Auburn before turning to professional baseball. (Author's collection.)

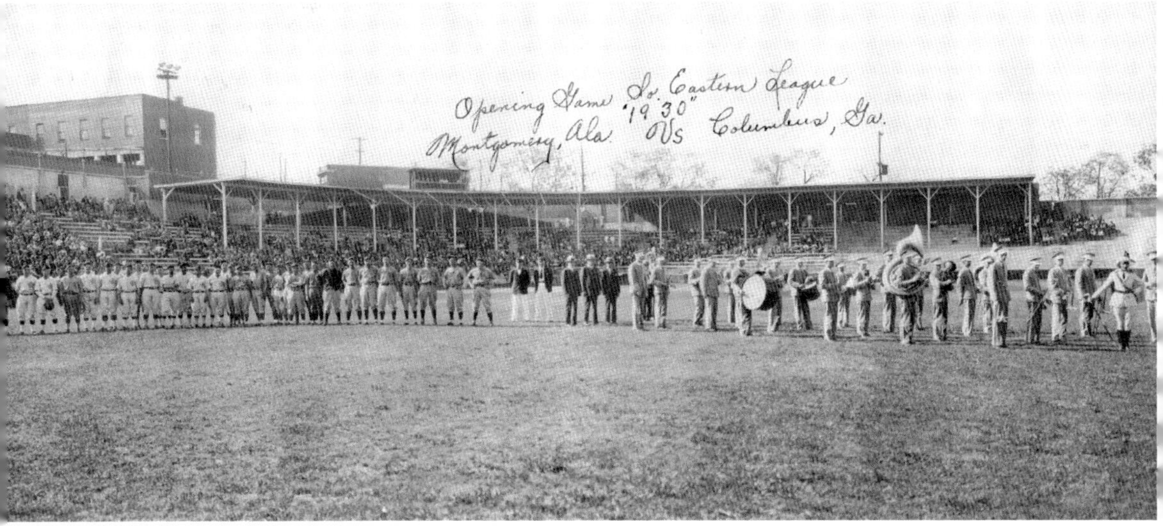

Opening day 1930 was a special day in Montgomery. The Lions had won back-to-back championships in 1928 and 1929, and fans were expecting more. The club and city officials wanted to win the President Cup, an award from the league president for the largest opening-day attendance. City and state employees got a half-day off, but not retail store employees with Easter being so close. The opening-day program was set. Gov. Bibb Graves and Mayor Bill Gunter formed the first pitch battery. The teams marched onto the field behind the always impressive Western Railway Band, led by majorette Margaret Paulin. The band marched to center field near the flag and played "The Star-Spangled Banner" before first-pitch ceremonies. Parts of this photograph are shown in greater detail in the following three images. (Courtesy of Skip Nipper.)

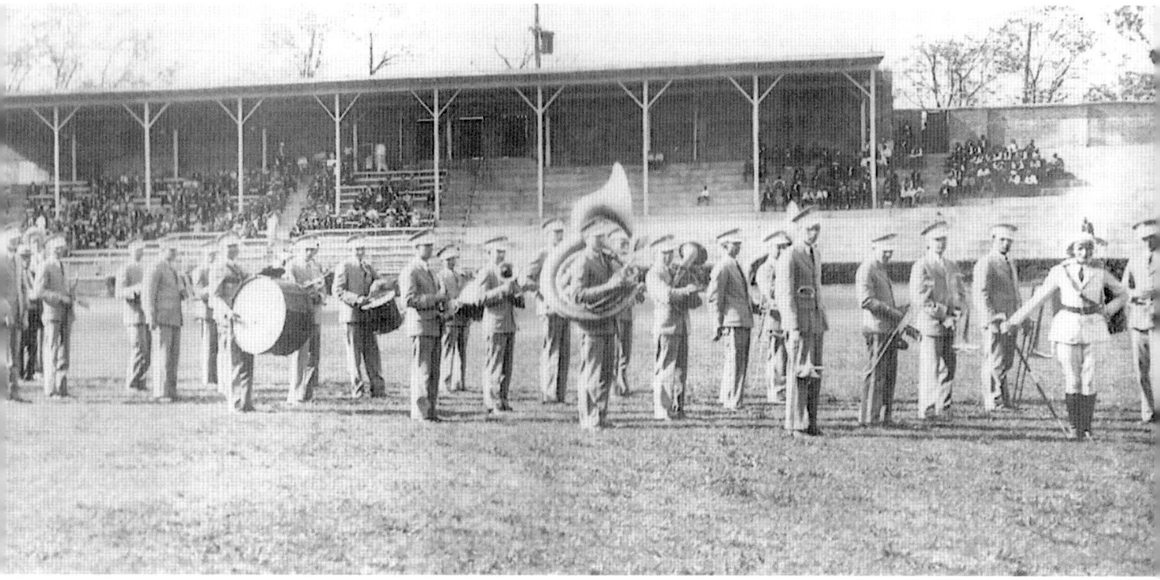

The panoramic image of opening day 1930 deserves a closer look. At one time, the Western Railroad Band was a very popular group in Montgomery. If there was a city or state function where music was required, the Western Railroad Band would be there to play "The Star-Spangled Banner" or whatever appropriate song was needed. The band was led by majorette Margaret Paulin. Her father, Howard Paulin, was a train engineer for the Western Railroad. In later life, Margaret became a statistician for the health department. (Courtesy of Skip Nipper.)

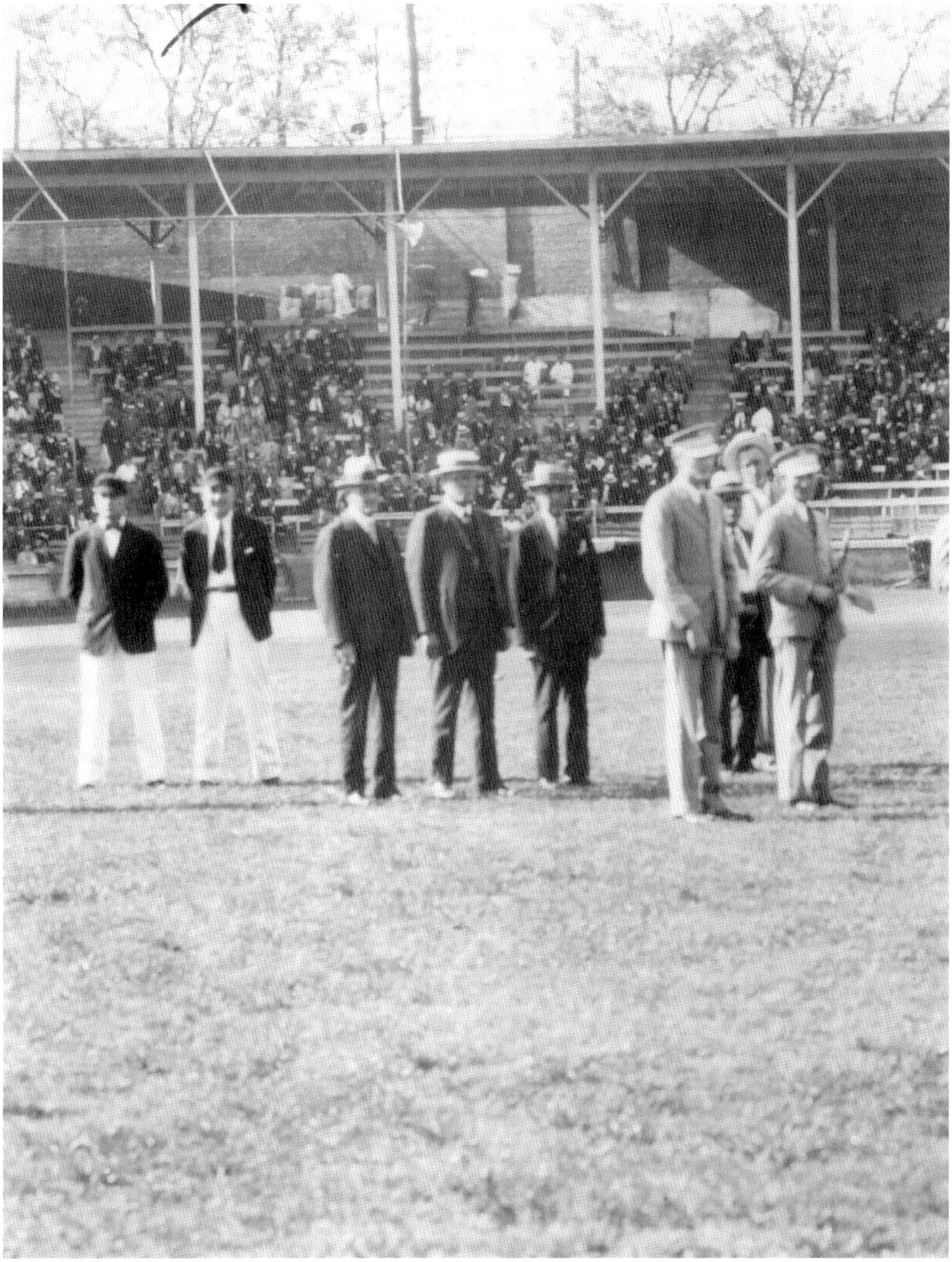

In the center are the dignitaries who cannot be identified individually, but from newspaper accounts, those at the opening day are known. Representing local government was the mayor of Montgomery, Bill Gunter, and governor Alabama Bibb Graves. The president of the league, Cliff Green, was also present. Also attending were team officials Zeke Lewis, club president, and Bob Compton, club vice president. Two of the men are obscured by members of the band. (Courtesy of Skip Nipper.)

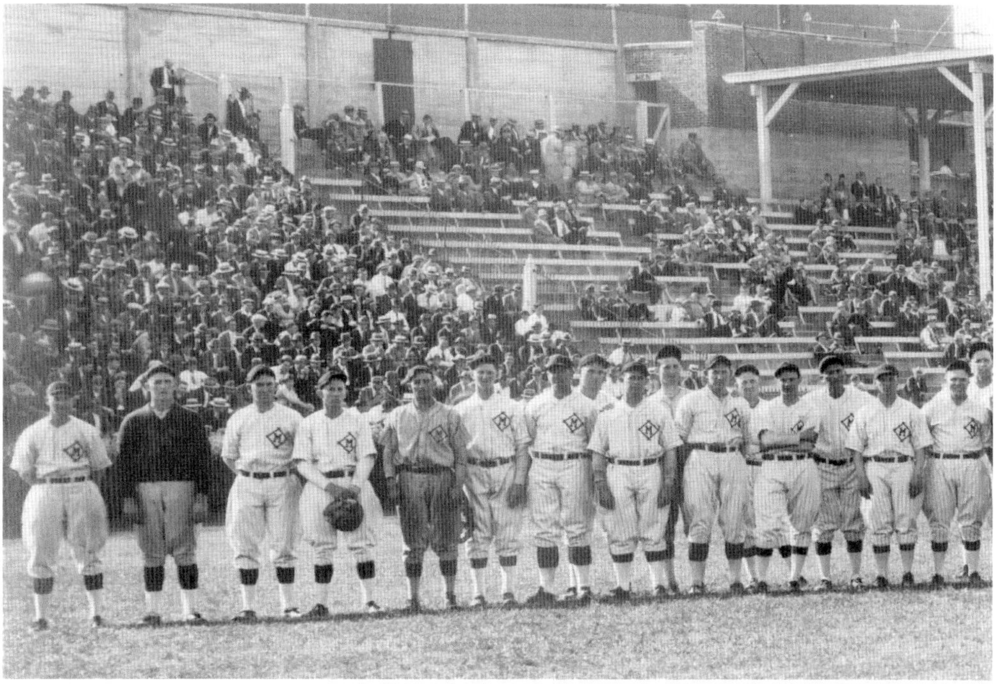

This section of the 1930 opening-day photograph shows the new Montgomery Lions for that season. Most of the players are wearing their freshly laundered white pinstripe uniforms. The few players in old, dark uniforms did not expect to play that day. Sadly, the team and newspaper were expecting a crowd of over 4,000, but only 2,900 showed up for the game. It was 1930, and the Great Depression was taking its hold on the economy, making a day at the ballpark dear to most fans. (Courtesy of Skip Nipper.)

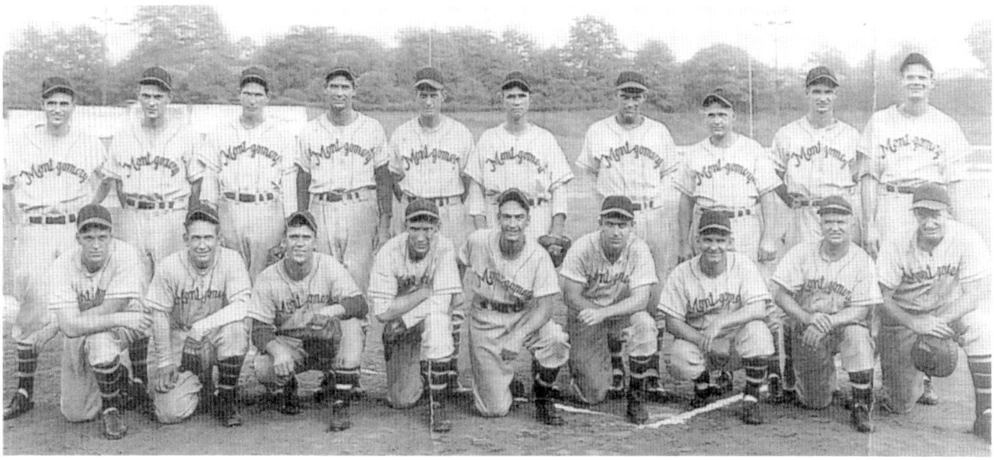

The four best years of Walker's pitching career, with 74 wins in four years, were at Jacksonville, Florida. Roy returned to Montgomery for three more seasons. The year of this photograph is not known, but it would have been taken between 1940 and 1942. Roy Walker is fourth from the left in the first row. Again, at the close of his time in Montgomery, the fans gave Walker a fan appreciation night. (Courtesy of Tommy Horn.)

Bill Pierre was born in Mobile, Alabama, in 1890. He played minor league ball from 1913 to 1929 and managed teams from 1919 to 1930. Pierre came to Montgomery in 1927, and by 1928, he had all the right players to make a run for a championship. Oddly enough, he left after the championship season of 1928 and moved down to a class D team in 1929. (Author's collection.)

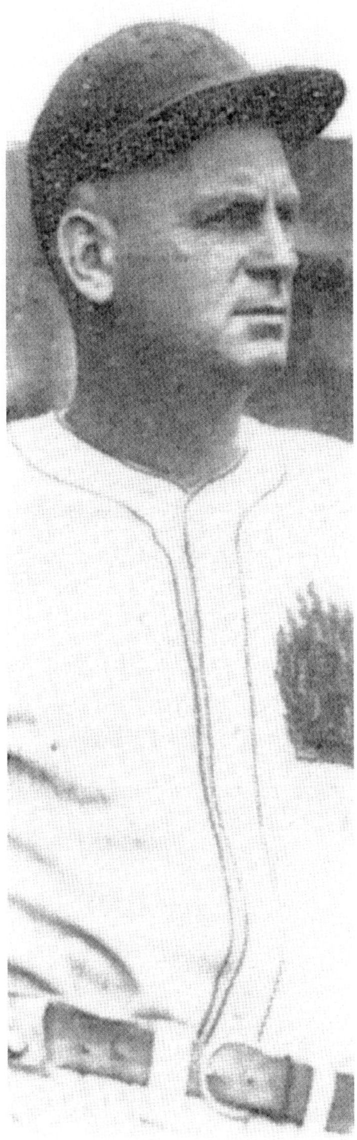

BILL PIERRE
Manager, 1930

Roy Ellam spent almost his entire 19-year minor league career with southern teams. In 1929 and 1930, he was a player-manager, a job title unheard of in professional baseball today. Ellam led the Lions to the second championship in 1929. The next year was supposed to be a repeat, but injuries and bad luck caught up with the Lions. (Author's collection.)

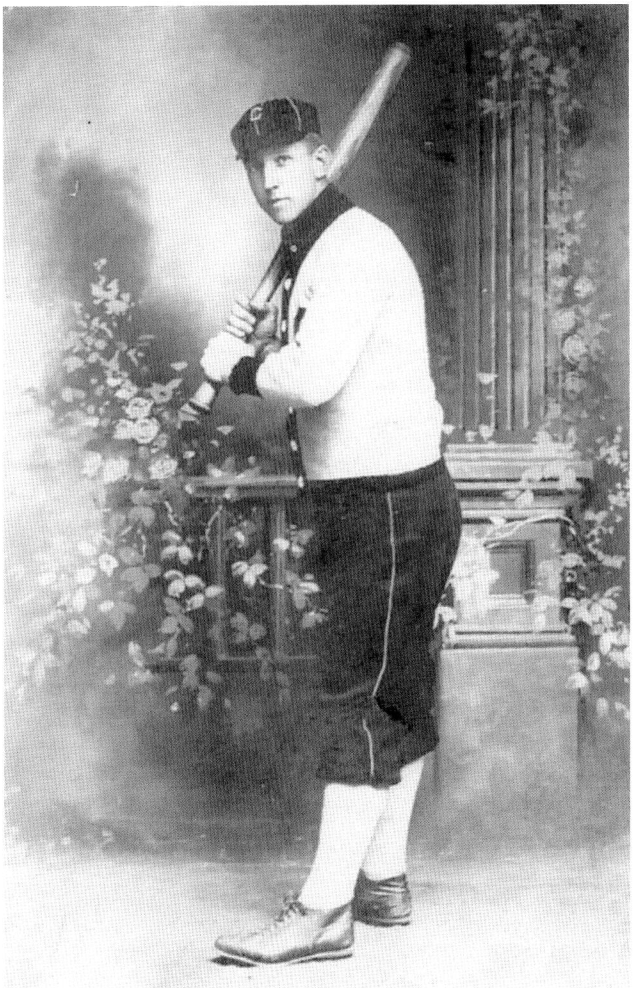

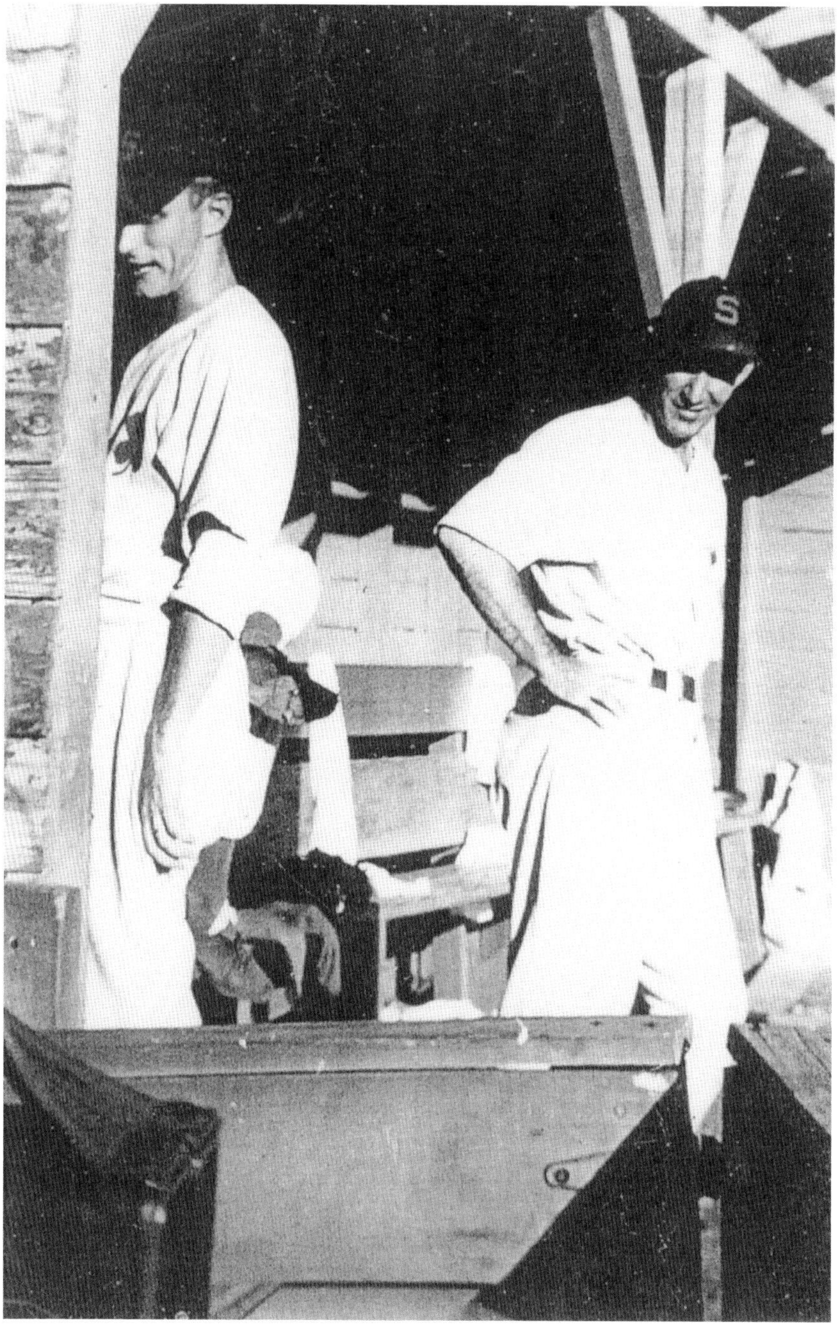

Roy Walker (left) last played for Montgomery in 1942. His career was finally coming to an end. After two injury-riddled seasons with Selma, Walker made one last attempt in 1950 to pitch. He made his first start for the Cloverleafs, only to be hit in the leg with a hard line drive. Fans in the stands heard the crack of the bone breaking! Walker's baseball career ended with him being carried off the field to the local hospital. He was 47 years old, which was well past the age of a minor league player. (Courtesy of Tommy Horn.)

5

Southern Negro Baseball Remembered

All throughout the South, Jim Crow laws denied blacks the right to participate in professional baseball. The black community in most cities took the next best option; they formed their own teams, and later, their own professional baseball leagues.

The earliest-known attempt to form a black baseball league was in 1886. Advertisements were placed in newspapers calling for colored baseball clubs to contact the Southern League of Colored Base Ballists in Jacksonville, Florida. At least 12 teams joined the league, with opening day being set for June 7, 1886. Montgomery's entry in the league was called the Blues. The league folded before the season's end. There was little or no press coverage.

A second attempt was the Colored Baseball League, organized in January 1905. The league held its organizational meetings in Montgomery. The Montgomery Hornets represented the city in this league. It, too, faded by July.

In February 1920, Rube Foster formed the Negro National League. Soon after, Southern black baseball teams met in Atlanta to form the Negro Southern League. Henry Hannon represented Montgomery at these meetings. This league would survive until 1951, and Montgomery was a major member from start to finish.

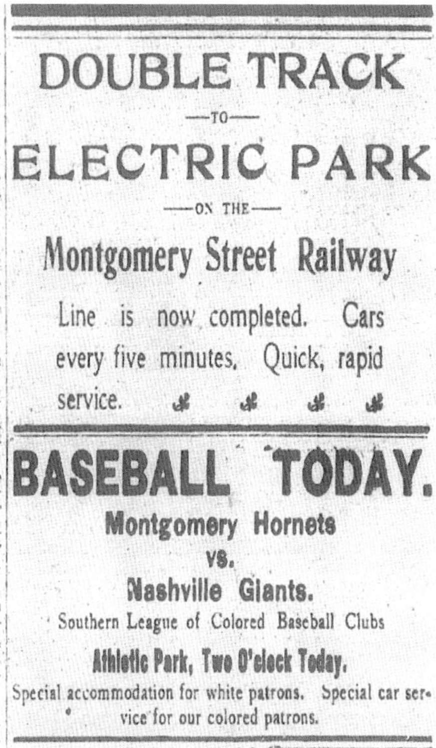

DOUBLE TRACK
—TO—
ELECTRIC PARK
—ON THE—
Montgomery Street Railway
Line is now completed. Cars every five minutes. Quick, rapid service.

BASEBALL TODAY.
Montgomery Hornets
vs.
Nashville Giants.
Southern League of Colored Baseball Clubs
Athletic Park, Two O'clock Today.
Special accommodation for white patrons. Special car service for our colored patrons.

Local newspapers did not cover the results of black baseball games, but they would run advertisements for their games. This advertisement ran in July 1905. Unfortunately, the league folded over a quarantine issue in relation to the team in New Orleans. (Author's collection.)

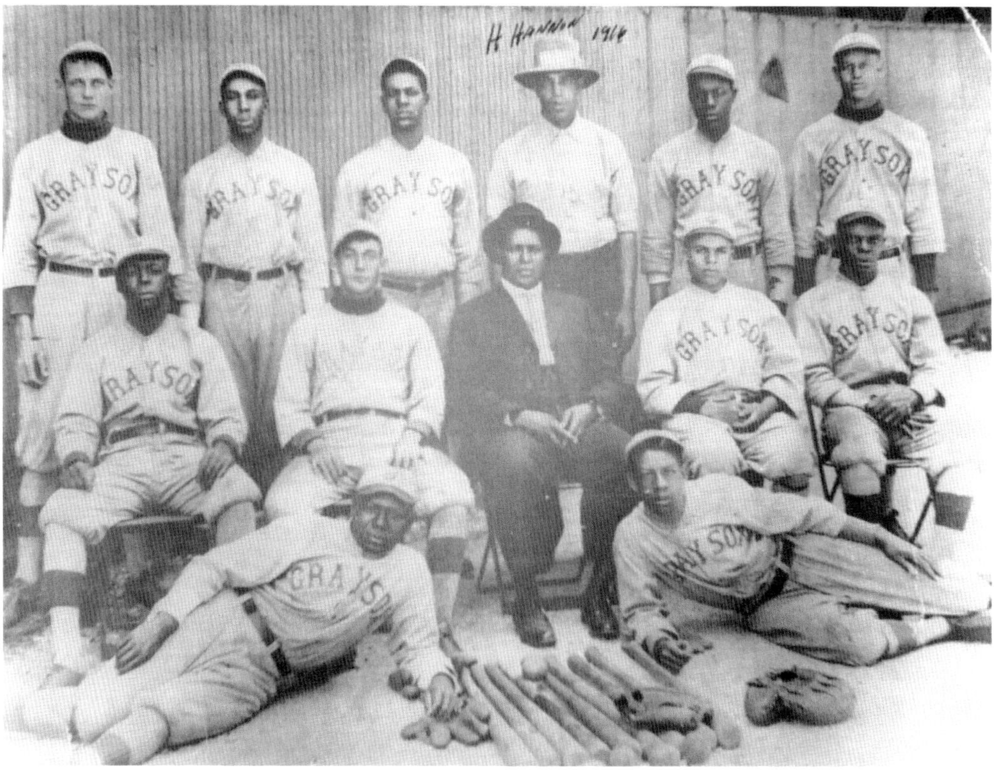

Baseball leagues do not appear overnight, but rather form when a group of well-established teams see the benefits of coming together to form a league to provide structure and stability to the game. This is a rare image of the 1916 Montgomery Grey Sox team, managed by Henry Hannon, one of the pioneers of African American baseball in Montgomery. (Courtesy of Bill Plott.)

John Patton was a major force in early-20th-century African American baseball in Montgomery. Both Patton and Henry Hannon played for the Philadelphia Giants in 1909. Patton was not just a local coach but also a former major league player on the national level. The fact that black players from the Deep South could find their way to professional baseball in the large cities of the Northeast speaks of a formal system of scouting and relationships between lower-level leagues. (Author's collection.)

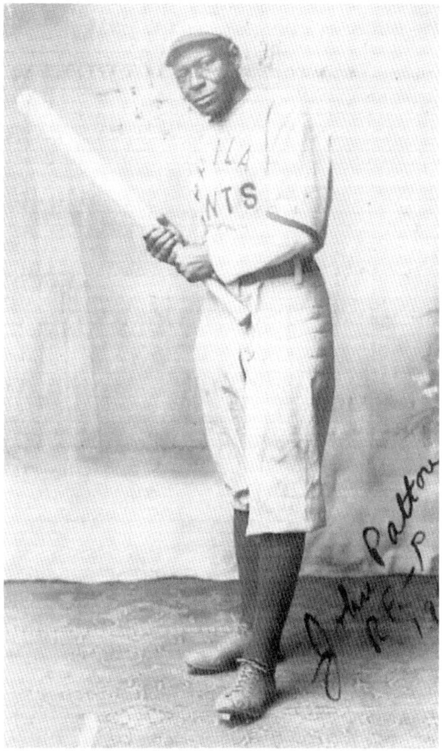

This early 1920s Montgomery Grey Sox team picture was taken in front of the South Holt Street Baseball Park. This is the only known image of club president John Staples (standing at center), the patriarch of African American baseball in Montgomery. The photograph also offers a rare glimpse of Marion "Daddy" Cunningham (seated, second from left) and his son Herman (seated second from right). (Courtesy of Bill Plott.)

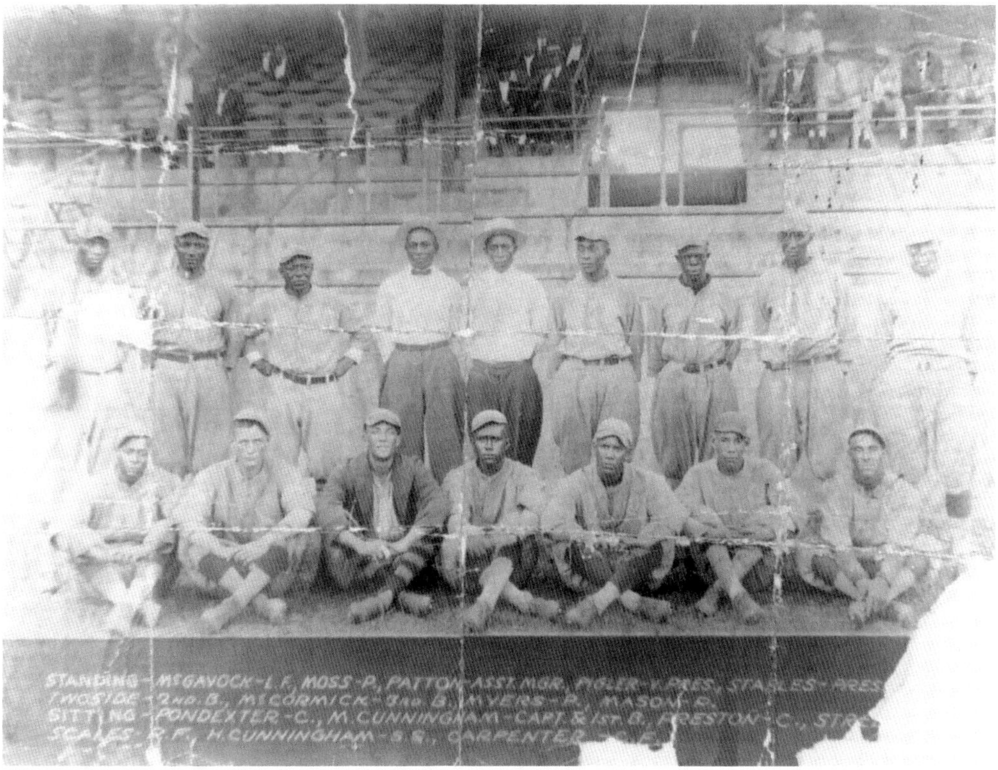

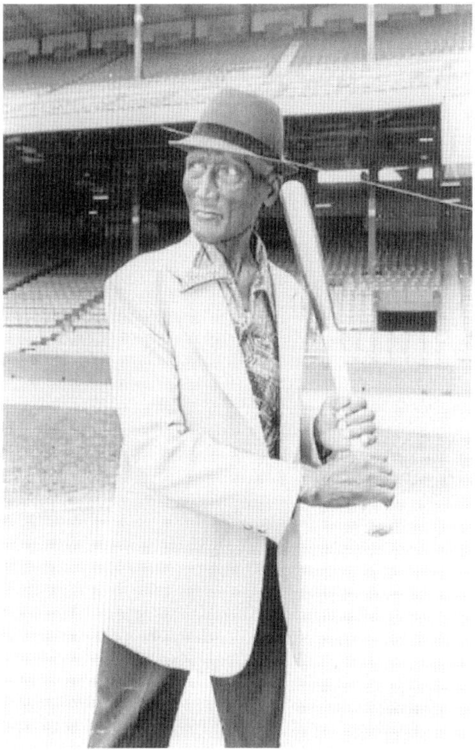

Norman "Turkey" Stearns was inducted into the National Baseball Hall of Fame in 2000. He is the all-time leader in Negro League baseball with 176 career home runs. After one season with the Nashville Giants of his hometown, Stearns played for the Montgomery Grey Sox before moving to the Detroit Stars. Bill James ranked Stearns as the 25th greatest baseball player of all time. That places Stearns in some very good company. (Author's collection.)

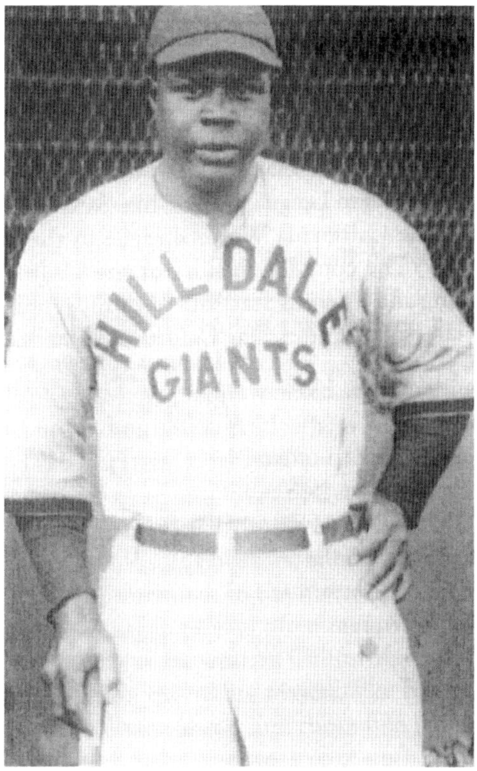

John Beckwith was one of the early power hitters in the Negro League. His professional career started with Montgomery in 1916. He soon returned to his hometown of Chicago to play for several area teams. He is remembered for his tape-measure home runs and his 38-inch bat. (Courtesy of the Center for Negro League Baseball Research.)

George "Tubby" Scales was born in Talladega, Alabama, in 1900. His professional baseball career would span over 30 years. Like many African American Alabama-born baseball players, Scales began his professional career with the Montgomery Grey Sox. Scales was admired for his ability to make hits off the really great curve ball pitchers. (Courtesy of the Center for Negro League Baseball Research.)

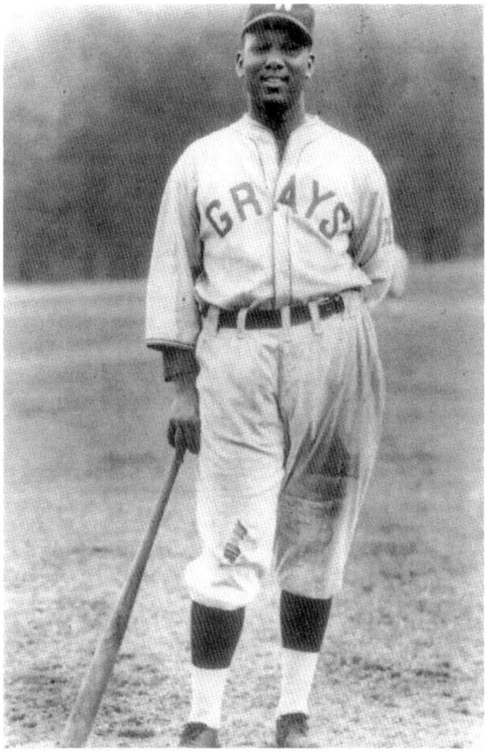

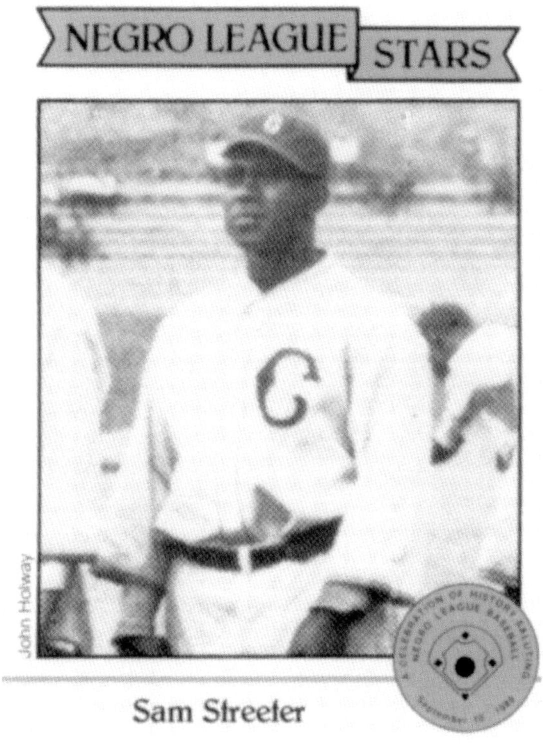

It is amazing how many accomplished baseball players played for Montgomery in just the two years of 1920 and 1921. Another of these exceptional players is Sam Streeter. In his first year of professional baseball with Montgomery at the age of 19, Streeter threw a no-hitter! He is well remembered as the starting pitcher of the East-West All-Star Game of 1936. (Author's collection.)

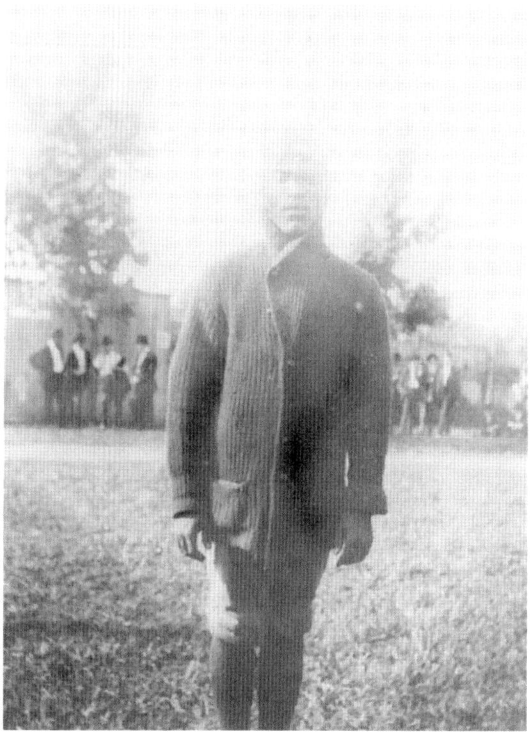

The story of Claude "Steel Arm" Dickey is a tragic one. After only three brief seasons in professional Negro League baseball, he was killed in a senseless act, dying at the age of 26. Dickey was destined for a long and productive career before being cut down in his prime. He was a member of the 1921 Montgomery Grey Sox. (Courtesy of the Center for Negro League Baseball Research.)

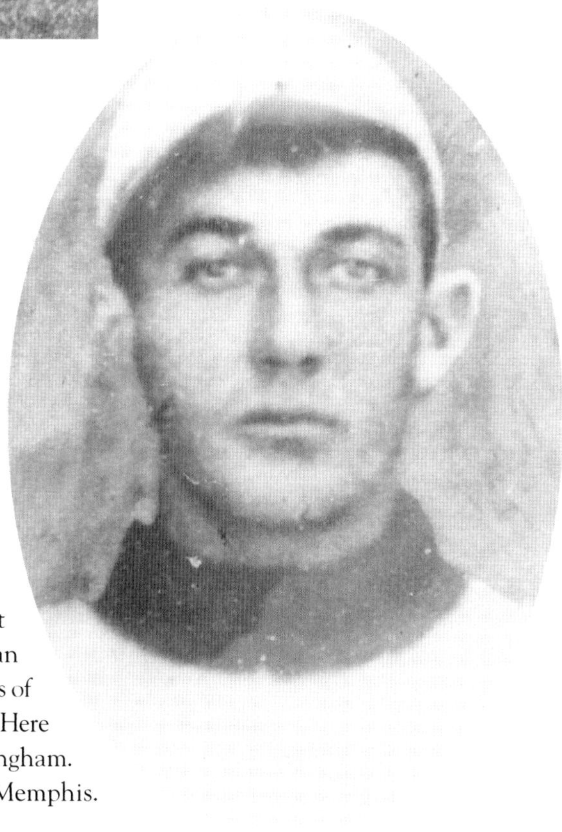

If Montgomery has a first family of Negro League baseball, it would be the Cunningham family, led by Marion "Red" Cunningham. He also played for the Memphis Red Sox. The 1921 Montgomery Grey Sox featured Marion at first, son Johnny at second, and son Herman at shortstop. Unfortunately, quality images of these early players are very difficult to find. Here is an early photograph of Johnny Cunningham. Like his father, Johnny also played for Memphis. (Courtesy of Bill Plott.)

Paul Hardy got his start with the Montgomery team in 1931. Hardy came from Meridian, Mississippi, and played 14 years in Negro League baseball. Six seasons were spent with the Black Barons of Birmingham as a catcher. (Courtesy of the Center for Negro League Baseball Research.)

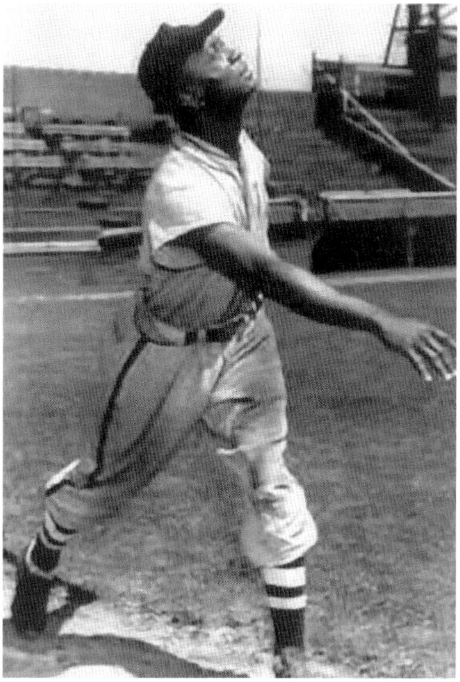

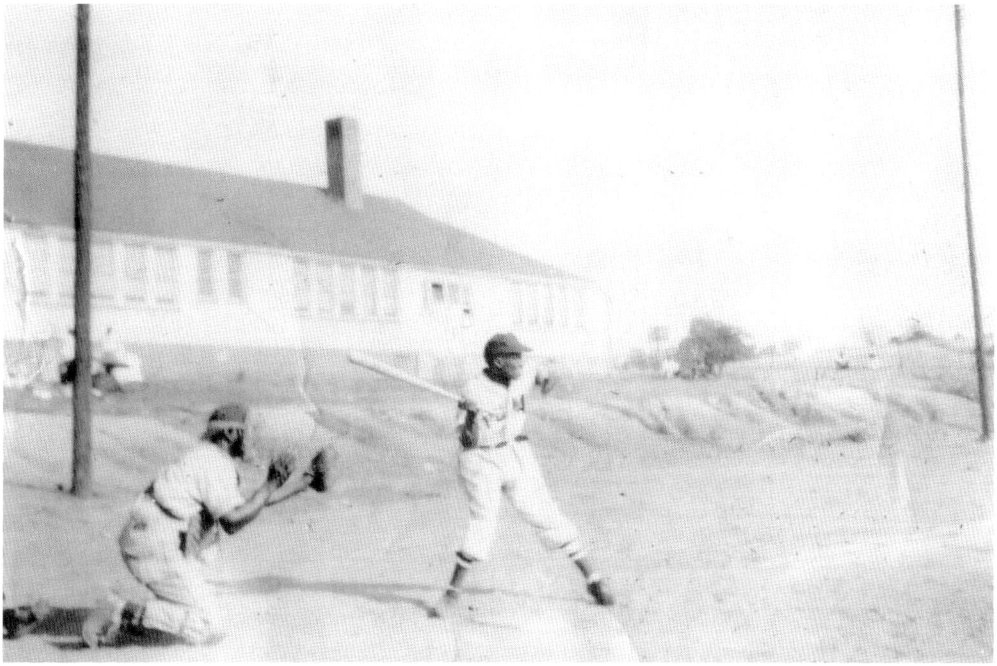

One of the most popular players in the Negro Southern League was Forest "One-Wing" Maddox. In 1922 and 1926, Maddox played for Montgomery. As a child, he lost his left arm in an accident. He pitched some, but mainly played the outfield. Fans delighted in watching him catch a fly ball, then throw the ball in the air, remove his glove, catch the ball, and throw it in one easy motion. Maddox died at the age of 31 in his native Atlanta. (Courtesy of Bill Plott.)

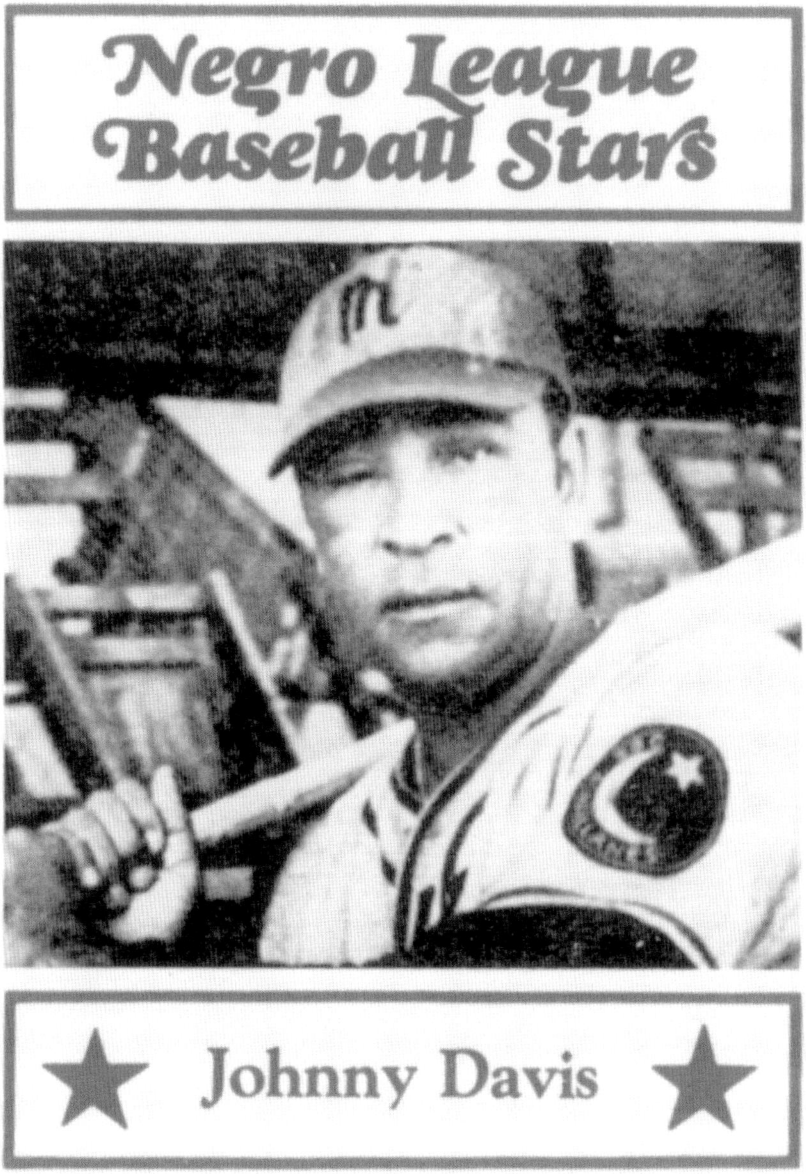

When it came to the integration of professional baseball in the South, the South Atlantic League led the way in bringing black players into the league. In 1953, the Jacksonville Braves were the first, adding Hank Aaron and Felix Mantilla. The Savannah Indians would follow less than a month later with Junior Reedy and Albert Israel. The next season, Montgomery chose two players to join the Montgomery Rebels, Johnny Davis, a big power-hitting outfielder, and George Handy, a sure-fielding second baseman who had played for the Memphis Red Sox in 1947. There were no major boycotts or protests to block their playing for Montgomery, but they still had to endure racial taunts and segregation in hotels and restaurants. Bad treatment would always be worse on the road. Unfortunately, there is no quality image of George Handy. (Author's collection.)

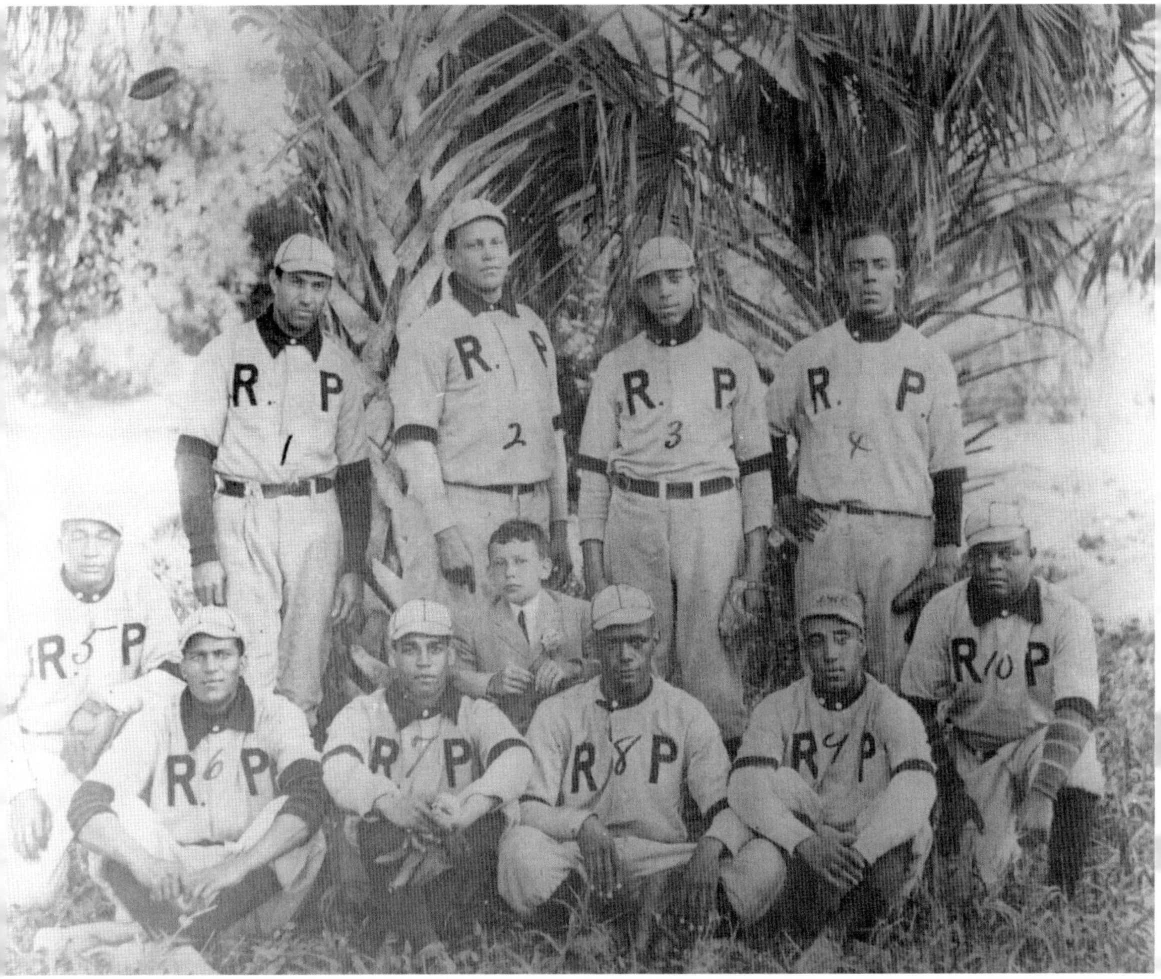

For most professional baseball players, the salary for playing baseball for a season was not sufficient to support them for the entire year. A second job or profession was required. For some players, like Montgomery's Henry Hannon, a winter job at a high-class hotel in Florida as a waiter was the perfect match to his baseball career. Hannon is pictured here seated third from the left, a player for the Royal Ponciana Hotel. At one time, the hotel was the world's largest wooden structure; during the Great Depression, it was closed and subsequently razed. (Courtesy of Bill Plott.)

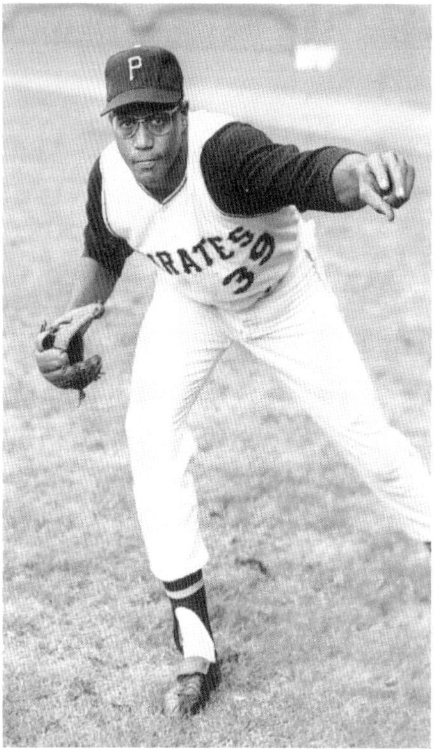

In 1931, Robert Veale was a pitcher for the Montgomery Grey Sox with mixed results. Veale also pitched for the Birmingham team. Little is known or remembered about Robert Veale's baseball career, but he left a legacy through his son. In the mid-1960s, Bob Veale Jr. pitched for the Pittsburgh Pirates. His performance was equal to or better than that of the most dominating pitchers of the time, like Sandy Koufax and Bob Gibson. (Author's collection.)

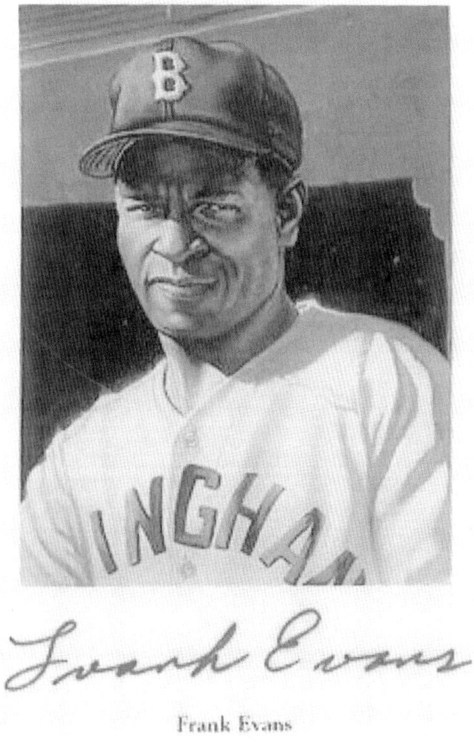

Frank Evans was born in Linden, Alabama. By age 16, he was playing baseball in the Negro League. Teams he played on included the Memphis Red Sox, Kansas City Monarchs, Cleveland Buckeyes, Birmingham Black Barons, Philadelphia Stars, and Chattanooga Choo-Choos. By 1954, Evans was playing minor league ball in the Evangeline League. He would later serve as a manager in the Negro League. After he retired as a player, Evans was an instructor, coach, and scout for several major league teams. Evans lived in Montgomery after he retired and was very active in the Alabama Negro League Ballplayers Association, which is a group for former Negro League baseball players, until his death in 2012. (Author's collection.)

6

Sluggers, Hurlers, and Rookies

The Baseball history of Montgomery spans a period of 124 years. During that time, the teams have had 12 different nicknames, not to mention the ones the press added. Montgomery has played in seven different baseball leagues. Unfortunately, many of those teams underachieved and do not merit mentioning in this book. At the same time, many individual players excelled during their time in Montgomery or went on to great success in the major leagues.

This chapter provides a basic biography of some of the most notable players and managers who passed through Montgomery. In all, Montgomery Minor League Baseball did what it was designed to do—give young players the opportunity to learn and mature while they improved their baseball skills enough to take them to the next level.

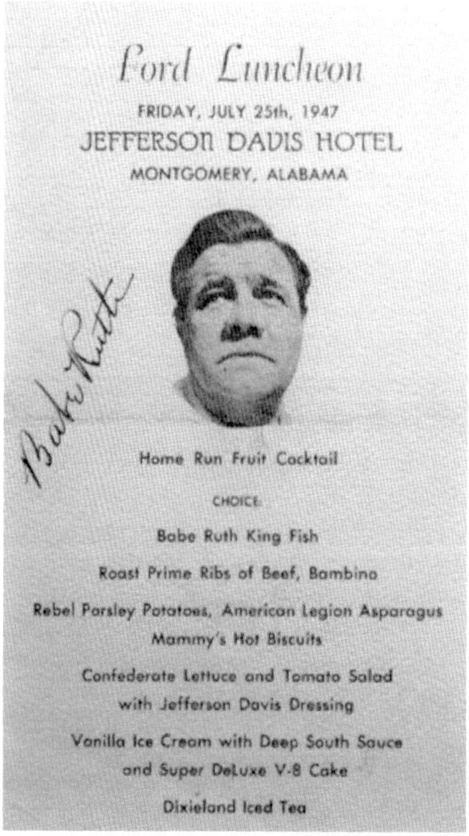

Ford Luncheon

FRIDAY, JULY 25th, 1947

JEFFERSON DAVIS HOTEL

MONTGOMERY, ALABAMA

Babe Ruth

Home Run Fruit Cocktail

CHOICE

Babe Ruth King Fish

Roast Prime Ribs of Beef, Bambino

Rebel Parsley Potatoes, American Legion Asparagus

Mammy's Hot Biscuits

Confederate Lettuce and Tomato Salad
with Jefferson Davis Dressing

Vanilla Ice Cream with Deep South Sauce
and Super DeLuxe V-8 Cake

Dixieland Iced Tea

Every baseball town has a Babe Ruth story. Ruth visited Montgomery several times, including once about a year before his death. Ruth came to speak at the state American Legion Championship, where he attended a luncheon at the Jefferson Davis Hotel, rode in a parade, and saw a game. At the airport, he was greeted by several hundred fans and was driven to the hotel in a special Lincoln convertible. As the car was leaving the airport, a young boy waved to Ruth, who had the car stop so he could shake the boy's hand. The newspaper mentioned this kind act by Ruth but did not include the boy's name. Among those who met Ruth at the airport was Eddie Wells, a Montgomery resident and old teammate of Ruth's. This place card from the luncheon was signed by Ruth. Note the baseball- and Southern-themed dishes, like "Home Run Fruit Cocktail" and "Confederate Lettuce and Tomato Salad with Jefferson Davis Dressing." One of these cards appeared on *Antiques Roadshow* in 2012 with an appraised value of $10,000. (Both, author's collection.)

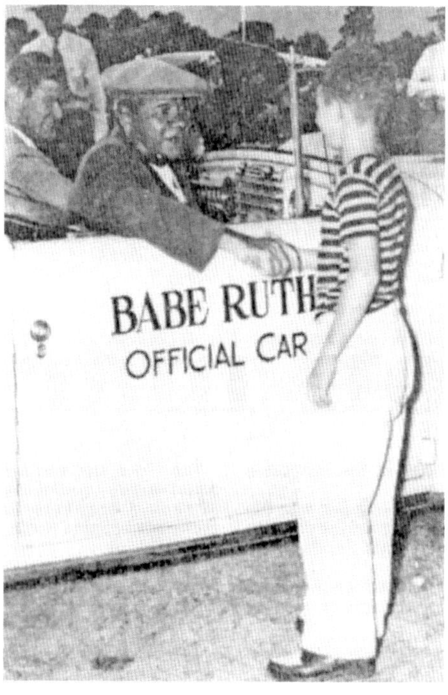

Harry Walker spent parts of two seasons with Montgomery in 1938 and 1939. He went on to win the National League batting title in 1947. His brother Dixie Walker also won a National League batting title in 1944, making them the only brothers to accomplish that amazing feat. Harry Walker (pictured) would later manage in the major leagues and was known for his ability to coach players needing batting instruction. After his retirement from professional baseball, he founded the baseball program at the University of Alabama at Birmingham. (Author's collection.)

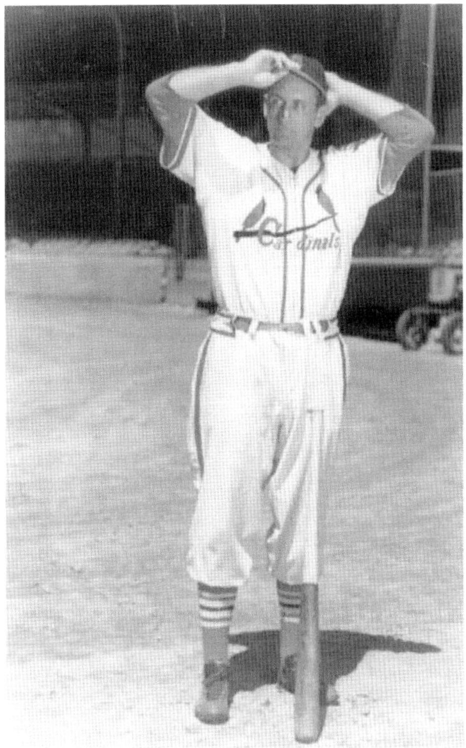

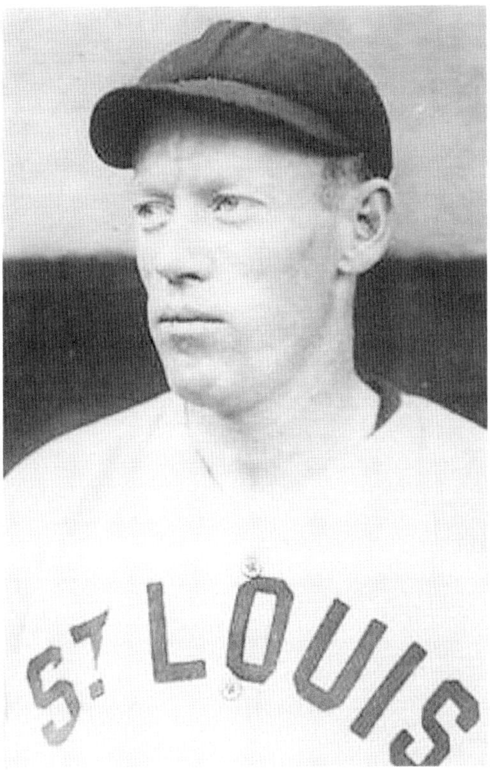

Most avid baseball fans are well aware of the famous brothers Dixie and Harry Walker. The famous Walker brothers were the second generation of their family to play Major League Baseball. Dixie and Harry's father, also known as Dixie, played in the major leagues. Dixie Sr.'s brother Ernie (pictured) also played for Montgomery in 1912 and 1913 before going on to play for the St. Louis Browns. Ernie's nephew Harry would also play for Montgomery in 1938 and 1939. The Walkers were a true Alabama baseball family. (Author's collection.)

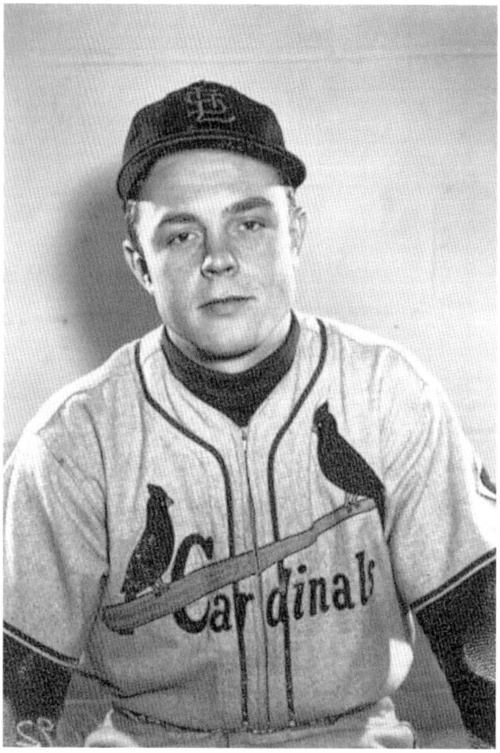

Montgomery baseball has produced its share of famous major league managers. After eight years of drifting around the minor leagues, Earl Weaver was with the Montgomery Rebels for the 1956 season. Around mid-season, the team was moved to Knoxville. Soon, the manager quit, and Weaver was named manager. Weaver never made it to the major leagues as a player, but he made it to the hall of fame as a manager. (Author's collection.)

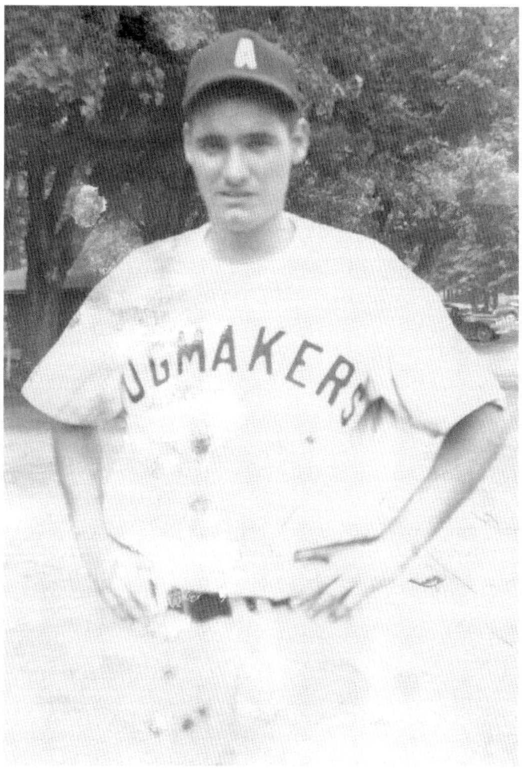

Larry Andersen was a backup catcher for the Montgomery team from 1954 to 1958. In 1955, the team had a knuckleball pitcher who was very difficult to catch for. The manager began letting Andersen catch the knuckleballs on all his starts. Andersen reasoned that his manager must have a lot of faith in his ability. Only later did his manager tell him he was more concerned about the number one catcher getting hurt! Baseball can be a humbling game. (Courtesy of Larry Andersen.)

Albert "Albie" Pearson was one of the smallest players to play Major League Baseball in the 1950s; he was only five feet, six inches tall. During his one season with the Montgomery team in 1955, Pearson hit .305, which earned him a promotion to the Pacific Coast League the next year. In October 1960, Pearson was drafted by the Los Angeles Angels, becoming part of the original Angels team. After his baseball career, Pearson became an ordained minister working with underprivileged youth. (Author's collection.)

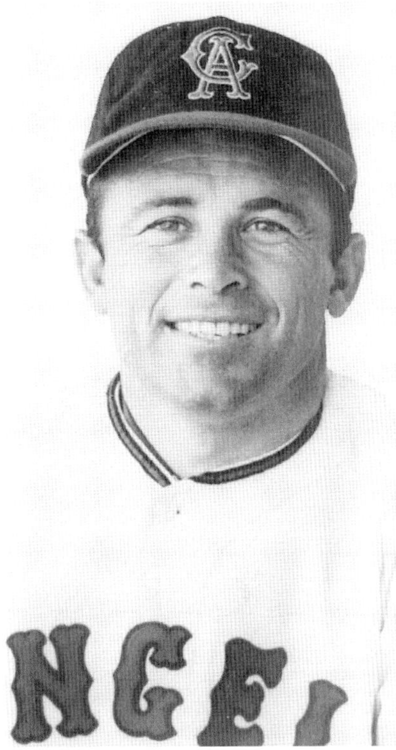

In 1955, Earl Wilson pitched for Montgomery in only his third season of professional baseball. He played for Montgomery during the 1950s when a black baseball player was not an everyday occurrence. In 1959, he became the second black player for the Boston Red Sox, the last major league team to integrate. He was the first black pitcher on the Red Sox team. In 1962, Wilson pitched a no-hit game and also hit a home run. Only two other players have accomplished this rare feat! (Author's collection.)

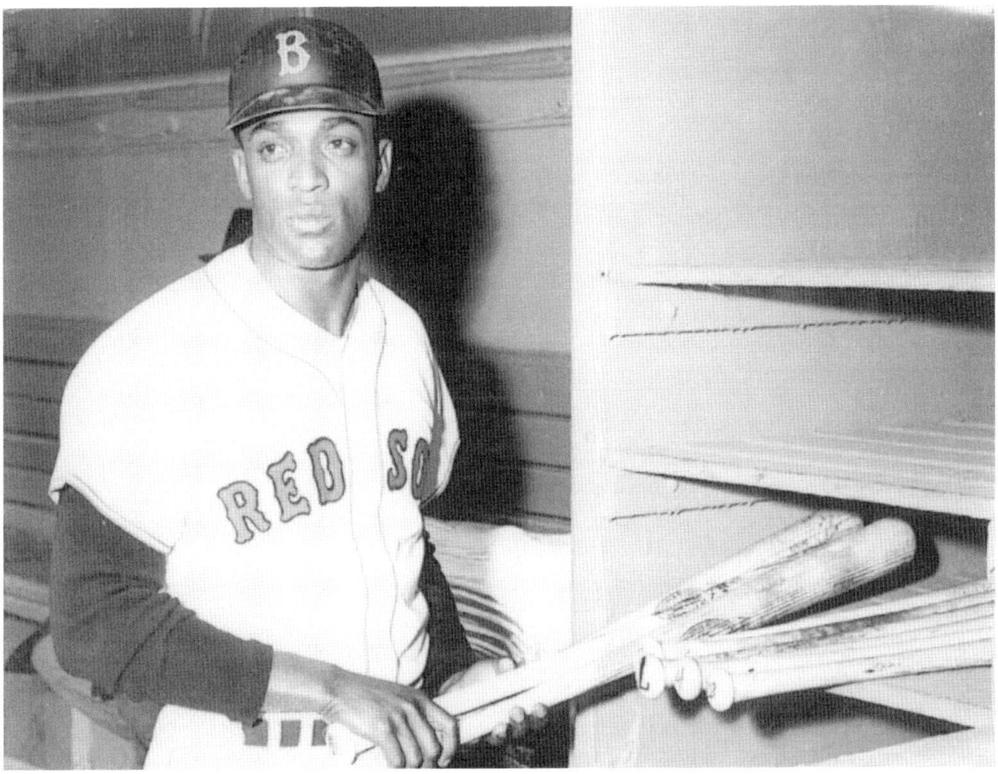

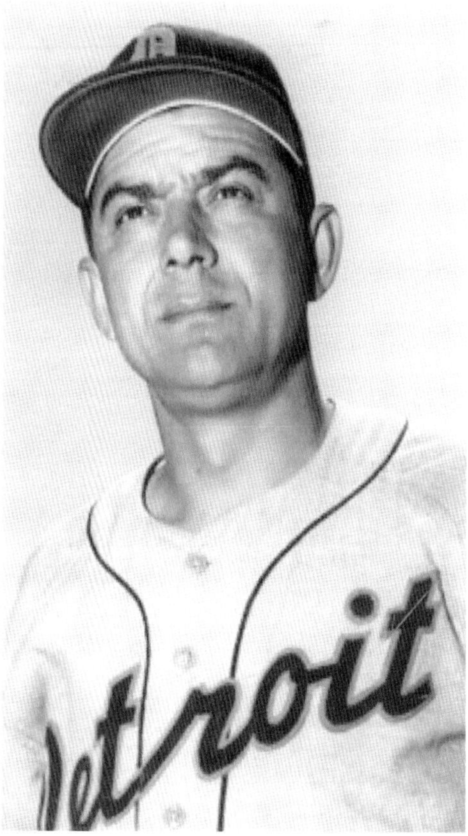

Charlie Metro had a short three-year career as a player in Major League Baseball. It was as a manager that Metro left his mark on professional baseball. Metro was a manager for 18 years, which included being manager of the Chicago Cubs and the Kansas City Royals. He was manager of the Montgomery team from 1950 to 1953. To last four years as manager of a team at any level is impressive. Metro helped guide many young players to successful careers in baseball. (Author's collection.)

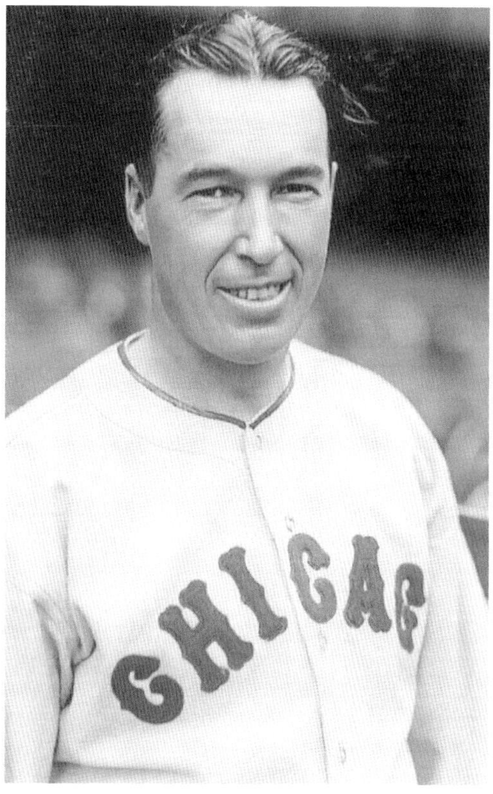

George "Mule" Haas had a very impressive 12-year career in Major League Baseball as part of a Philadelphia Athletics team that rivaled the New York Yankees in the late 1920s and 1930s. His most memorable accomplishment came in the 1929 World Series against the Chicago Cubs. In game four with Philadelphia down 8-0, Haas hit a three-run inside-the-park home run to spark a rally by the Athletics, who scored 10 runs to win the game. He also hit a home run in the ninth inning of game five, which Philadelphia went on to win. Haas came to Montgomery in 1949 to manage the Rebels. This was only his second year as a manager. He was also known as one of the best bench jockeys in his time. (Author's collection.)

Ray Berres came to Montgomery in only his second year of professional baseball in 1930. He was known as a fine defensive catcher. After Montgomery, Berres moved up to Birmingham and then to the Brooklyn Dodgers. He had an 11-year career in the majors followed by 17 seasons as the pitching coach for the Chicago White Sox. (Author's collection.)

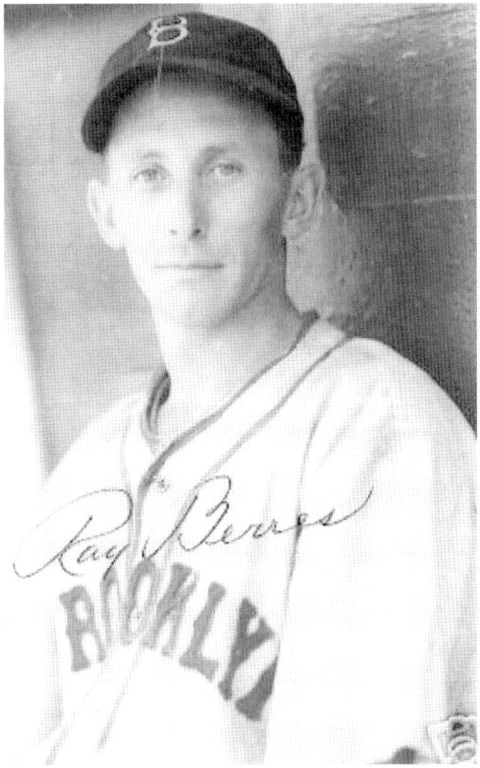

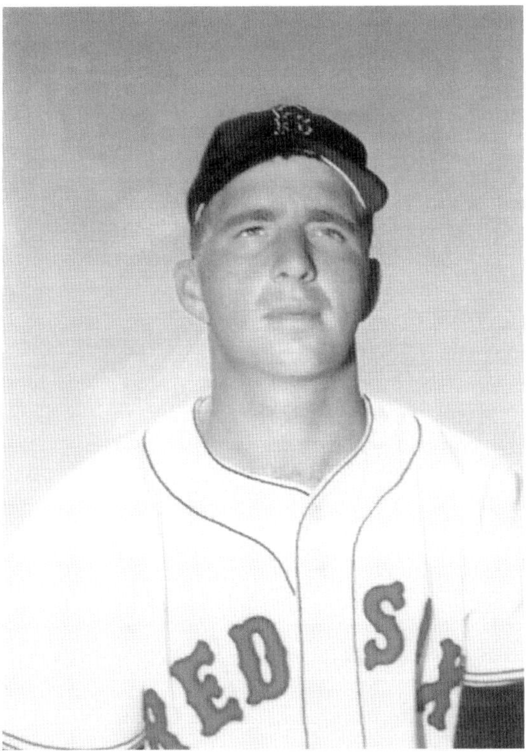

Guy Morton Jr. (pictured) was the son of Guy Morton Sr., a pitcher for the 1920 Cleveland Indians and teammate of Jim Bagby. Guy Jr. also became a professional baseball player. After a very good year at Greensboro in the Carolina League, he was called up by the Boston Red Sox at the end of the season. He was sent into a game as a pinch hitter and struck out. This would be his only time at bat in the major leagues. In 1954, Morton was sent to Montgomery, where he had a good year. Unfortunately, he spent the rest of his career with several different Southern Association teams until 1960, when he retired. After baseball, Morton became a Baptist minister in Ohio. At least he got one at-bat. (Author's collection.)

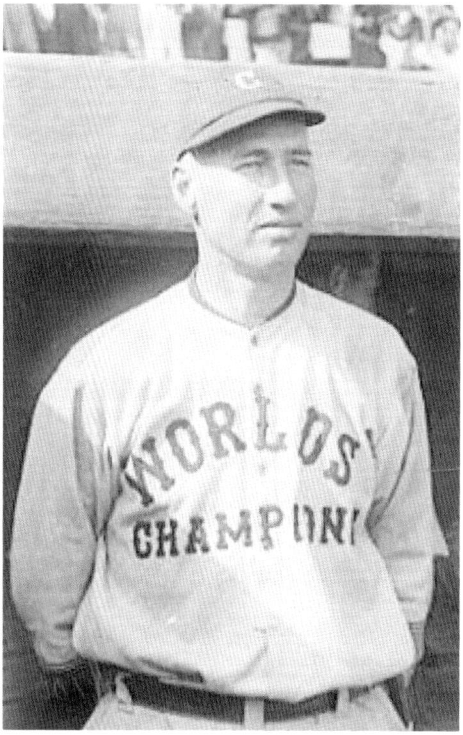

Jim Bagby Sr. spent parts of three seasons learning the art of pitching in Montgomery from 1911 to 1913. By 1916, he was a starter for the Cleveland Indians. His finest season was 1920, when he not only won 31 games but also helped Cleveland win the World Series over Brooklyn. Jim's son Jim Bagby Jr. also played Major League Baseball. After Bagby Sr.'s baseball career was over, he was an umpire and referee in sports. (Author's collection.)

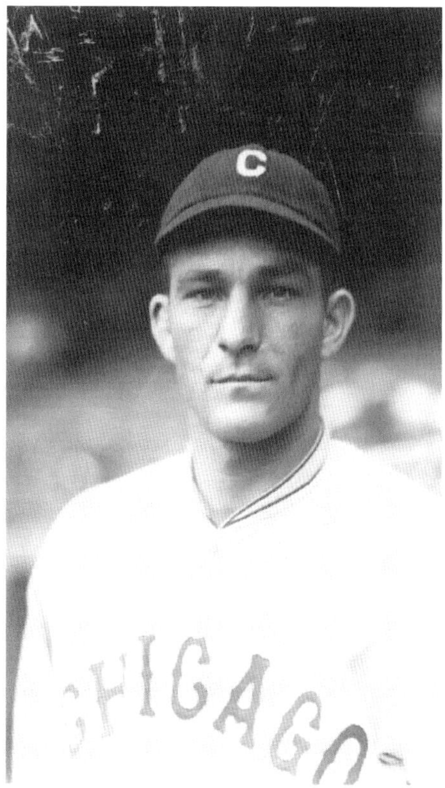

Riggs Stephenson was known as the "Southern Gentleman." In Alabama, he is remembered as one of the greatest fullbacks ever to play college football. The 1920 Alabama football team produced seven future Major League Baseball players. Stephenson played 14 seasons in the majors with a lifetime batting average of .336, certainly a hall of fame–type career. Stephenson ended his baseball career by managing the Montgomery team in 1939. He also inserted himself as a pinch hitter a few times that season. (Author's collection.)

Kirby Higbe had a 12-year major league career as a pitcher. His best years were with the Brooklyn Dodgers. Higbe had a bittersweet year in 1941. During the regular season, he won 21 games and led the National League in almost all pitching categories; however, the fourth game of the World Series is why he is remembered. In his only World Series start, Higbe had a 4-3 lead over the Yankees in the ninth inning. Then, tragedy struck when catcher Mickey Owens allowed a third strike to get past him, which allowed Tommy Henrich to reach first base and the Yankees to win the game and the series. In 1951, Higbe found himself trying to pitch his way back to the major leagues. He played in 1951 and 1952 with Montgomery. There would be no return to the majors for Higbe, and 1953 was his last year in professional baseball. (Author's collection.)

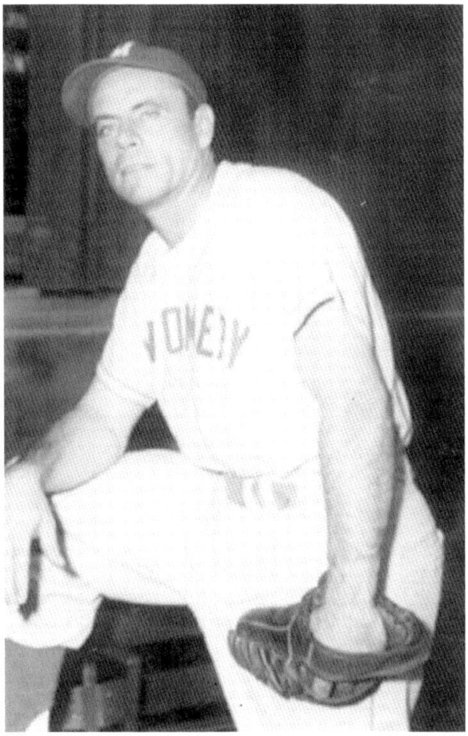

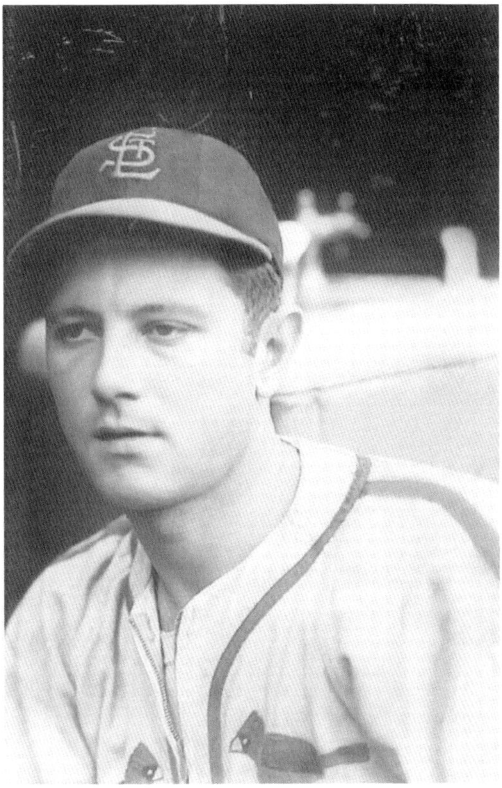

Johnny Beazley was born in Nashville, Tennessee. At age 21, he was with the Montgomery team in 1939. In three short years, he won 20 games for the St. Louis Cardinals. Beazley won two games in the World Series against the New York Yankees, including the deciding fifth game. A sore arm greatly shortened his career. (Author's collection.)

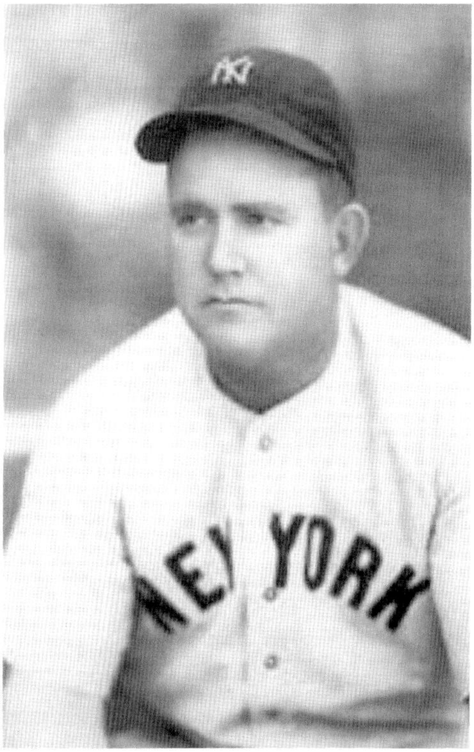

Ivy Paul Andrews from Dora, Alabama, pitched in the major leagues for parts of 10 years. Of course, his nickname was "Poison Ivy." His best season was 1935 with a 13-7 record for the St. Louis Browns. The most memorable time of his career was his first three years with the New York Yankees, being a part of the great Yankee team of Ruth and Gehrig. Andrews came to Montgomery in 1940. He went on to coach and manage a few years before returning to Walker County to retire from baseball. (Author's collection.)

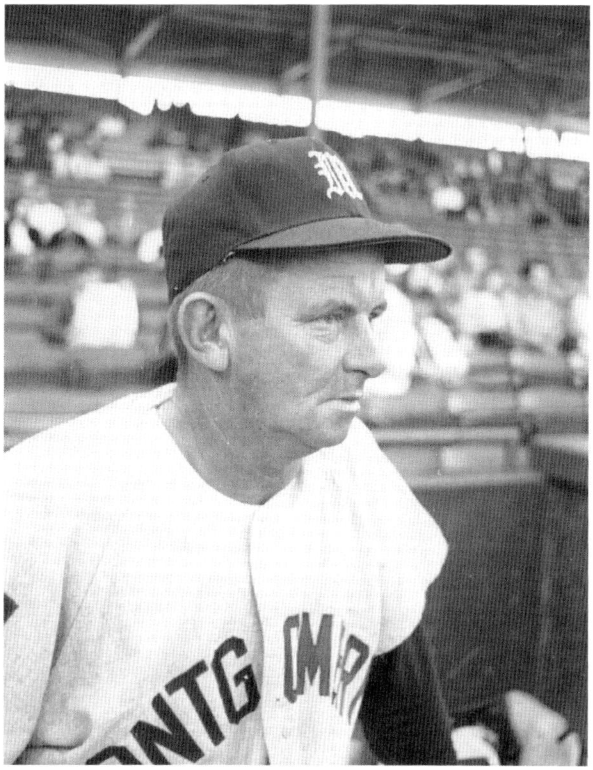

Wayne Blackburn was a career minor league player, as were many players who became managers. Blackburn was the manager of the Montgomery Rebels for two seasons in 1965 and 1966. Montgomery was part of the Detroit Tigers farm system, and 1965 was their first year back in the Southern League. Sadly for Blackburn, Detroit did not have the quality of players during his time with the Rebels. They would soon shuffle through Montgomery. After two losing seasons, Blackburn moved to the Florida League for Detroit. (Author's collection.)

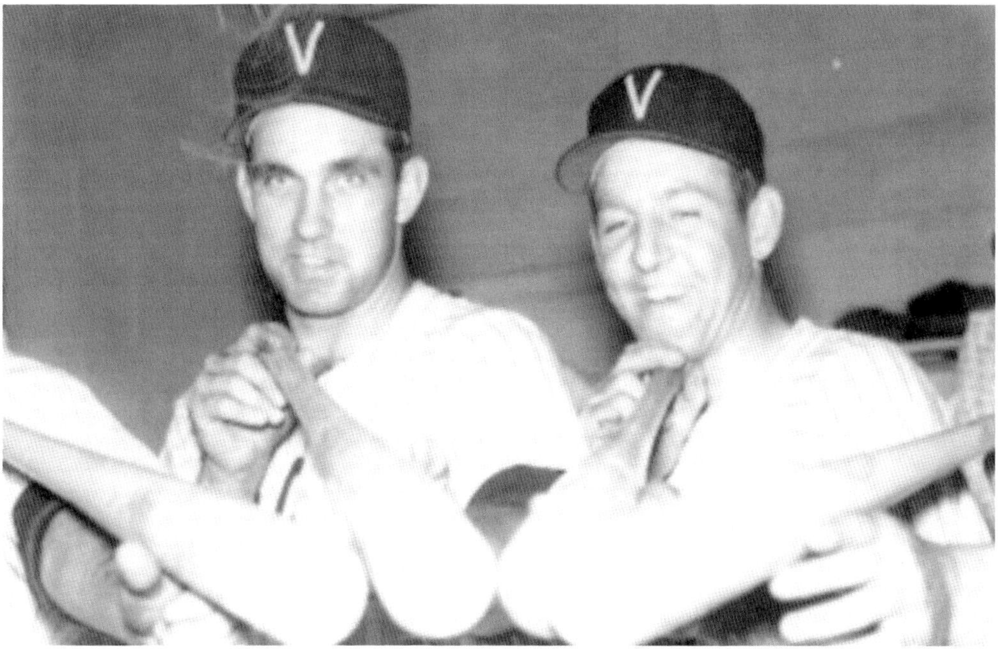

Dick Greco's baseball career spanned 12 seasons, all in the minor leagues. Two of his best years were with the Montgomery Grays of the South Atlantic League. In 1951 and 1952, he led the league in home runs, and in 1952, he was the league's most valuable player. In all, Greco hit 333 home runs, never getting a chance in the major leagues. While playing for Tacoma, his hometown team in 1950, Greco was married at home plate to Evelyn Moore. Like many World War II–era players, Greco may have lost his best years serving his country. He is on the right in this image. (Author's collection.)

One of the most fascinating careers noted in this book was that of Bud Lively. He was the son of a former major league pitcher, Jack Lively, who roomed with Ty Cobb. Bud was signed to play baseball while still a teenager. He spent part of the 1942 season with Montgomery and then started the 1943 season at Birmingham, leaving soon after to enlist in the army. During World War II, he served under Gen. George Patton. When the war was over, he spent three seasons with Cincinnati, which included a one-hit game pitched against a Jackie Robinson–led Brooklyn Dodgers. After baseball, Lively went to work for NASA in Huntsville and worked on the team with Dr. Wernher Von Braun, helping to put a man on the moon. His accomplishments in his amazing life are too many to include. (Author's collection.)

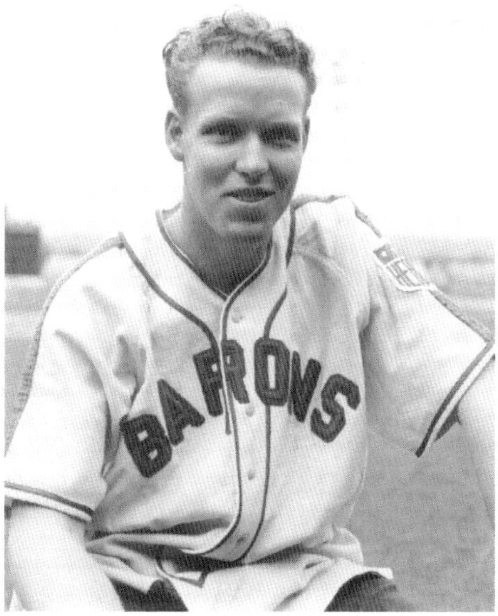

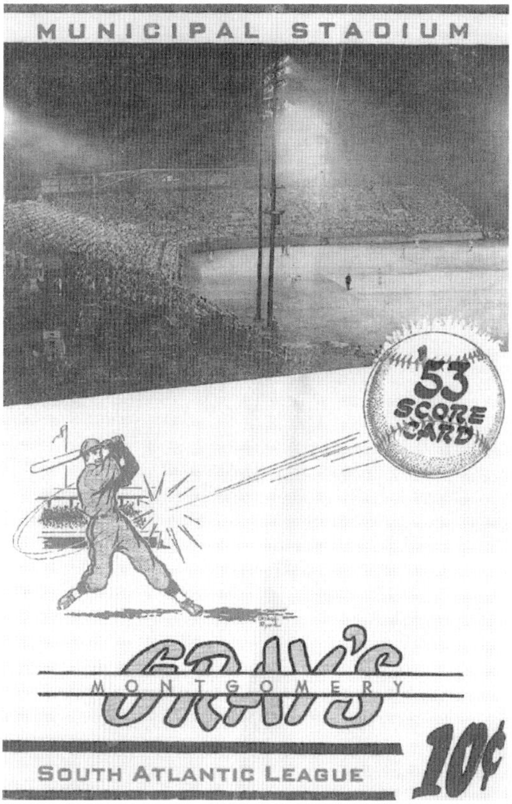

The 1953 scorecard at left speaks of a special event that happened that year. It would be 1954 before the Montgomery team would have a black player, but another important event happened in 1953 when, for the first time, a black player performed in a game in Montgomery against the Grays. That player was Hank Aaron. This 1953 Grays scorecard shows a packed house at Patterson Field. The image below shows Hank Aaron with the Jacksonville Braves as he looked during the season he played against Montgomery. Note that Aaron was an infielder when he originally broke into professional baseball. (Both, author's collection.)

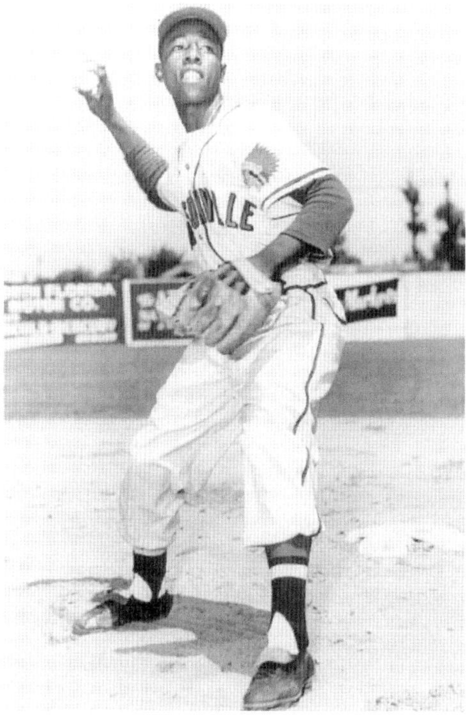

7

THE DYNASTY

A sports dynasty is often a once-in-a-lifetime event. It can be taken for granted when it is happening and only truly appreciated years later. Major League Baseball dynasties are rare, and a Minor League Baseball dynasty is even more remarkable. Too many factors can change a minor league team, preventing its continued success. There is far too much player movement and no guarantee that the next group of players will perform as well for a dynasty to happen.

Looking back, the Montgomery Rebels' accomplishments from 1972 to 1978 are most impressive. The impact of the Montgomery dynasty continued for years on the parent club, the Detroit Tigers. It was many of the same very talented players who won all those championships at Montgomery who moved up to Detroit to be part of the 1984 Tigers world championship team.

The Montgomery teams of the 1970s dynasty provided Detroit with both functions of a minor league team. First, they provided the talented players to fill their roster, and second, they provided an excess supply of talent that could be traded to obtain the missing pieces for a World Series contender. Montgomery was very successful in both.

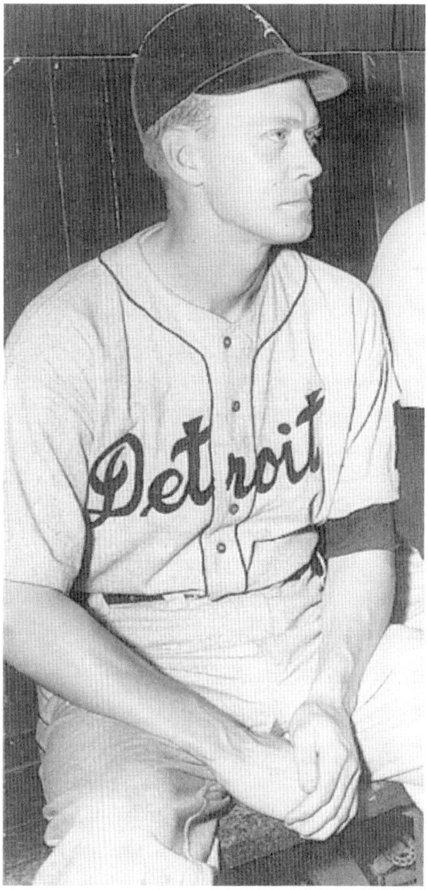

Hoot Evers was a former outfielder for the Detroit Tigers. In 1971, he came back to the Tigers as director of player development. It was during Evers's tenure from 1971 to 1978 that the Detroit farm system produced a bumper crop of talented future major league players. Most of these players came through Montgomery to learn the finer points of the game and, as a by-product, produce a minor league dynasty. (Author's collection.)

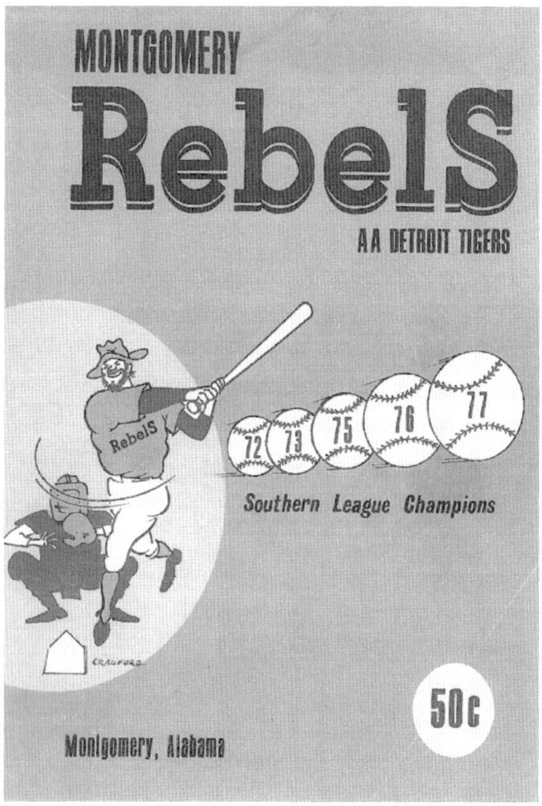

This 1978 Montgomery Rebels program cover says it all: an unheard-of run of five championships in six years! Nothing had happened like this since the Nashville Volunteers of 1939–1944. Dynasties in any sport are difficult to produce, but in Minor League Baseball they are almost impossible. The needs of the parent club too often come before the wishes of a farm club to keep a winning team together. This makes what Montgomery accomplished in the 1970s even more amazing. (Author's collection.)

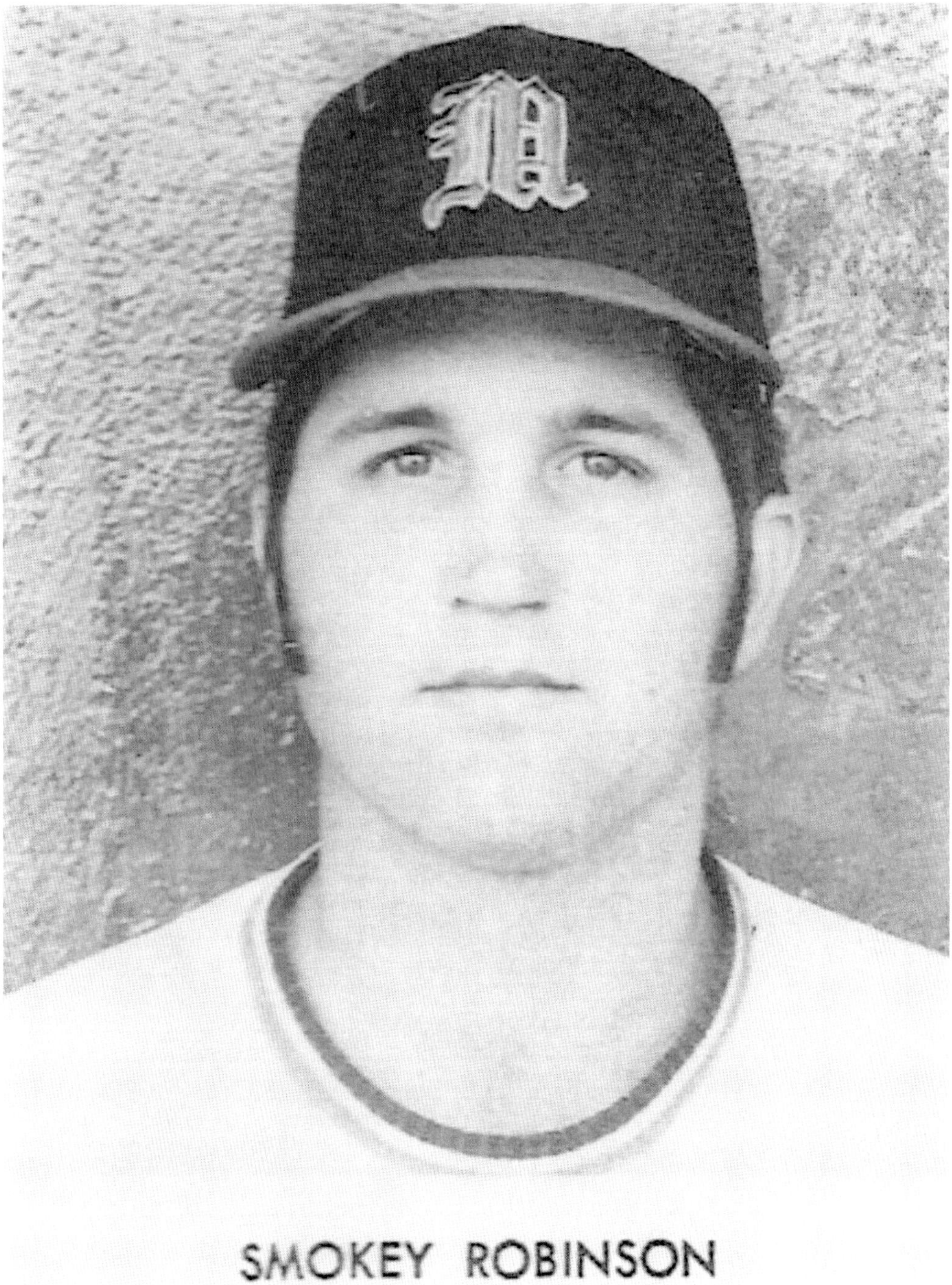

Many of the successful Rebel players who made major contributions to the championships of the Montgomery teams went on to major league careers. Unfortunately, some never got that opportunity. Bob "Smokey" Robinson was a huge factor in Montgomery's success in 1972 and 1973, but it never translated to time with the Tigers. In 1973, Robinson hit 28 home runs and batted in 94 runs with an average of .352. (Author's collection.)

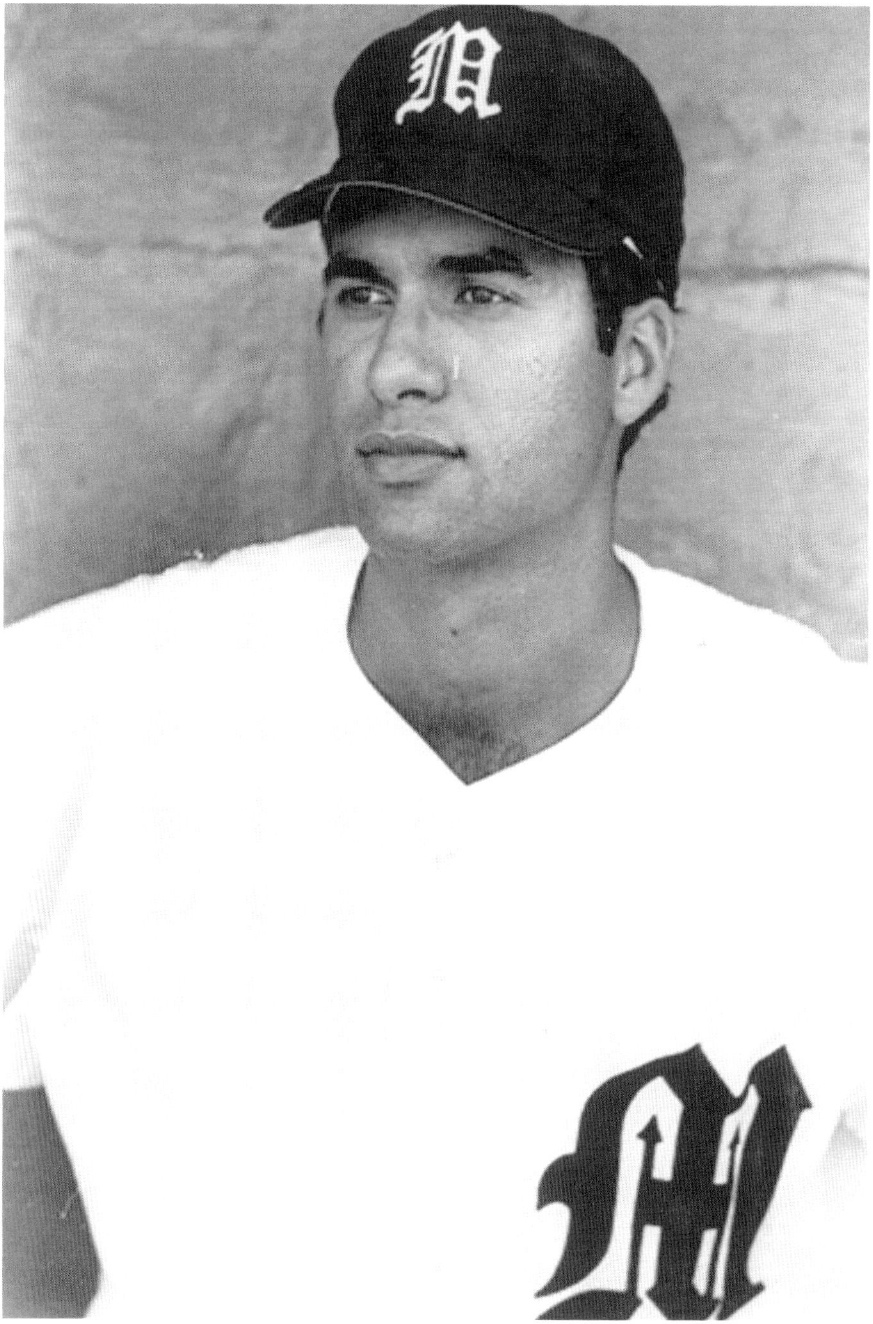

George Kalafatis never made it to the major leagues, but on a July night in 1969, he was the best in a 13-0 victory over the first-place Birmingham A's; Kalafatis hit four home runs, the first time a Montgomery player had accomplished this in any league. In Kalafatis's fifth at-bat, he could only single, ending his night with eight RBIs. What made this even more special was that he did it at home at Patterson Field. It would be 2014 before another Southern League player would match this feat. (Author's collection.)

Charles "Chip" Swanson played for the 1972 and 1973 Montgomery championship teams, but it is his 1970 perfect game for the Montgomery Rebels that he is remembered for. On August 14, Swanson pitched the first perfect game in Southern League history against Savannah. The perfect game earned him a promotion to Triple-A Toledo, but Swanson never got the call to the major leagues. (Both, author's collection.)

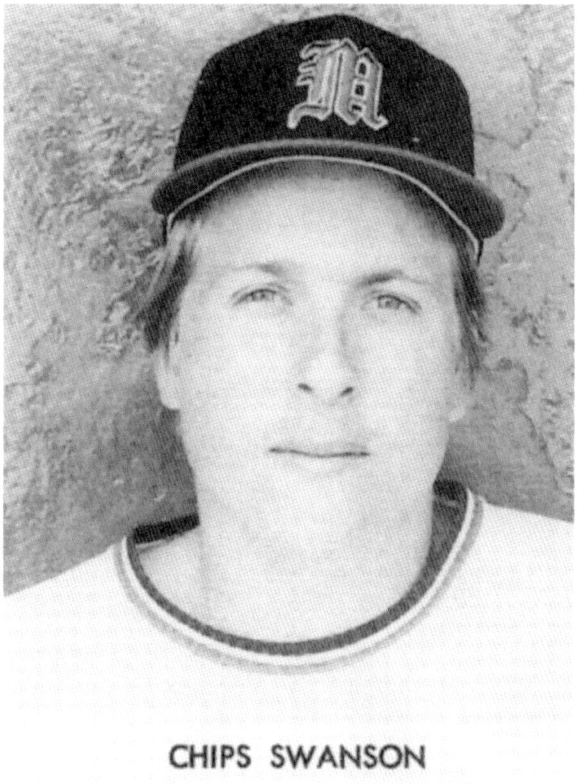

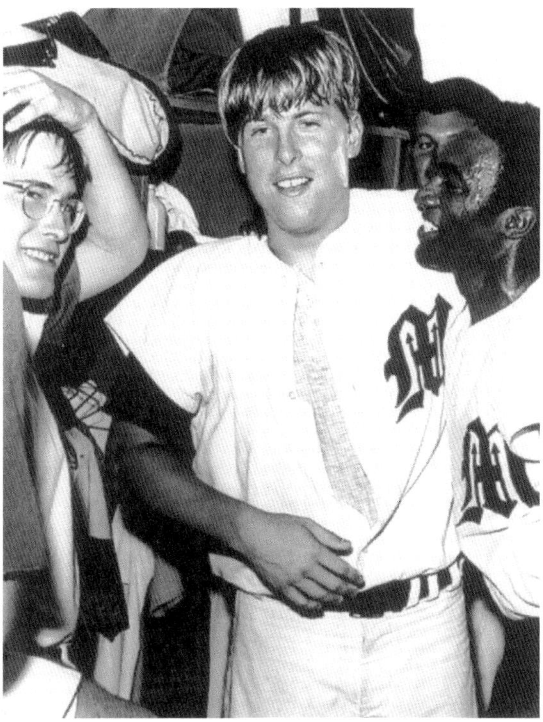

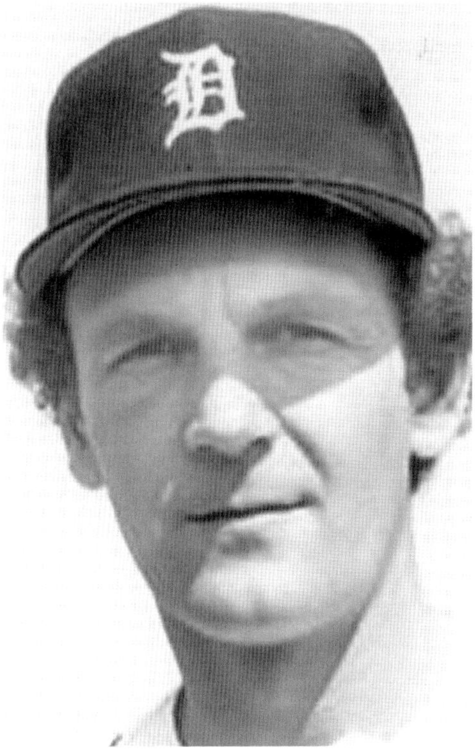

Jim Leyland came up in the Detroit Tigers farm system, playing parts of four seasons for Montgomery. Detroit realized his potential as a future manager. To no one's surprise, Leyland returned to Montgomery in 1974 to manage the Rebels right in the middle of the dynasty run. Unfortunately for Leyland, early season injuries for the Tigers led to the call-up of several promising pitchers, which left Montgomery very short of talent. The 1947 season would be just a blip on the radar for the Rebels, who returned to championship form in 1975. (Author's collection.)

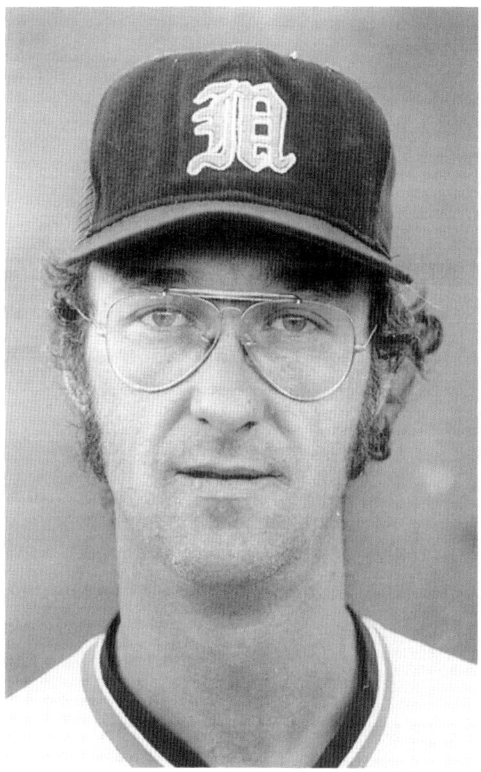

After Les Moss moved on to manage Triple-A Evansville, Detroit named Ed Brinkman to manage Montgomery. Brinkman continued Moss's successful ways, winning the 1977 championship. It was also a very wise move to have a former gold-glove shortstop as Montgomery's manager, as Brinkman played an important role in the development of Alan Trammell and Lon Whitaker. Brinkman grew up in Cincinnati and played high school baseball with Pete Rose. (Author's collection.)

Fred Hatfield's professional career spanned 21 years, with 10 years in the major leagues. In the mid-1960s, Hatfield was coach of the baseball program at Florida State. By the early 1970s, he was on track to be considered for a major league managerial position. As part of the Detroit organization, he won back-to-back championships at Montgomery. His two seasons as manager of the Triple-A Evansville club netted him American Association Manager of the Year. His career stalled after losing seasons and being continually passed over for several different positions, and Hatfield ended as a scout. (Author's collection.)

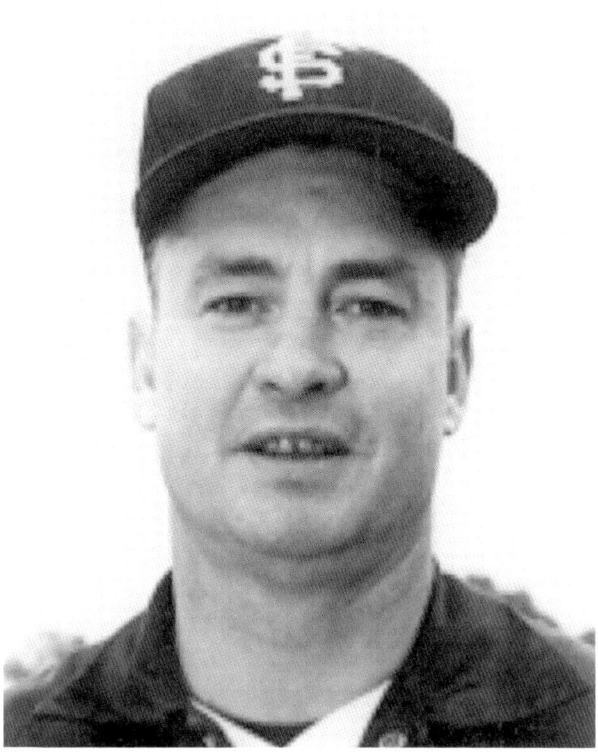

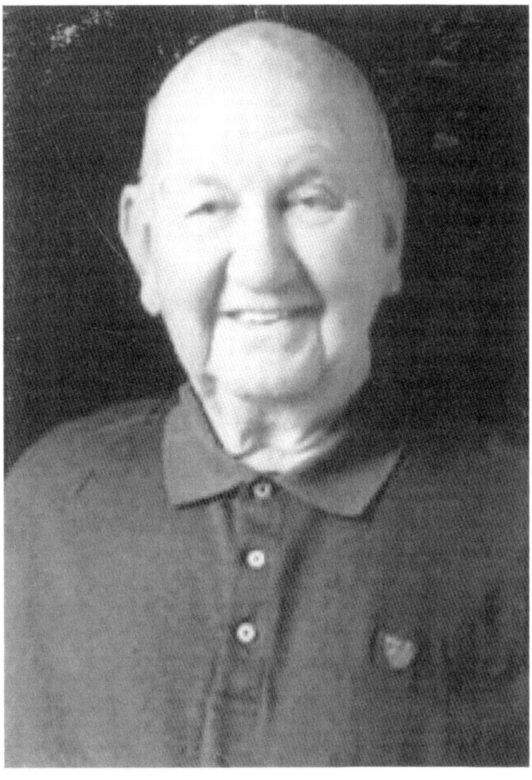

No one has been more a part of Montgomery baseball than Mack McWhorter, who played for Montgomery from 1948 to 1951 and also coached and managed Montgomery teams. In the 1970s he was part of the ownership, serving both as president and vice president of the franchise. After McWhorter's playing days, he and his wife, Mariah, settled in Montgomery, where he was president of the Dexter Propane Gas Company and a Montgomery County commissioner. (Author's collection.)

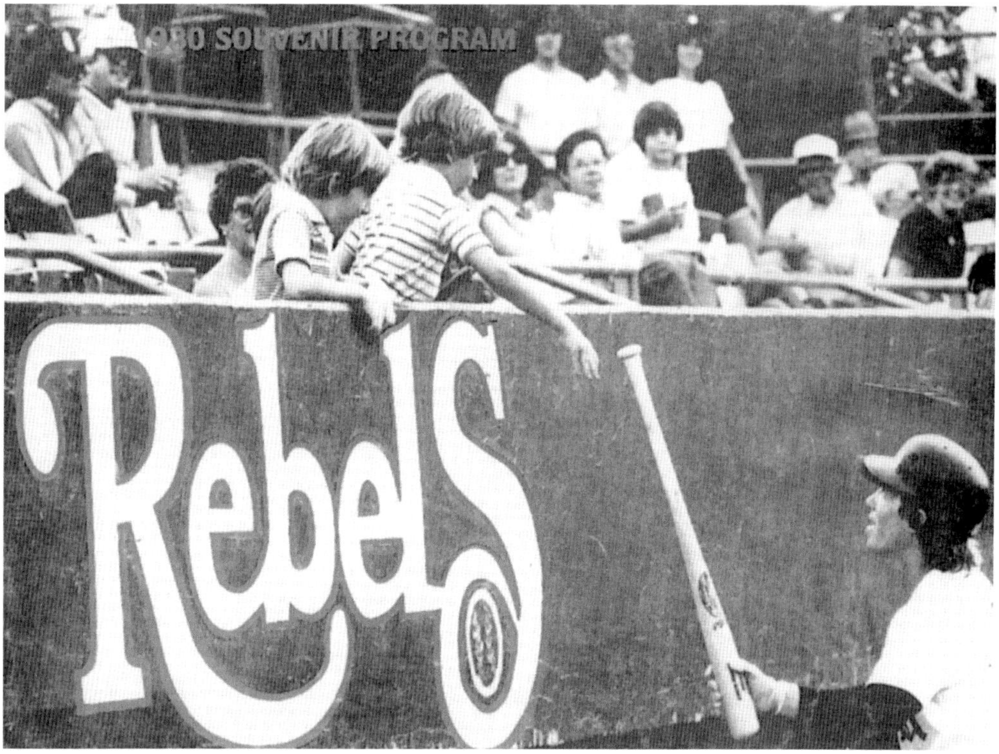

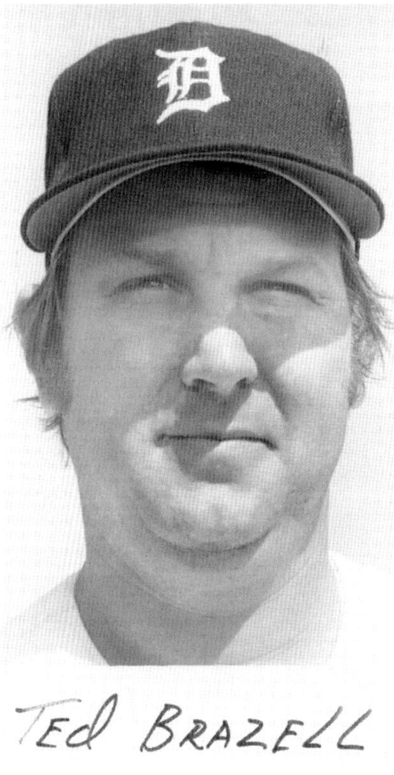

After the dynasty was over, baseball would soon leave Montgomery. This 1980 Montgomery Rebel program cover tells a bittersweet story about the retirement of fan-favorite player Ted Brazell. As the fans honored Brazell with a player appreciation night at the close of the season, Brazell gave his bat to one of the owner's sons. A few years later, when Brazell's son was born, the former owner of the team returned the bat for Ted's son Craig. Looking back now, knowing that 1980 was the last season of Minor League Baseball until 2004, the cover also seems to say, "We might as well give the equipment away because we won't be back next year." (Author's collection.)

Ted Brazell played six seasons with the Montgomery Rebels. In 1979 he retired as a player, but stayed on with Montgomery as a coach. Brazell's experience as a catcher made him ideal to help bring along rookie pitchers. After baseball, Ted and his wife, Mary, settled in Montgomery. Their son Craig also played professional baseball, enjoying a career with the New York Mets and several years in Jackson. (Author's collection.)

Dave Rozema was the pitching leader for the 1976 team. He led all pitching in most complete games, most shutouts, most wins, and lowest earned run average. Rozema was part of the Tigers' 1984 world championship team. (Author's collection.)

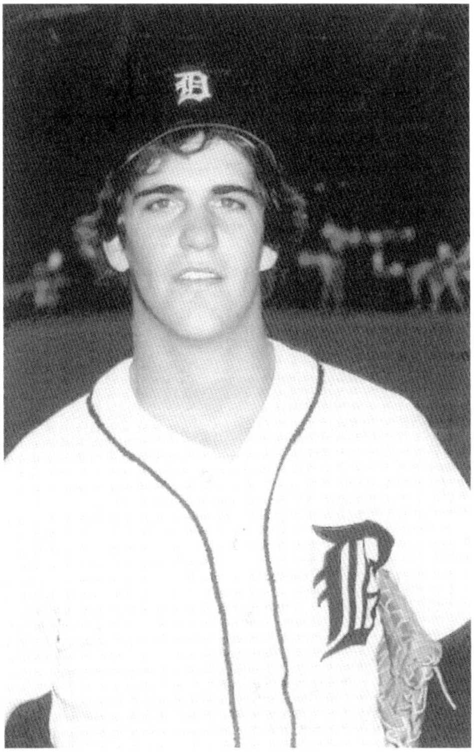

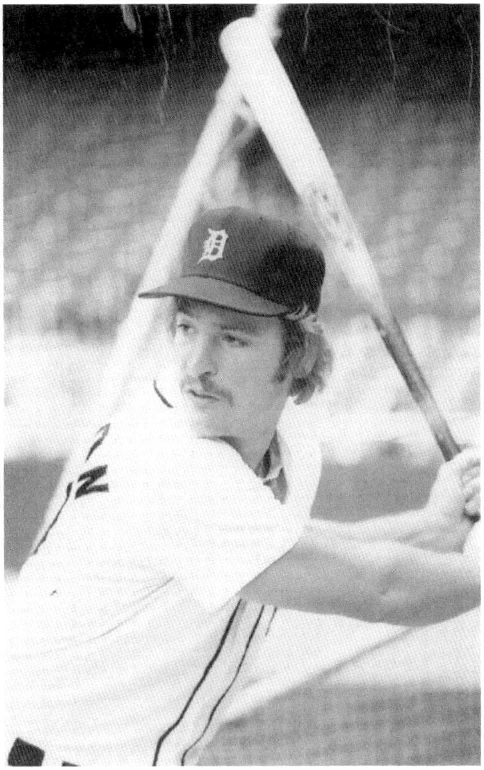

Jason Thompson showed the Detroit management he had power. After only one season at Montgomery, Thompson became the regular first baseman for the Tigers. He went on to have an 11-year major league career, hitting over 200 home runs. (Author's collection.)

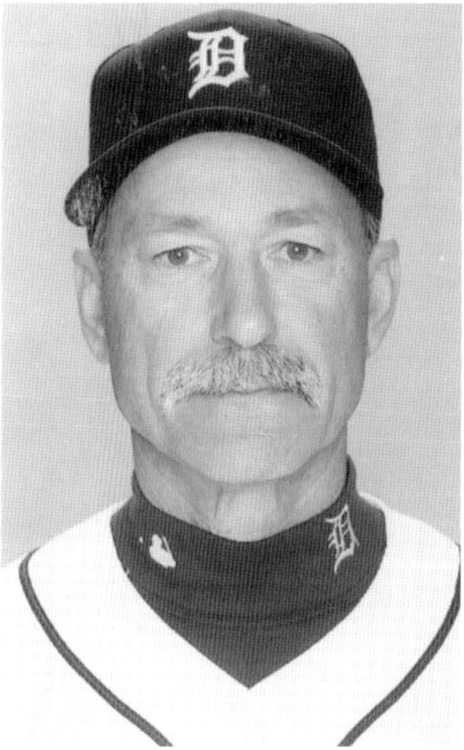

Tom Brookens was a mainstay of the 1976 championship team. He led the team in most games played, most at-bats, and most triples. Brookens went on to be the Tigers' third baseman for the next 10 years. (Author's collection.)

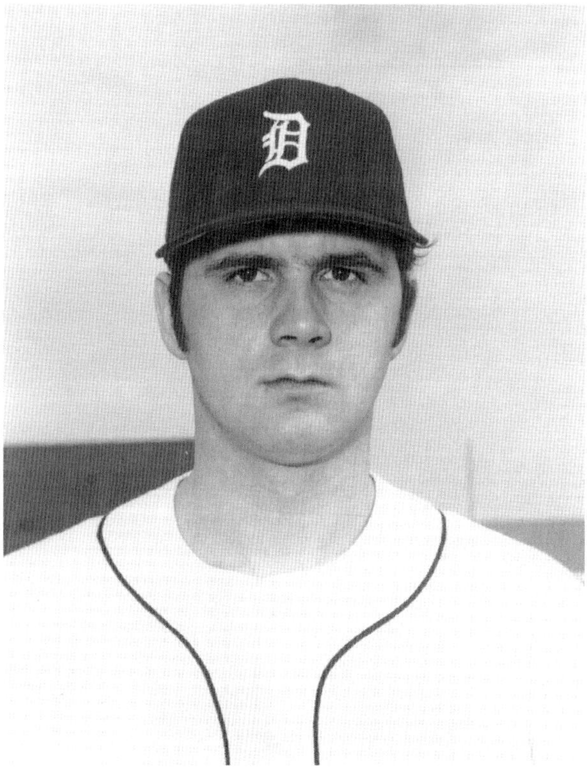

Daniel J. Bootcheck posted double-digit wins for Montgomery in both 1971 and 1972. In 1973, he was plagued with sore arm problems that limited his ability to pitch regularly. Bootcheck called it quits after 1973, returning to his home in Indiana where he opened the Sand Trap Sports Bar, which he managed until his death in 2015. (Author's collection.)

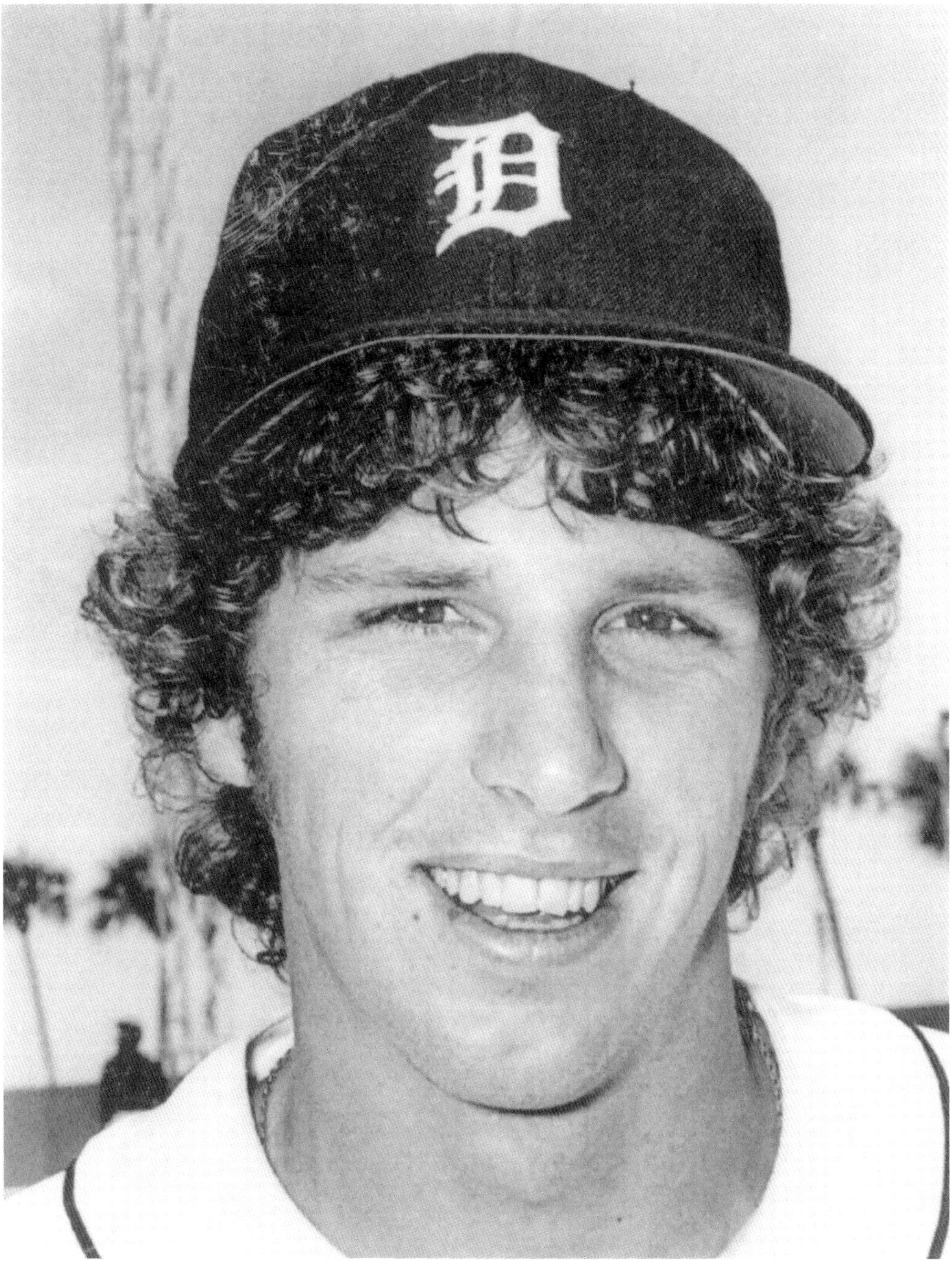

Mark Fidrych was one of those rare baseball players who breathed new life into the game; however, his career in the sport was brief due to an injury. Fidrych only spent two weeks with the Montgomery Rebels before he was called up to Triple-A. According to a *Rolling Stone* magazine article about him, it was an unidentified coach at Montgomery who first started calling Mark "the Bird." The hair, the lanky build, the large beak, and the high-pitched voice all contributed to that nickname. Like the article stated, "Mark Fidrych is rock and roll." (Author's collection.)

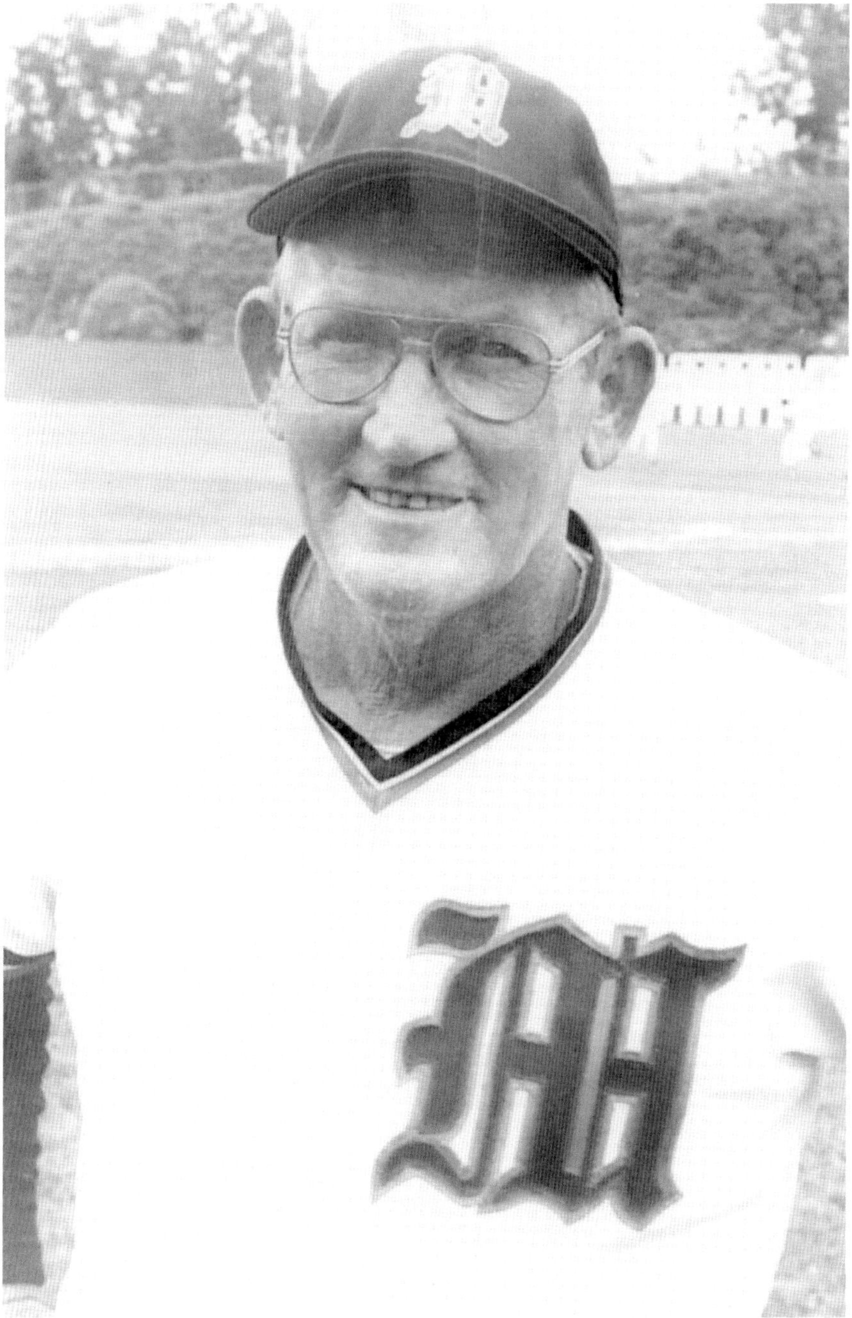

Les Moss had a 13-year career as a catcher, all in the American League. He briefly managed the Chicago White Sox in 1968. Moss came to Montgomery in 1975 and produced back-to-back Southern League championships. His old-school style worked well with the young players. In 1977 and 1978, he was promoted to the Detroit Triple-A team in Evansville. After being named Minor League Manager of the Year in 1978, Moss was named Detroit Tigers manager in 1979. (Author's collection.)

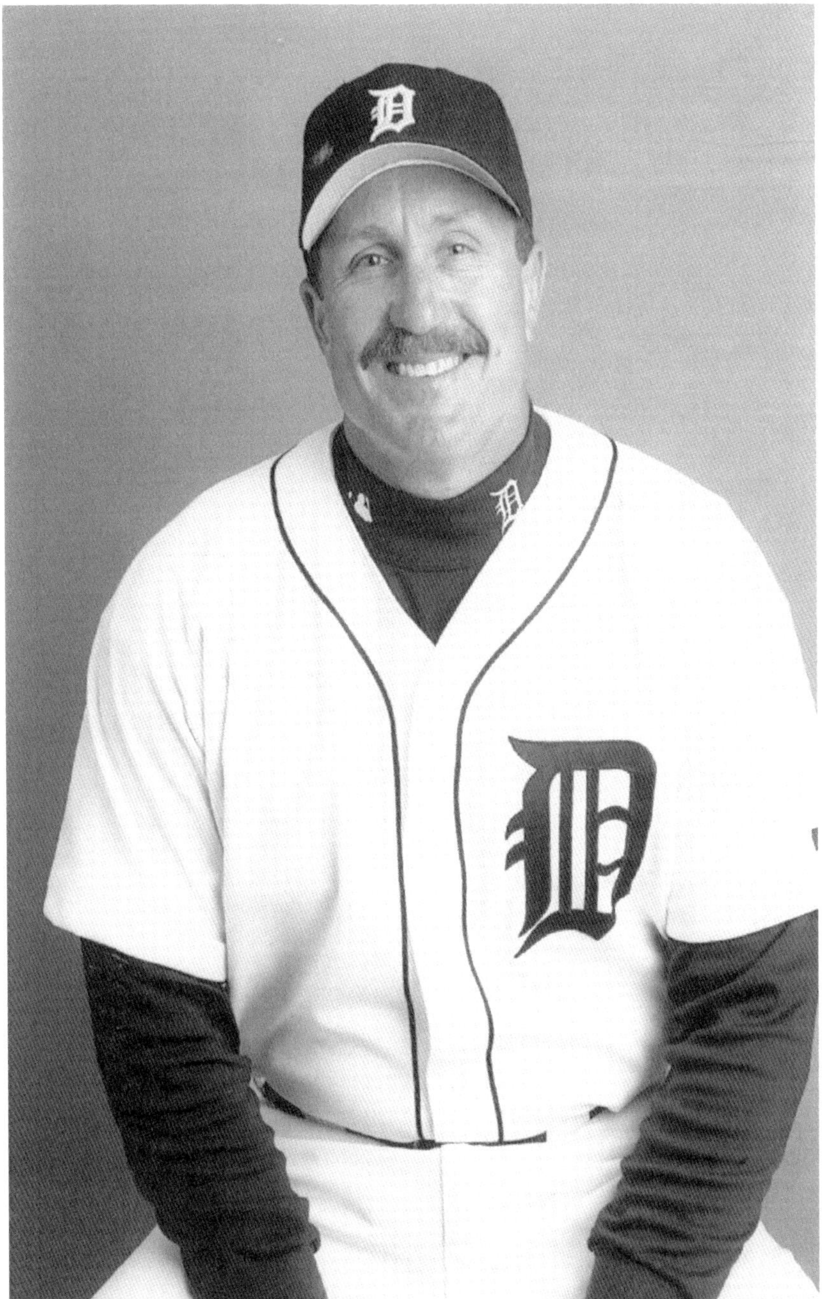

Lance Parrish was drafted by the Detroit Tigers as a third baseman in 1974. At Lakeland in 1975, Detroit decided to make Parrish into a catcher. Parrish stated in an interview that his manager at Montgomery, Les Moss, played a big role in his becoming an All-Star catcher. Moss had been a catcher in his playing days. Parrish had a very productive 10-year career with Detroit, continuing to play in the majors until 1995. His career highlights and statistics made him a potential hall of fame candidate. (Author's collection.)

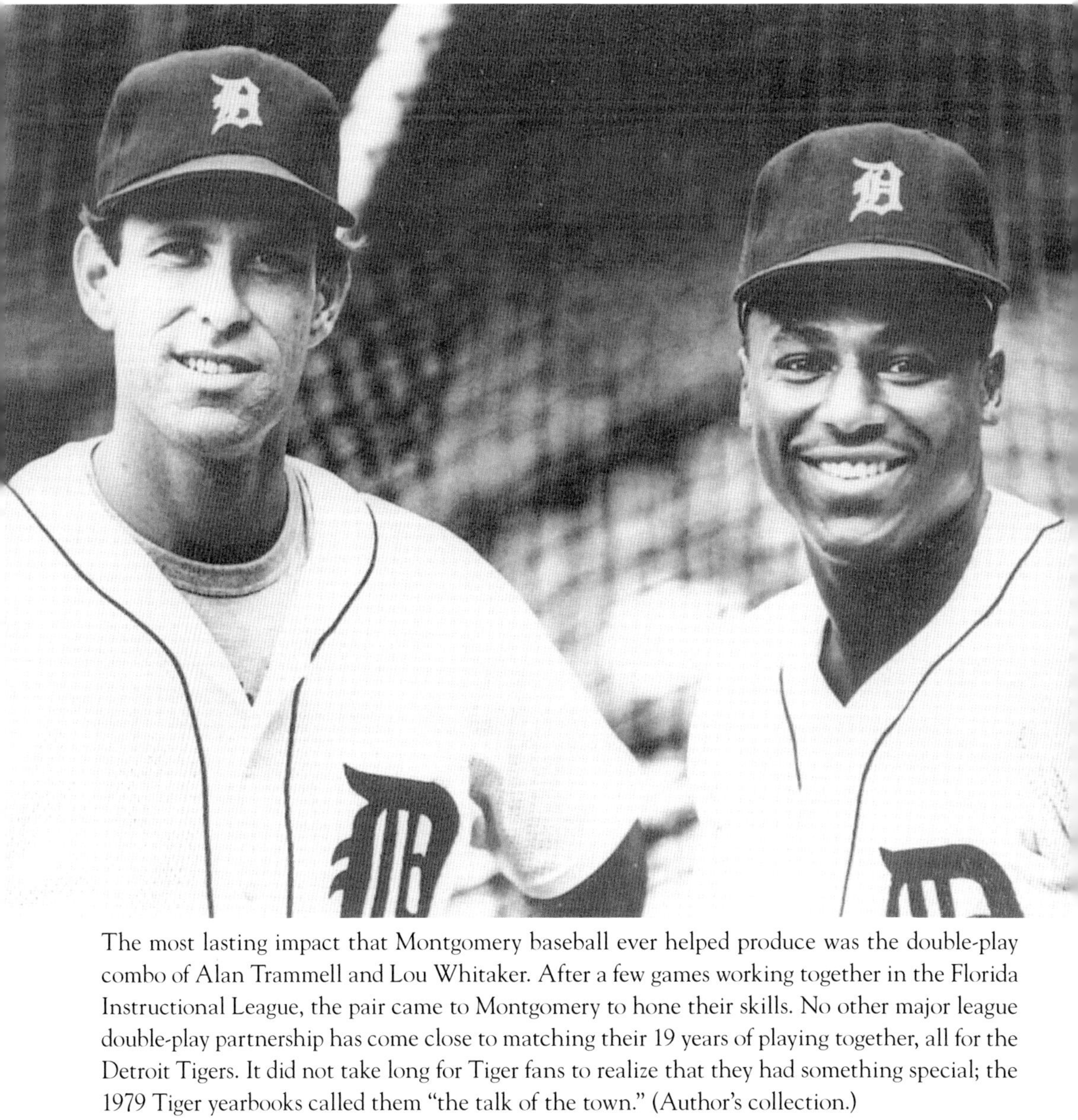

The most lasting impact that Montgomery baseball ever helped produce was the double-play combo of Alan Trammell and Lou Whitaker. After a few games working together in the Florida Instructional League, the pair came to Montgomery to hone their skills. No other major league double-play partnership has come close to matching their 19 years of playing together, all for the Detroit Tigers. It did not take long for Tiger fans to realize that they had something special; the 1979 Tiger yearbooks called them "the talk of the town." (Author's collection.)

8

The Biscuits

The city of Montgomery's decision to select Tom Dickson and Sherrie Myers to bring baseball back to Montgomery seemed to be a very wise move. Many people looked at building a new stadium and bringing a new team to Montgomery as a huge money pit. It would be a big expenditure for tax payers with very little in return. Instead, Montgomery has become the model for other cities on how it is to be done successfully.

Minor League Baseball was last played in Montgomery in 1980. Alabama's other large cities, Birmingham, Huntsville, and Mobile, all had successful minor league teams. It was time for Montgomery to join the league. The ownership group purchased an Orlando team to bring to Montgomery in 2004. A contest for a team name resulted in the "Biscuits." At the first announcement, this produced a few giggles and the thought that this might not be a good idea after all. The idea for unique names for minor league teams began in Columbus, Georgia, where the team changed its name to the Mudcats and reaped a windfall of revenue. Team owners Dickson and Myers did the same in Lansing, Michigan, naming the team there the Lugnuts, which proved to be a great success. The question became, would the Biscuits be a boom or bust? After the first year of over a million dollars in sales in team merchandise, the answer was clear.

The next step was placing a competitive team on the field. The Biscuits would be a farm team of the Tampa Bay Rays. Up until 2004, the Rays had not been a success as a major league team or in their minor league development. New ownership in 2004 revamped the minor league system, which brought quick results.

The Montgomery Biscuits began to produce bumper crops of major league–quality players. That would prove evident in Tampa Bay's appearance in the World Series in 2008.

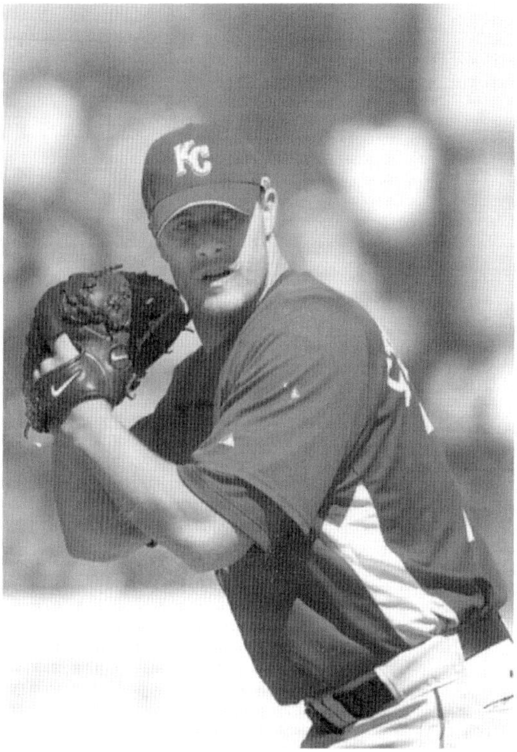

Jason Standridge had been in the Tampa Bay farm system since its beginning. He was a first-round draft pick and had already had several call-ups to Tampa. For the new Montgomery Biscuits, he was the first player to be called up to the major leagues. Standridge went on to play in the majors until 2007, when he began playing baseball in Japan. He was part of championship teams in 2014 and 2015. (Author's collection.)

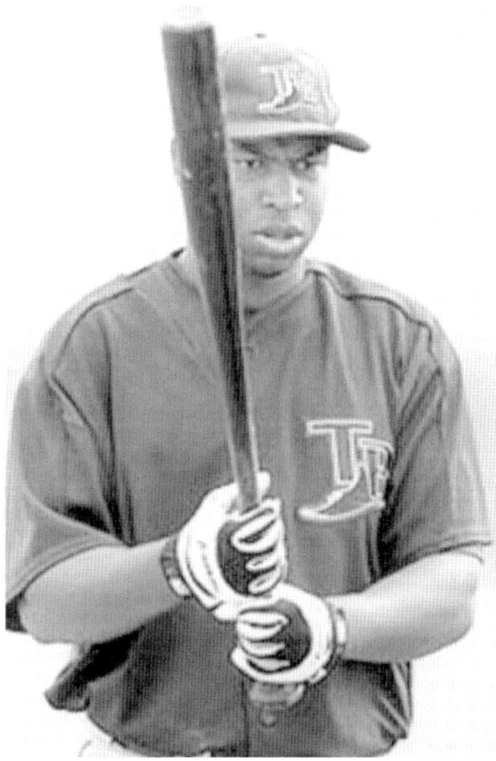

Delmon Young was Tampa's first overall pick in the 2003 draft. Young was the first Biscuit player to win the league's Most Valuable Player award. After playing for a variety of other major league teams, Young signed with Tampa for the second time in 2013. After a few games at Montgomery, he was back with the Rays for September. (Author's collection.)

B.J. Upton was only in Montgomery for 29 games, but he made the most of his time with the Biscuits. His .327 average earned him a trip to Tampa Bay, making him the second Biscuit player to be called up. Upton was not yet 20 years old when he made his major league debut on August 2, 2004. (Author's collection.)

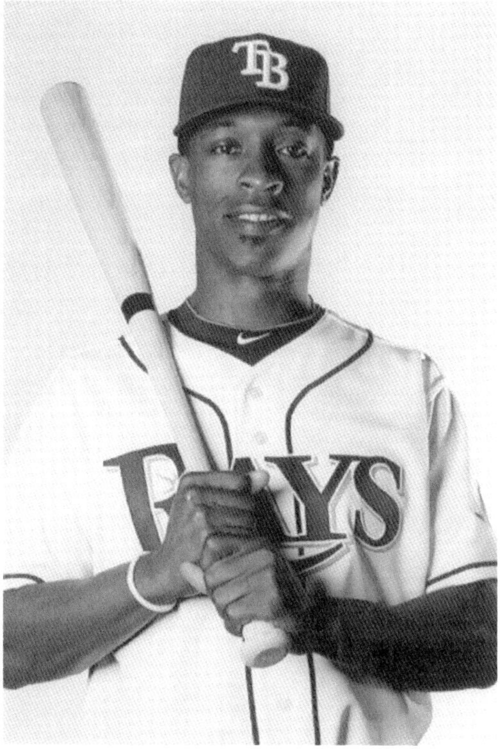

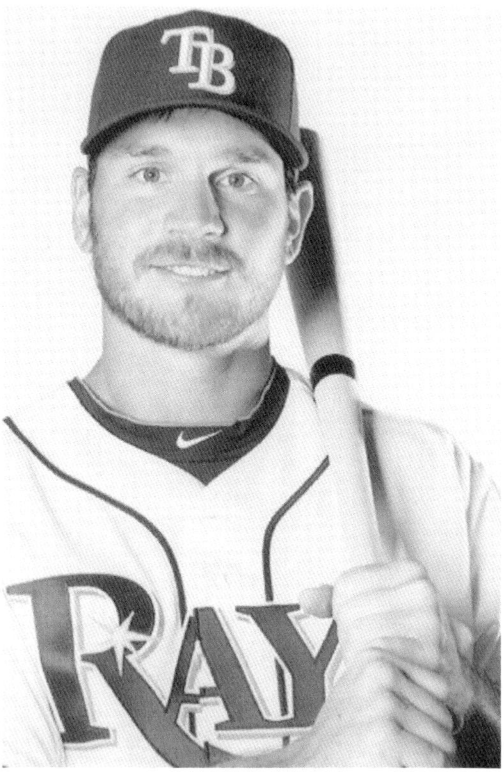

John Jaso was the starting catcher for the 2007 championship team. He is the only Biscuit player to appear in two Southern League All-Star games. As of 2016, Jaso was still playing Major League Baseball, primarily as a first baseman for the Pittsburgh Pirates. (Author's collection.)

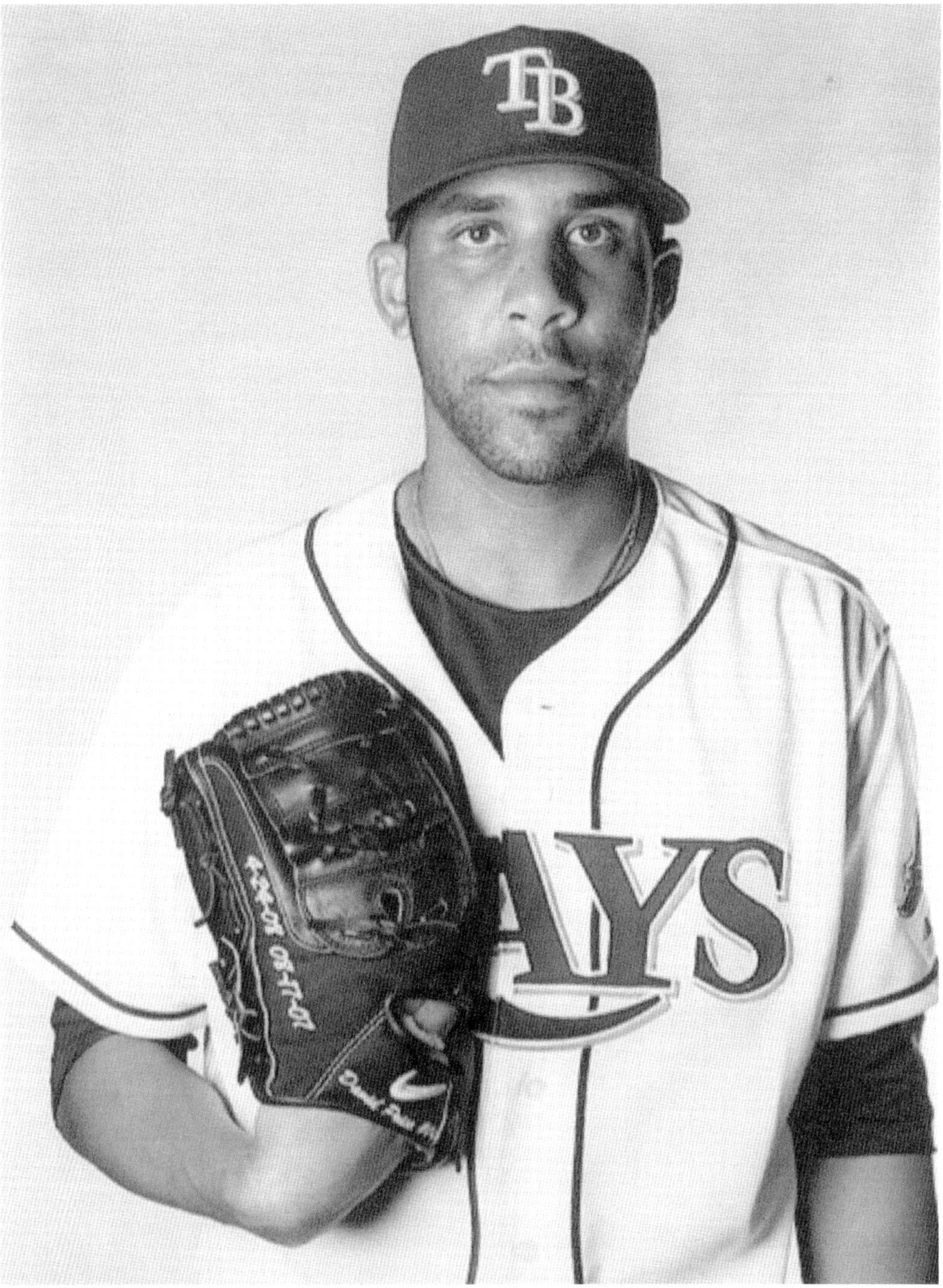

After an amazing pitching career at the college level at Vanderbilt University, David Price was the top overall pick in the 2007 player draft. In 2008, he made only 19 starts; nine of those were with Montgomery, where he posted an impressive 7-0 record. By the end of the year, Price had pitched in two games of the 2008 World Series. (Author's collection.)

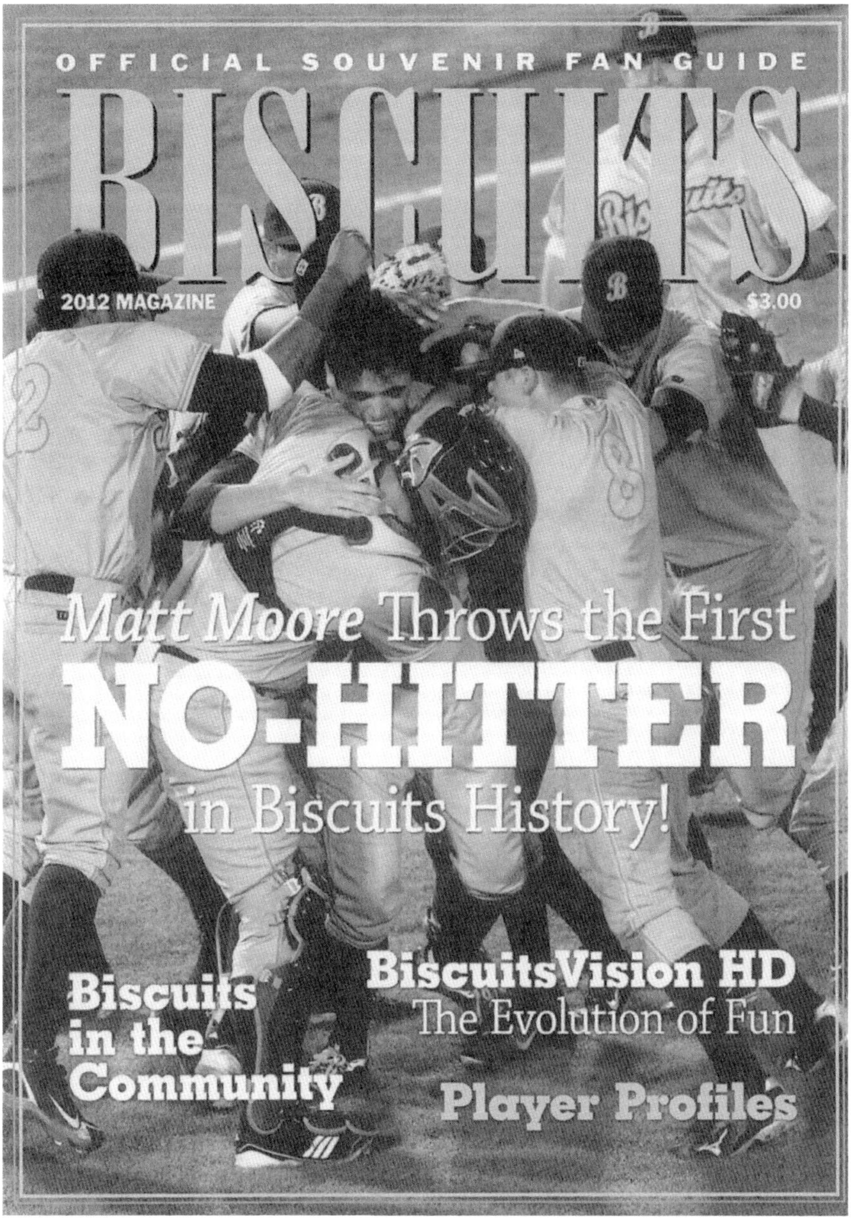

Starting in 2007 in rookie league, Matt Moore worked his way up to the Montgomery Biscuits in 2011. Then, on June 16, he performed the most impressive start of his pitching career. The Biscuits were in Mobile to play the Bears. Moore's family had traveled from Arizona to see him pitch and to celebrate his birthday. After lunch with his family, Moore prepared for his start that evening. On this hot and humid night, before less than a thousand fans including his family, Moore pitched a no-hitter. His team got him two runs before he even threw his first pitch. The final out came on a ball hit straight back to him. This masterful performance led to Moore's promotion to Triple-A Durham and then to his first major league start in September against Baltimore. (Author's collection.)

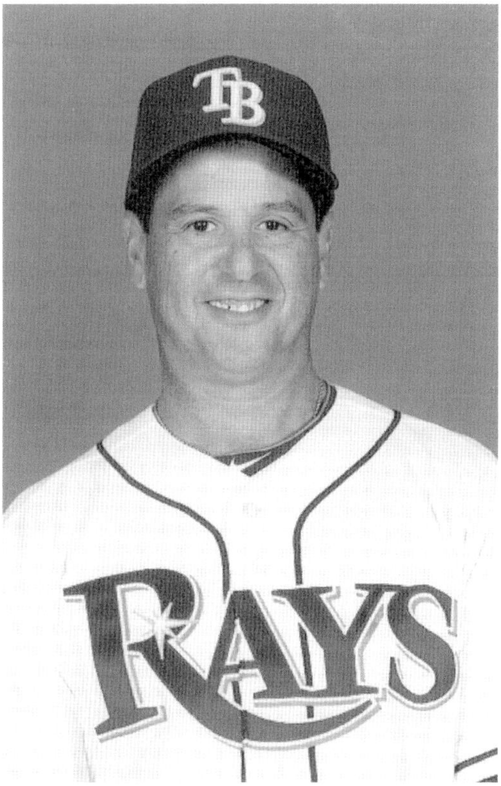

Charlie Montoyo is from Florida, Puerto Rico. He played college baseball at Louisiana Tech University. His major league career consisted of four games with the Montreal Expos in 1993. He was the Orlando manager in 2003 and continued to manage the team when it moved to Montgomery. In 2006, he managed Montgomery to the Southern League championship. In 2007, he was promoted to manager at Triple-A Durham for Tampa Bay. In 2015, he was a prime candidate to manage the Tampa Bay team but had to settle for the third base coaching position.(Author's collection.)

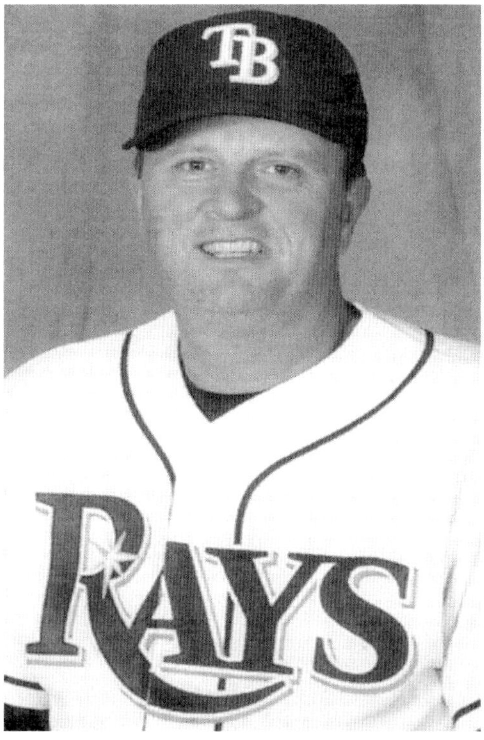

Billy Gardner Jr. managed the Biscuits for seven years. That type of longevity can be seen as a curse or a success. Gardner was manager of the Biscuits when they won their second of back-to-back championships in 2006 and 2007. Gardner was no stranger to Montgomery baseball. In 1973, he was in his father's dugout when the Rebels defeated the Jacksonville team managed by Billy Gardner Sr. (Courtesy of the Montgomery Biscuits.)

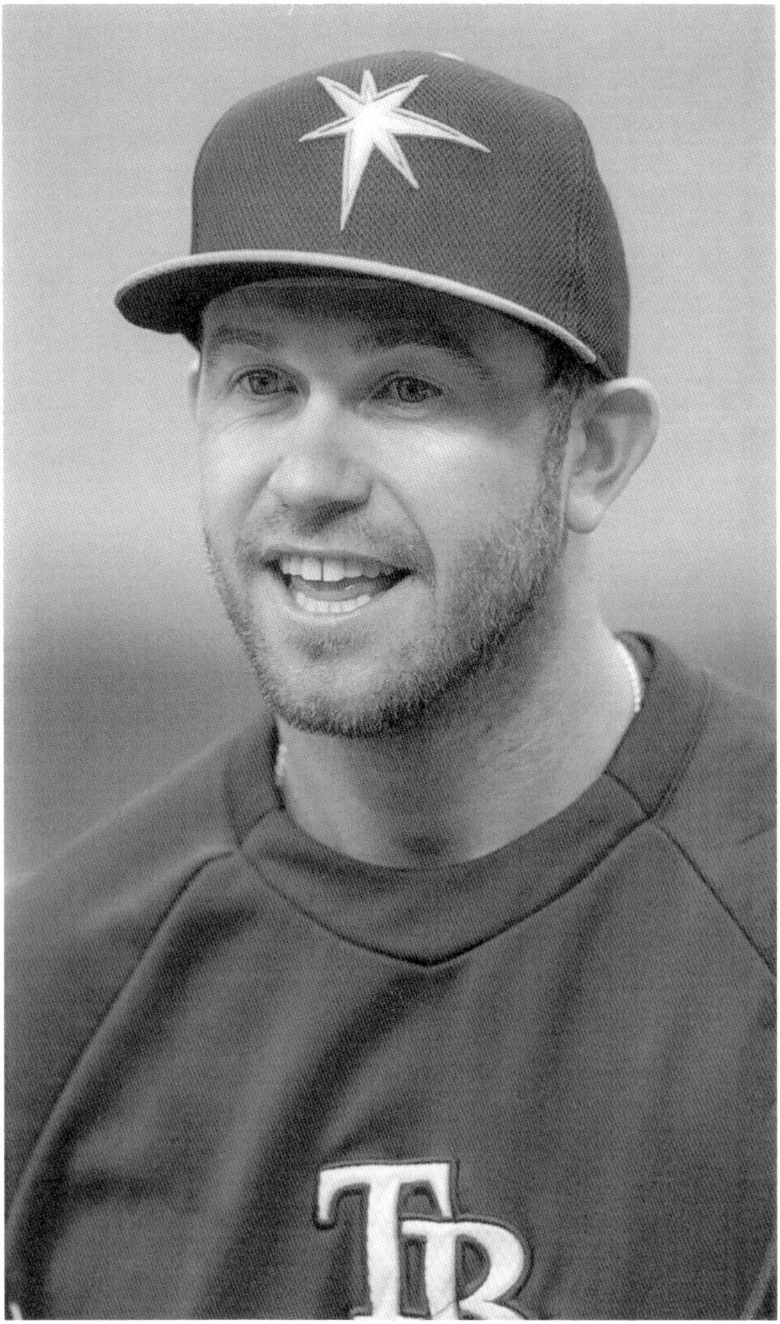

Evan Longoria quickly moved through the Tampa Bay farm system, arriving in Montgomery ahead of schedule. He was named the Most Valuable Player for the Southern League in 2007, even though he missed the last month of the season due to being called up to Durham. He gave Montgomery fans something to remember him by when he hit a grand slam in his last at-bat as a Biscuit in the 10th inning in a game against Birmingham. In 2008, he was Rookie of the Year in the American League. (Author's collection.)

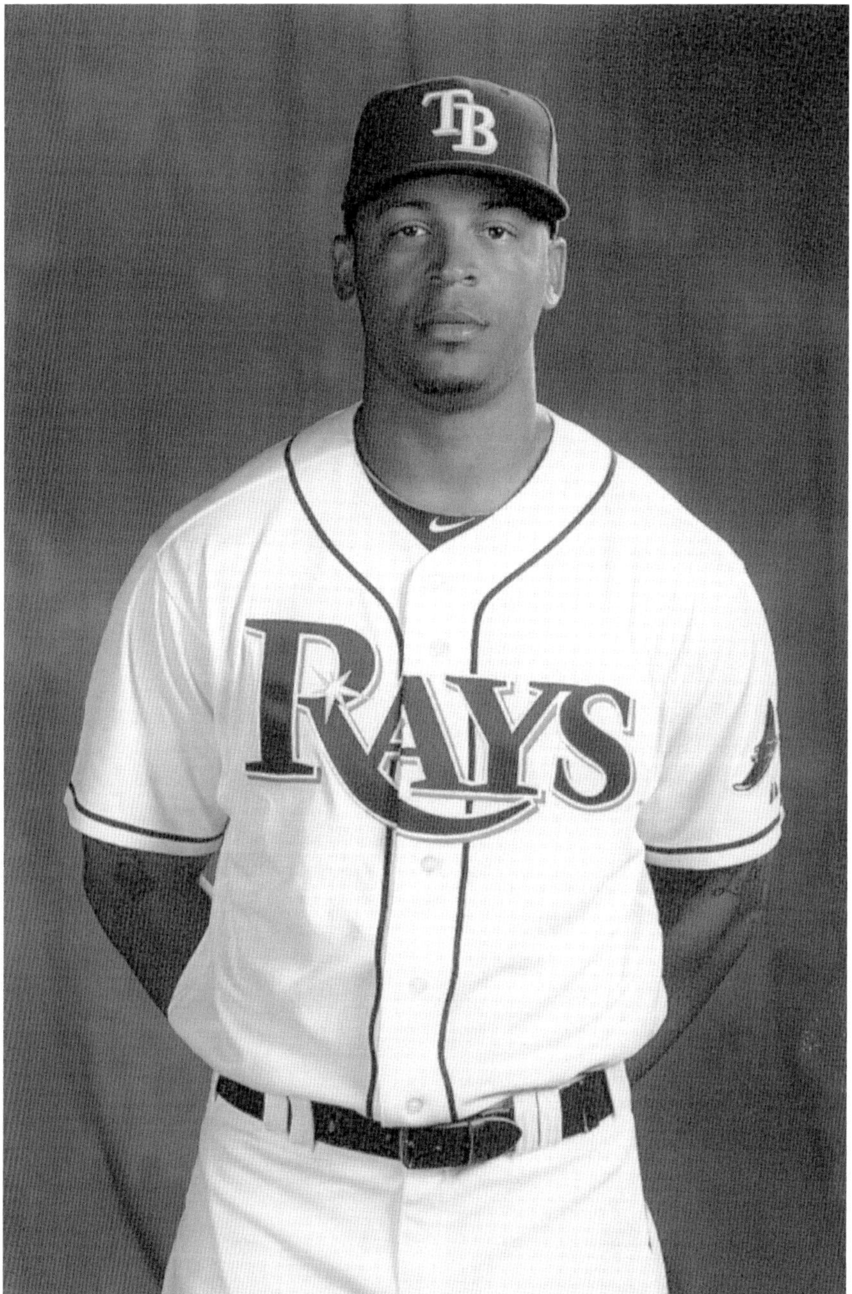

Desmond Jennings, from Pinson, Alabama, was drafted 10th by Tampa Bay in 2006. He spent only one season, 2009, with Montgomery, but what a season he had with the Biscuits. He was voted the league's Most Valuable Player and finished in the top five of seven different offensive categories. His speed resulted in 37 stolen bases and helped his defense, committing only one error in 92 games. Not many players are considered to be five-tool players, but Jennings's numbers say he is. (Author's collection.)

The Tampa Bay Rays obtained Scott Kazmir in a trade with the New York Mets in July 2004. Tampa sent him to Montgomery, where he started only four games but pitched so well that he was called up to Tampa Bay in August, never playing at Triple-A Durham. He had a 2-3 record at the end of the 2004 season, but coaches could see progress in his performance. In 2006, he was the opening-day starter for Tampa, becoming the youngest pitcher (22 years old) to achieve that honor since Dwight Gooden in 1985. (Author's collection.)

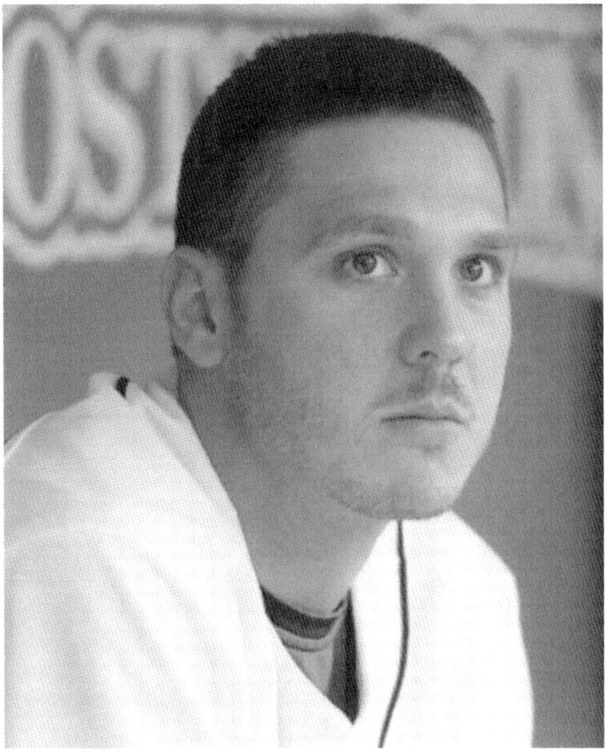

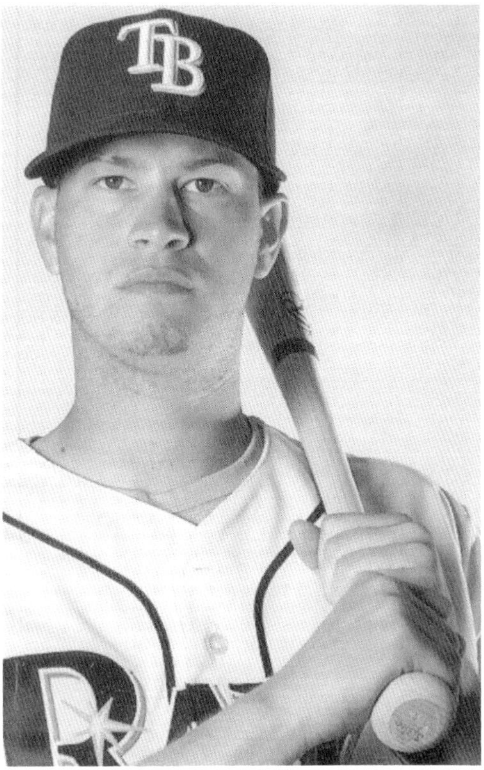

Reid Brignac came to Montgomery at the same time as Evan Longoria in 2006. The next year, Brignac was the starting shortstop for the whole season. Injuries and the talent ahead of him slowed his chances of making the big league club. In 2010, he stayed with Tampa Bay the complete season. In 2016, Brignac is playing for the Atlanta Braves. (Author's collection.)

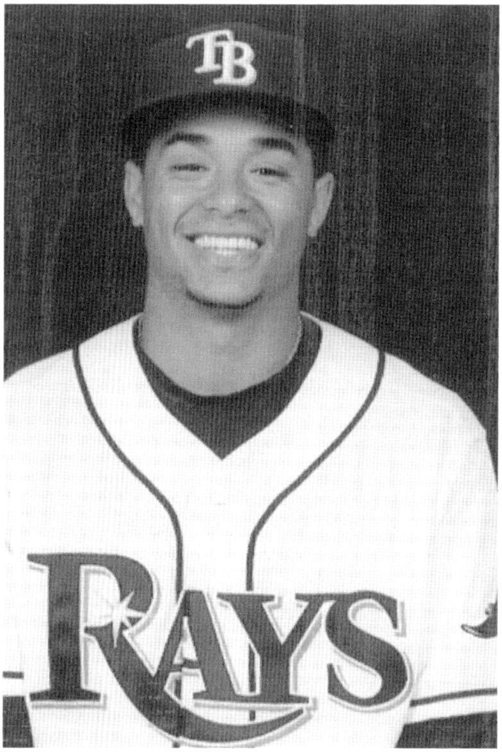

Chris Archer came to Montgomery in a roundabout way. He was signed by the Cleveland Indians in 2006. In 2008, he was traded to the Chicago Cubs. In 2010, Archer was named Best Minor League Pitcher in the Cubs organization. Then, in January 2011, he was traded to Tampa Bay. Tampa sent Archer to Montgomery for the 2011 season. He pitched poorly during the first half of the season, but then improved in the second half, which caused him to be promoted to Triple-A Durham. (Author's collection.)

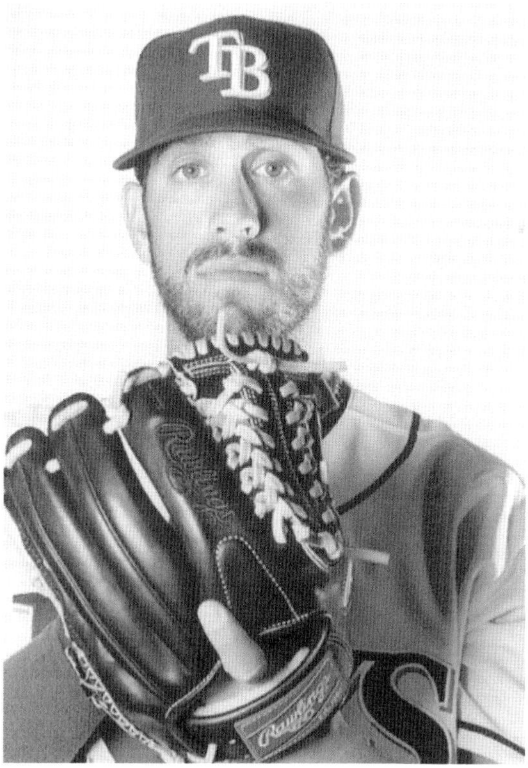

James Shields came to Montgomery mid-season in 2004. He had a difficult time adjusting to Double-A baseball. Much of his problem was due to the shoulder surgery he had in 2001, which caused him to miss the entire 2002 season. His shoulder healed nicely, and he turned in a 7-5 record. He continued to progress to the big leagues, going to Durham in 2006 and making his major league debut on May 11, 2006, with Tampa. (Author's collection.)

Jason Hammel was part of the steady stream of quality pitchers that Montgomery was sending Tampa every year. At Montgomery, he had an impressive 8-2 record. Hammel made his major league debut on April 11, 2006. (Author's collection.)

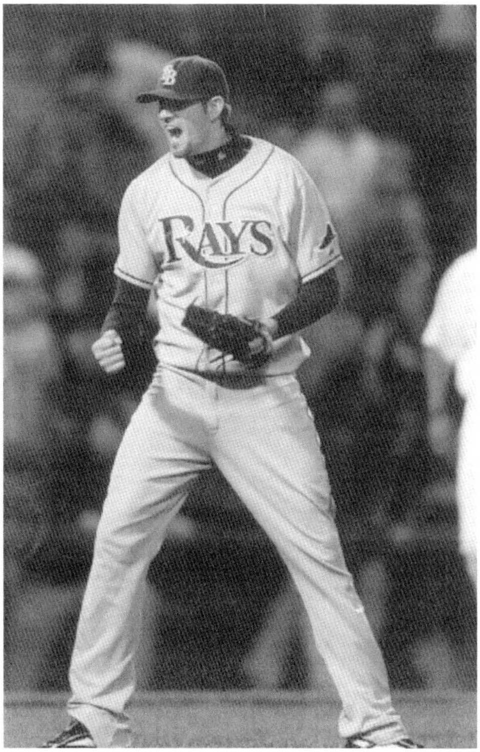

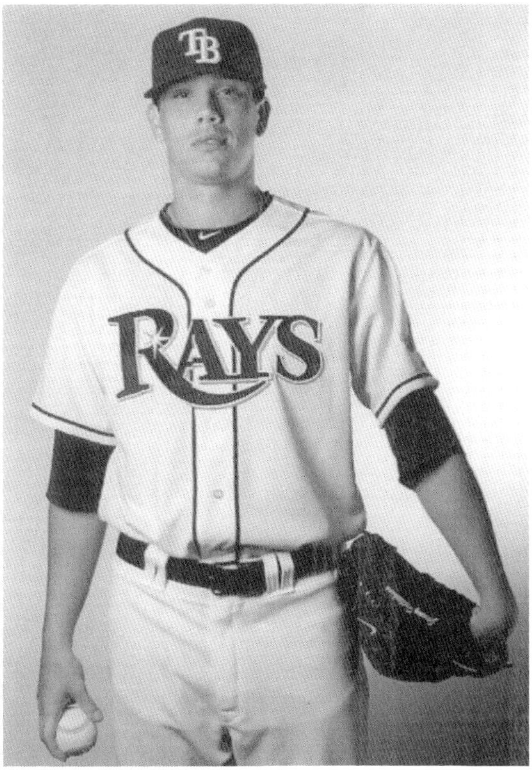

Jeremy Hellickson pitched for the Montgomery Biscuits in 2008 and 2009. He made his major league debut on August 2, 2010, pitching a great game, limiting Minnesota to two runs in seven innings. Afterward, Hellickson was optioned back to Durham, but was called back up to Tampa later the same month. His second major league start was even more impressive. Hellickson pitched seven shutout innings against Detroit. (Author's collection.)

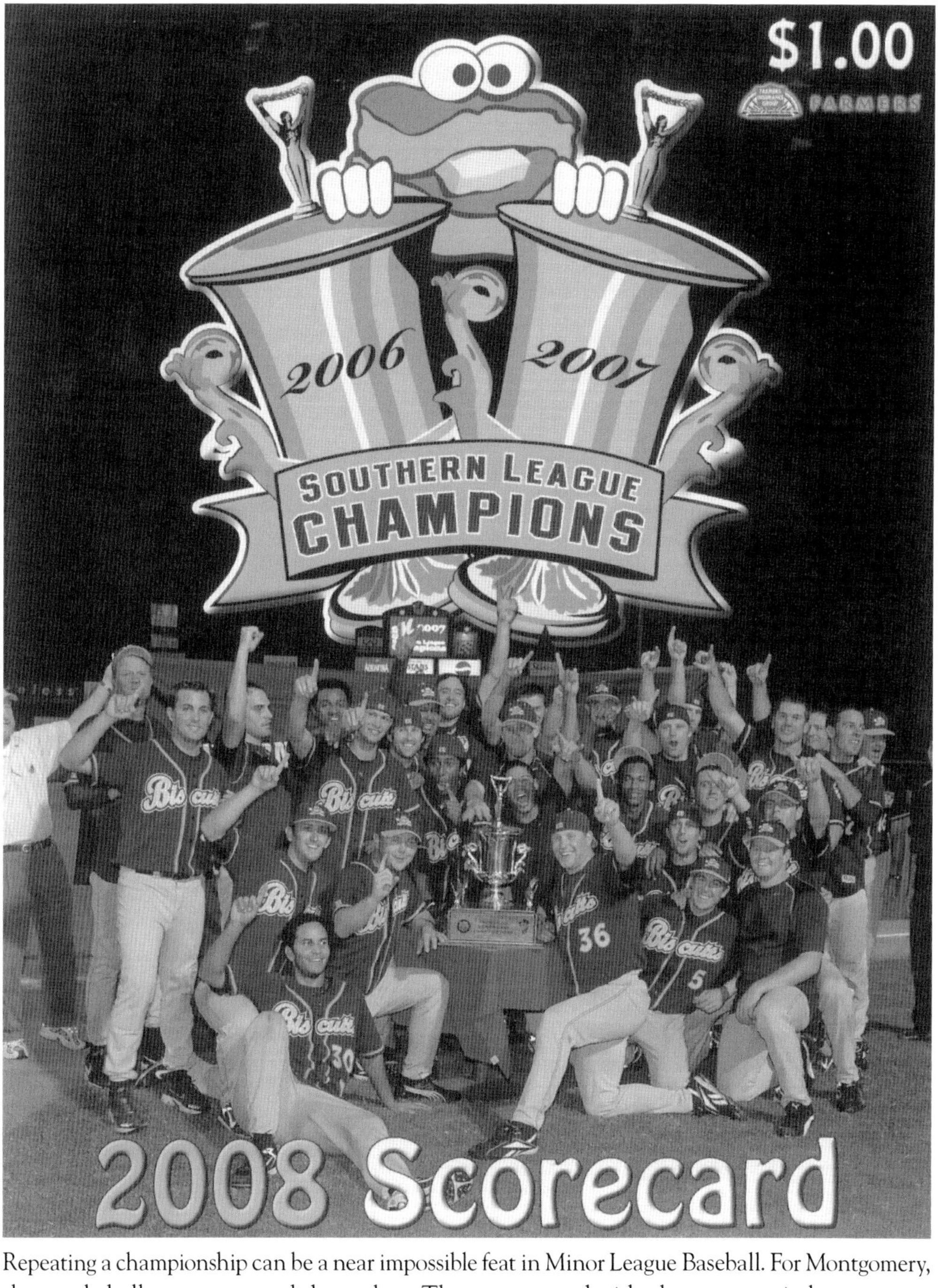

Repeating a championship can be a near impossible feat in Minor League Baseball. For Montgomery, the usual challenges presented themselves. The team started with almost an entirely new roster every year. Charlie Montoyo was gone, and Billy Gardner Jr. was new at running the club. In all, the 2007 season was very similar to 2006. The team spent the first half learning to play together, and once Evan Longoria and Reid Brignac arrived, the rest was history. The cover of the 2008 scorecard speaks to the pride Montgomery has in its Biscuit baseball. (Author's collection.)

9

RIVERWALK STADIUM

Riverwalk Stadium is considered by many as the finest minor league ballpark in the nation, and who could argue with that? Riverwalk was designed by HOK and Sport, the same firm that built Camden Yards in Baltimore. It was Camden Yards that changed baseball park design forever. Overnight, baseball stadiums built in the last year became obsolete. New ballparks are often designed to remind fans of the old stadiums of the early 20th century. Symmetrical fields are out. Riverwalk has all that and more. It incorporates an old railroad building, has an active train track running past it, and is close to the Alabama River. It has all the retro features and all the modern amenities fans demand today.

Riverwalk reminds patrons of the ballparks of yesteryear, which helps them to ease into their seats and make a new old-timey memory.

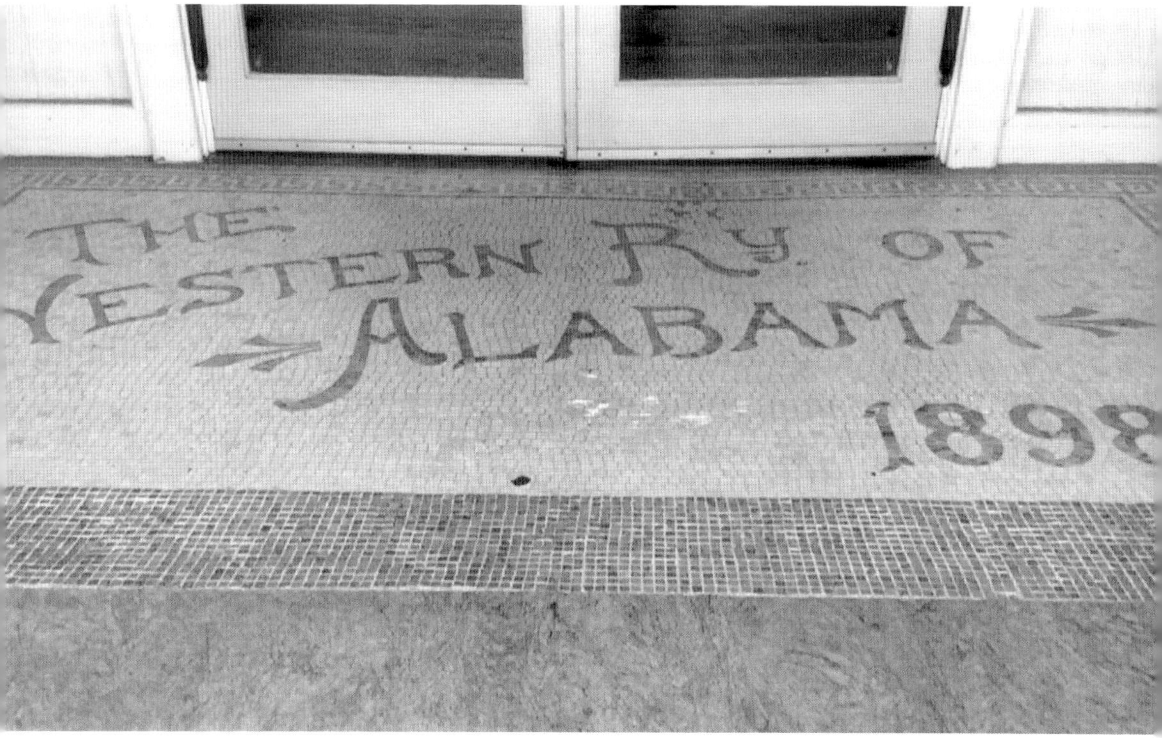

Entering the office of the Montgomery Biscuits, the history of the building is immediately apparent. The tile entrance hints at the story of the Western Railway of Alabama building. It was built in 1898 when trains were the main mode of transportation between cities. (Author's collection.)

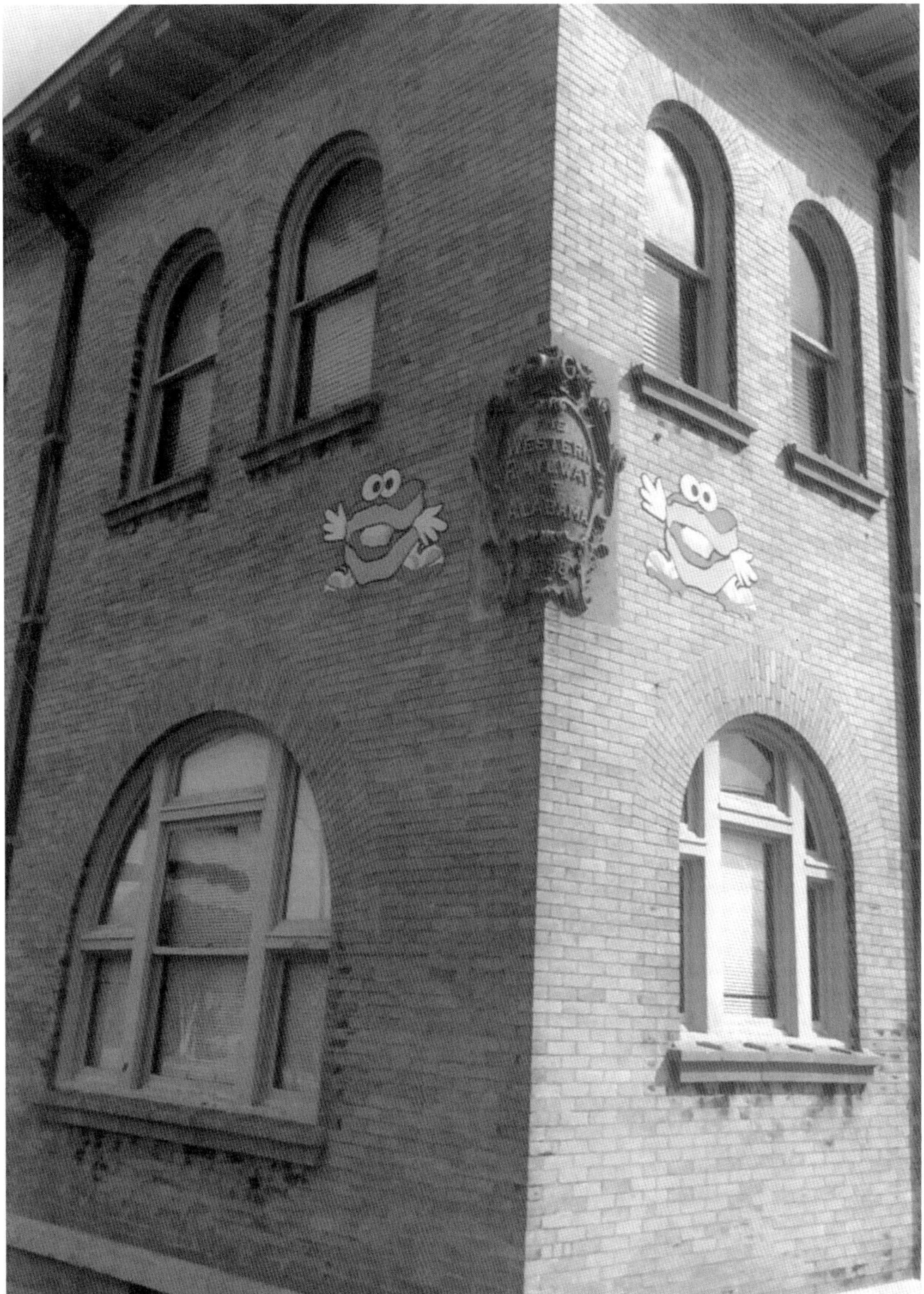

The corner of the Western Railway building still displays a cornerstone with the same basic information that the entrance contains. The Western Railway of Alabama was a rail line that connected Montgomery with East Point, Georgia. (Author's collection.)

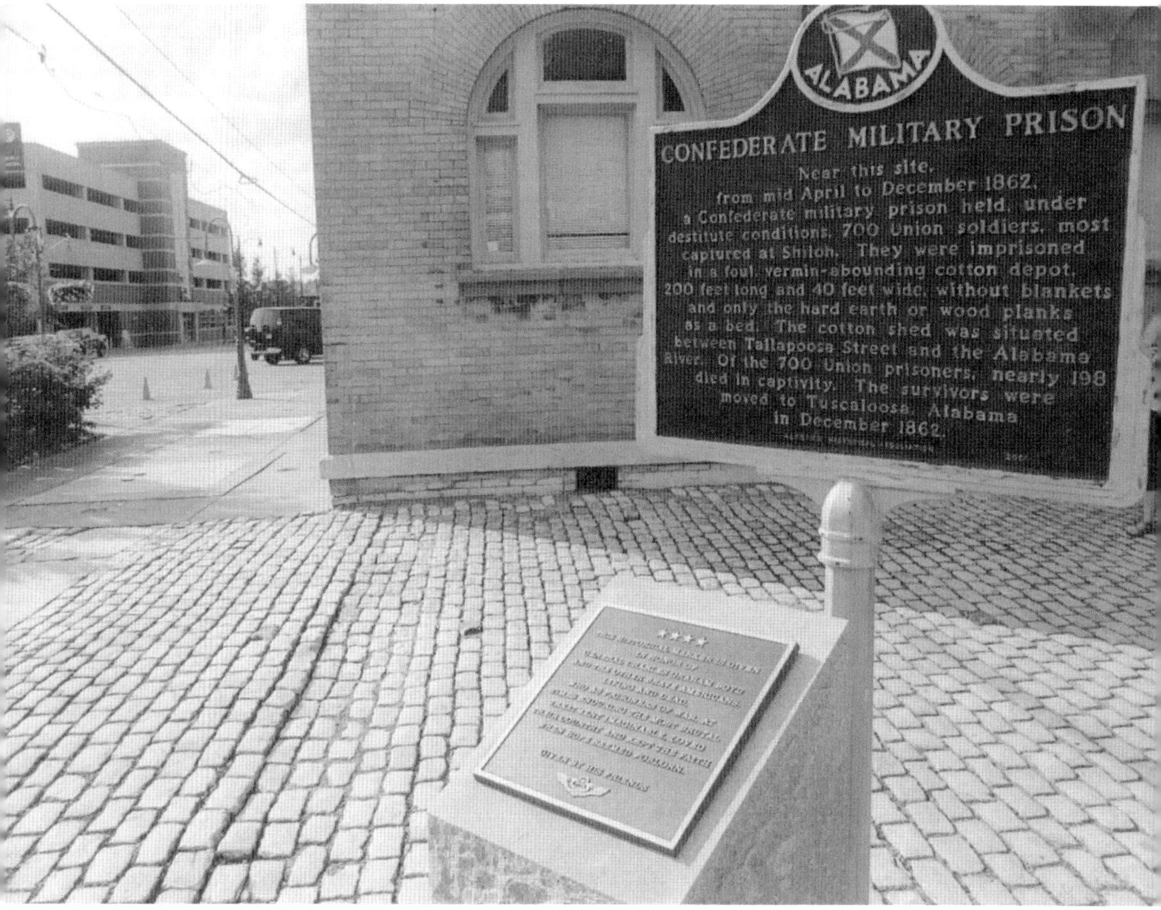

Riverwalk Stadium contains even more historical significance. During the Civil War, this site was a prisoner-of-war camp where Union soldiers were held. Riverwalk is like the city of Montgomery in that there is history that needs to be preserved and stories that need to be retold. (Author's collection.)

Outside the ballpark, down the first base side, stands the end of the old railroad shed. Where trains and cargo were once located, fans now enjoy concessions in the Club Car Bar and suites on the second level. It is possible to build a new ballpark, but the character of the ballpark is defined by its past. (Author's collection.)

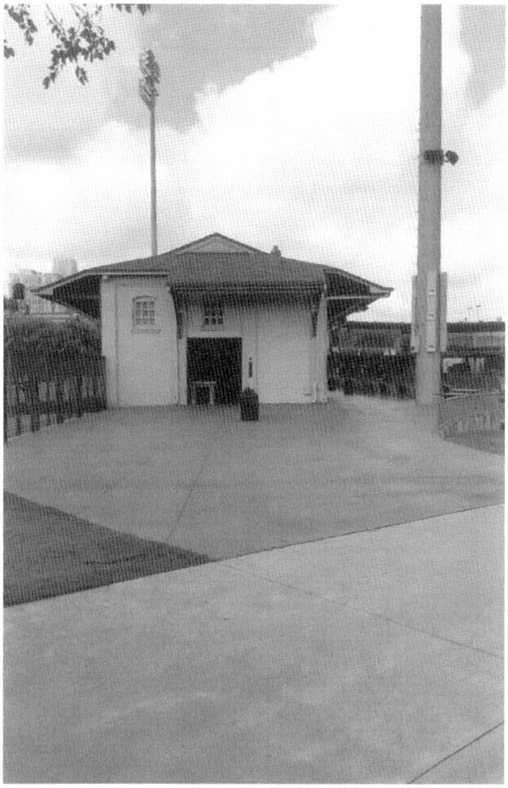

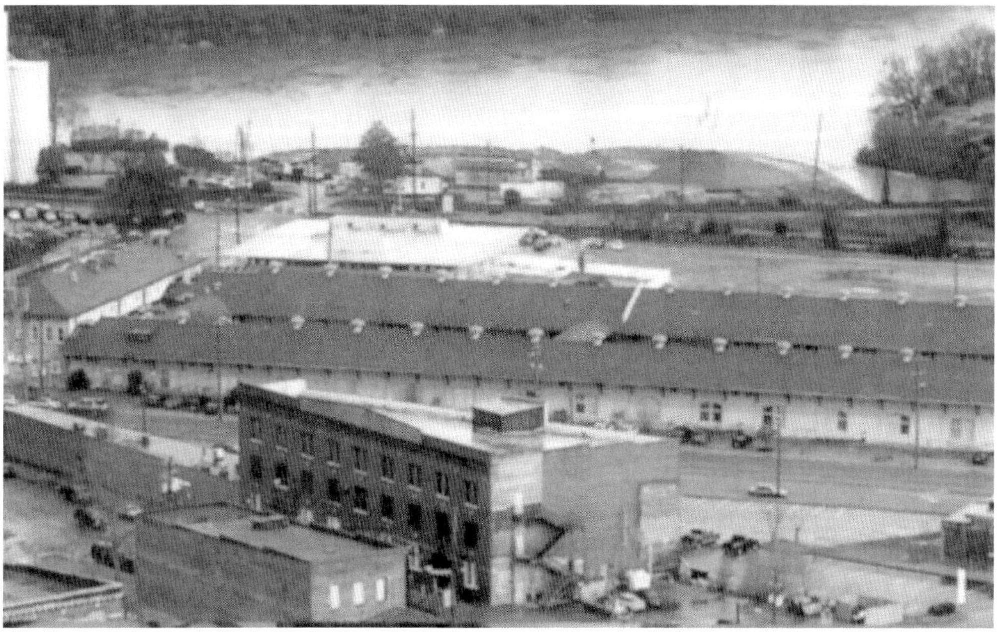

It is easy to forget what the site of Riverwalk Stadium looked like before construction began. There were other structures on the site that had to be removed. The ballpark has brought redevelopment to the surrounding area. (Courtesy of the Montgomery Biscuits.)

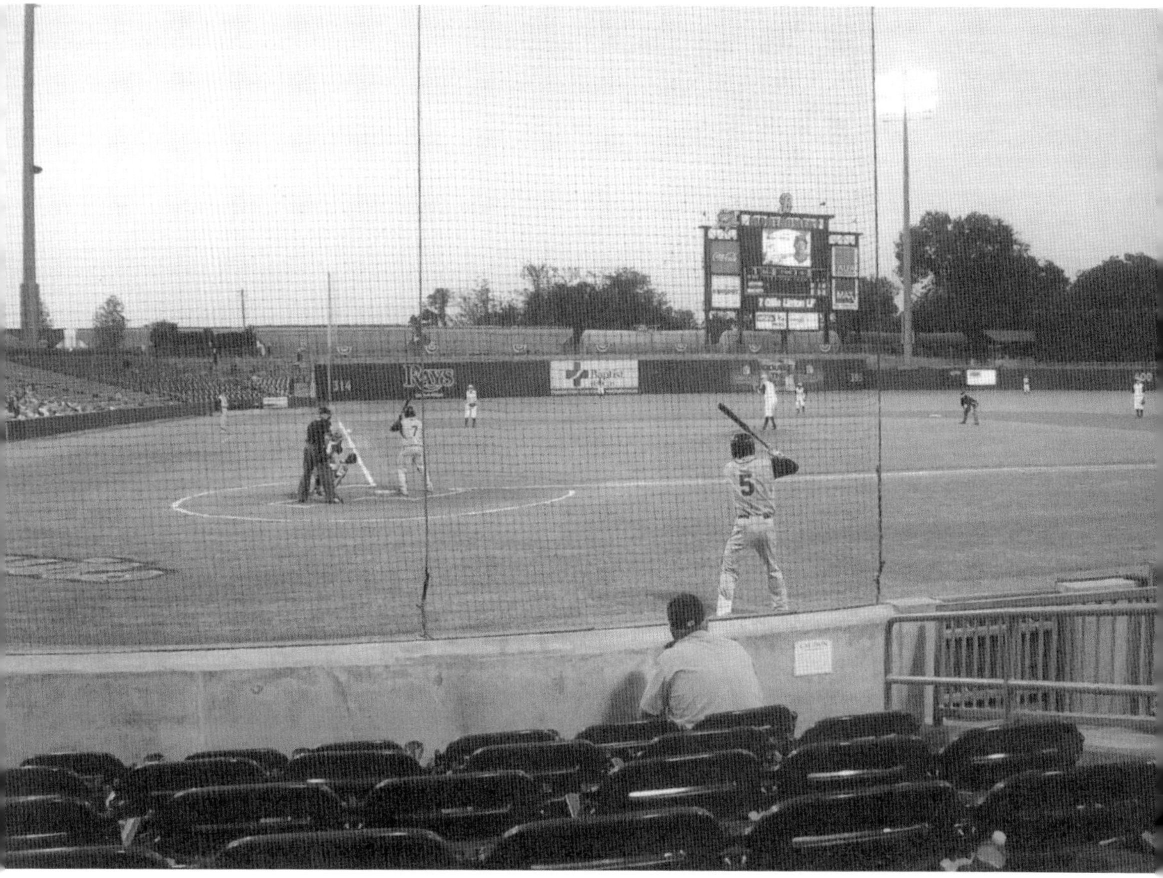

Above the left field wall, a train is slowly going by. Montgomery's mayor Bobby Bright said he would give $1,000 to the first Biscuit player who hit a home run off a train car. On August 13, 2004, Iker Franco did just that; the next day, Mayor Bright paid up. (Author's collection.)

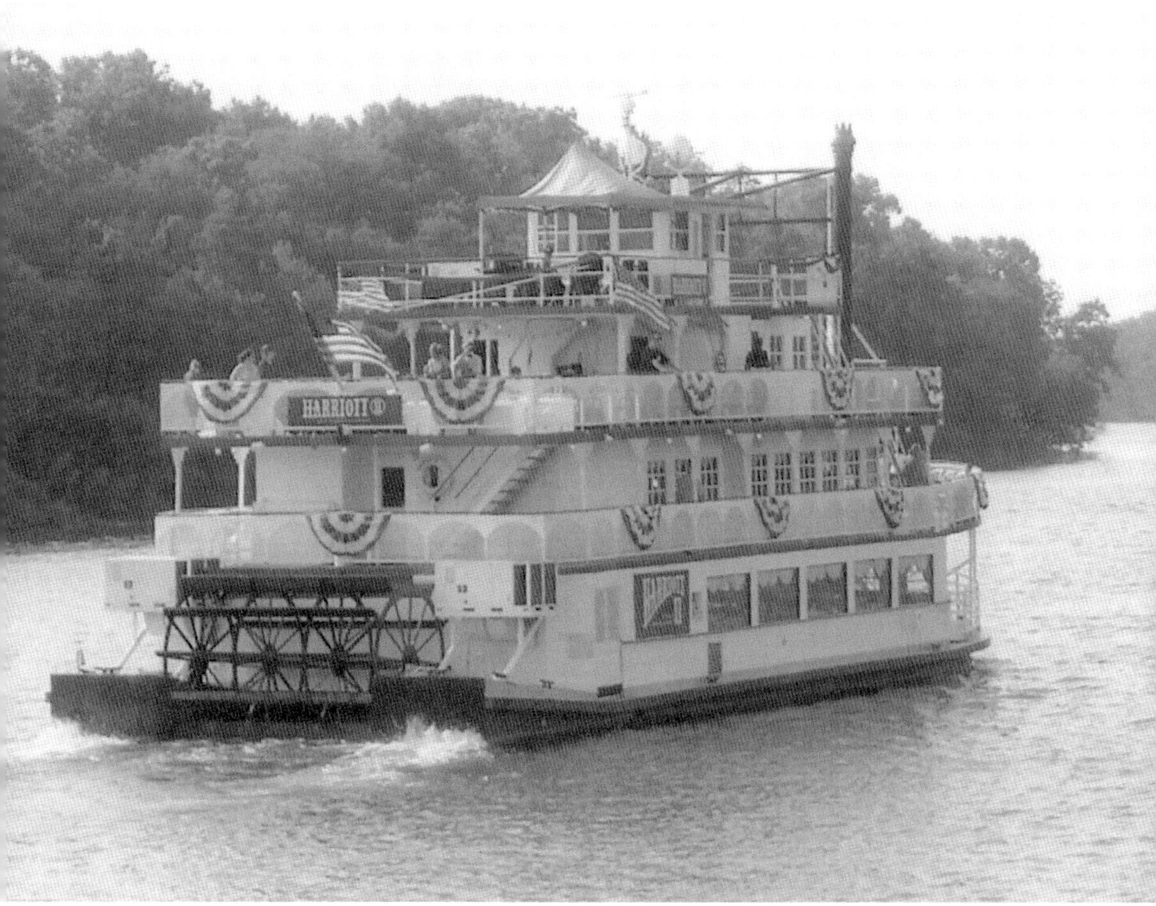

If seeing a train slowly rambling past the ballpark is not enough, there is also a chance to see the paddleboat *Harriott II* steaming by during a game. Next time the Biscuits are on the road, a dinner cruise would give the opportunity to see Riverwalk Stadium from the vantage point of the Alabama River. (Author's collection.)

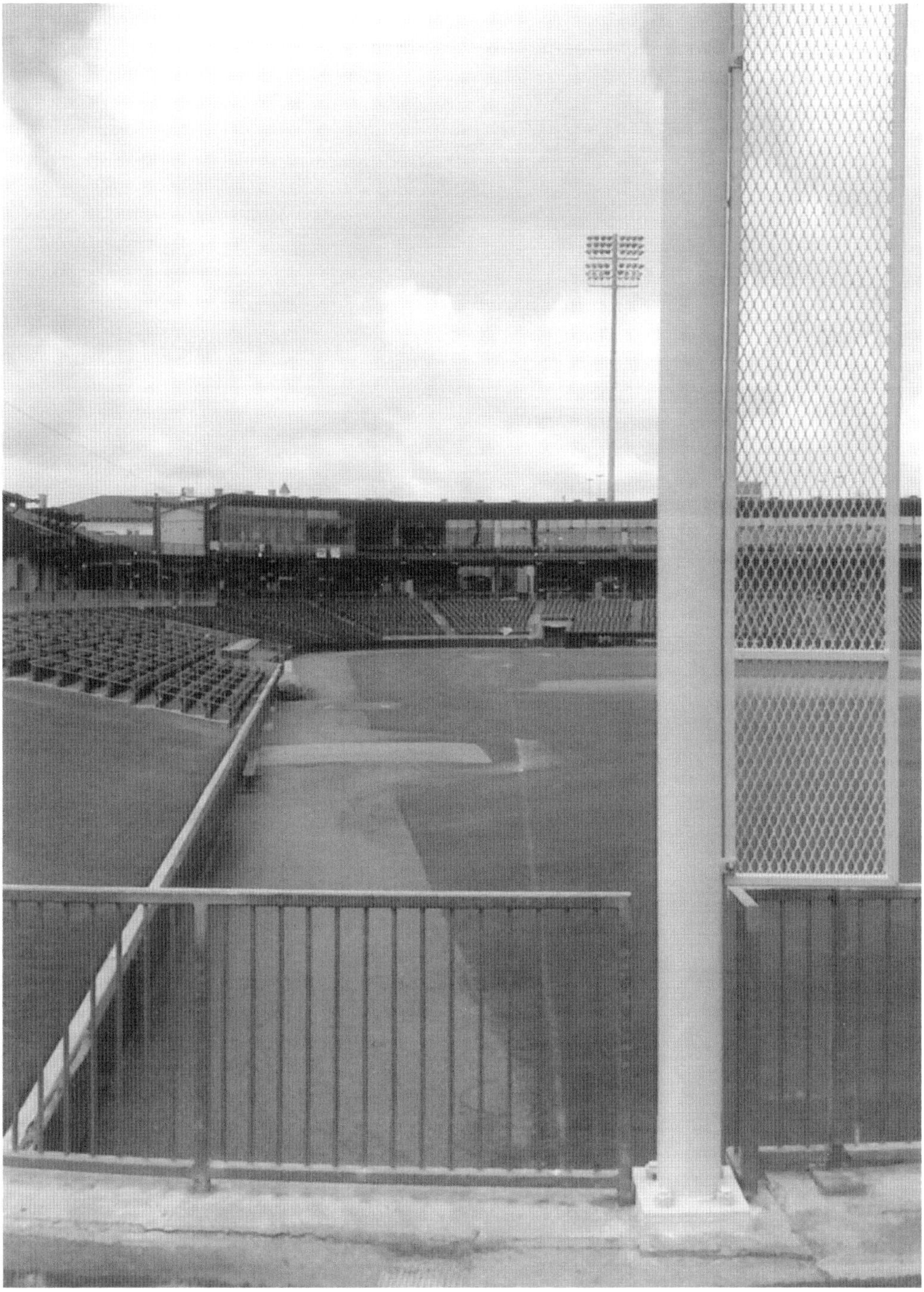

Riverwalk Stadium gives fans the opportunity to view a game from many different angles. Many minor league parks have no access to outfield viewing. At Riverwalk, visitors can spend an inning walking completely around the field and see the game from many different viewpoints. A home run really looks awesome from the outfield. (Author's collection.)

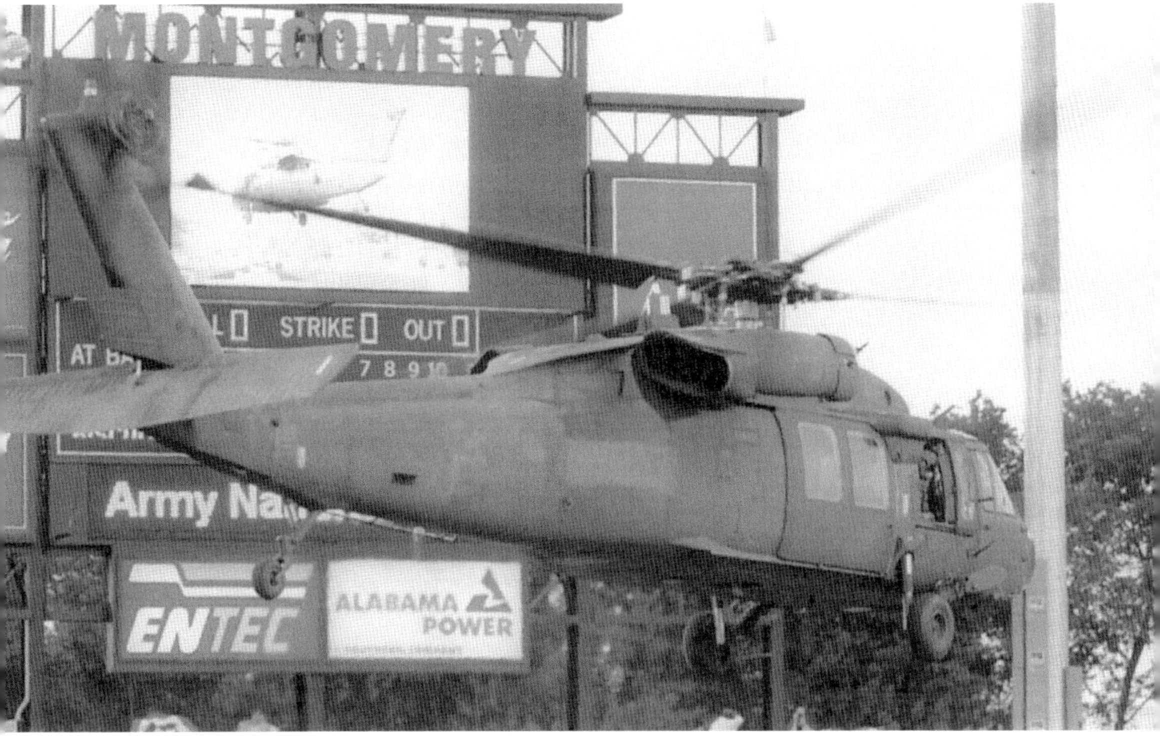

On opening day at Riverwalk Stadium, April 16, 2004, a Blackhawk helicopter delivered the game balls. It had been 24 years since the last Rebels' last game at Patterson Field. Two generations of Montgomery's youth had missed out on the pleasure of growing up with Minor League Baseball. Opening day was a complete success. The Biscuits won their first game against the Huntsville Stars, and Riverwalk Stadium was the talk of the town! (Courtesy of the Montgomery Biscuits.)

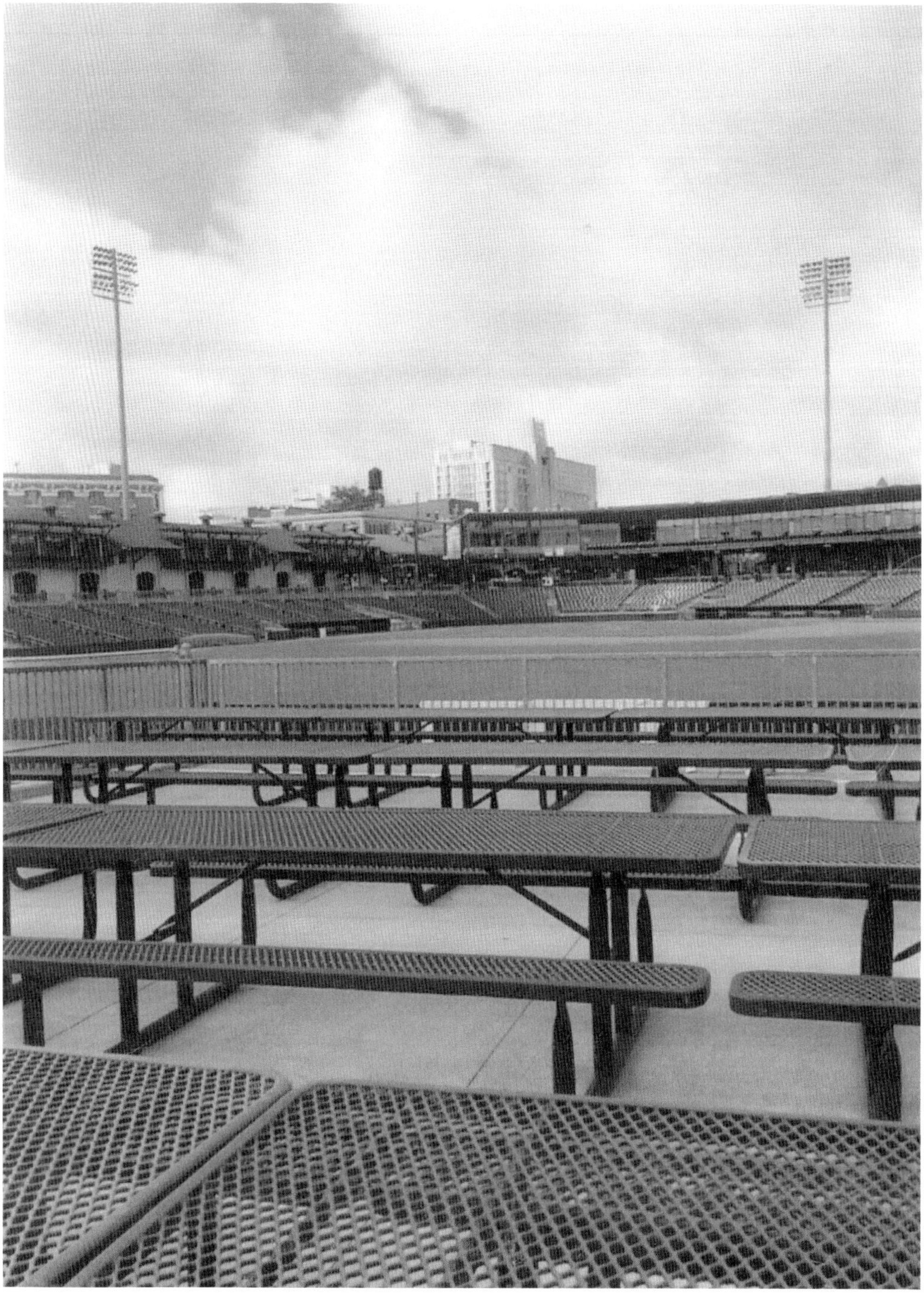

Over 4,000 fans can picnic at a Biscuit game. Baseball only gets better when it is combined with other traditional American favorite pastimes, like picnicking and spending time with friends and family. Riverwalk provides the fans with an array of different settings to enjoy a game. (Author's collection.)

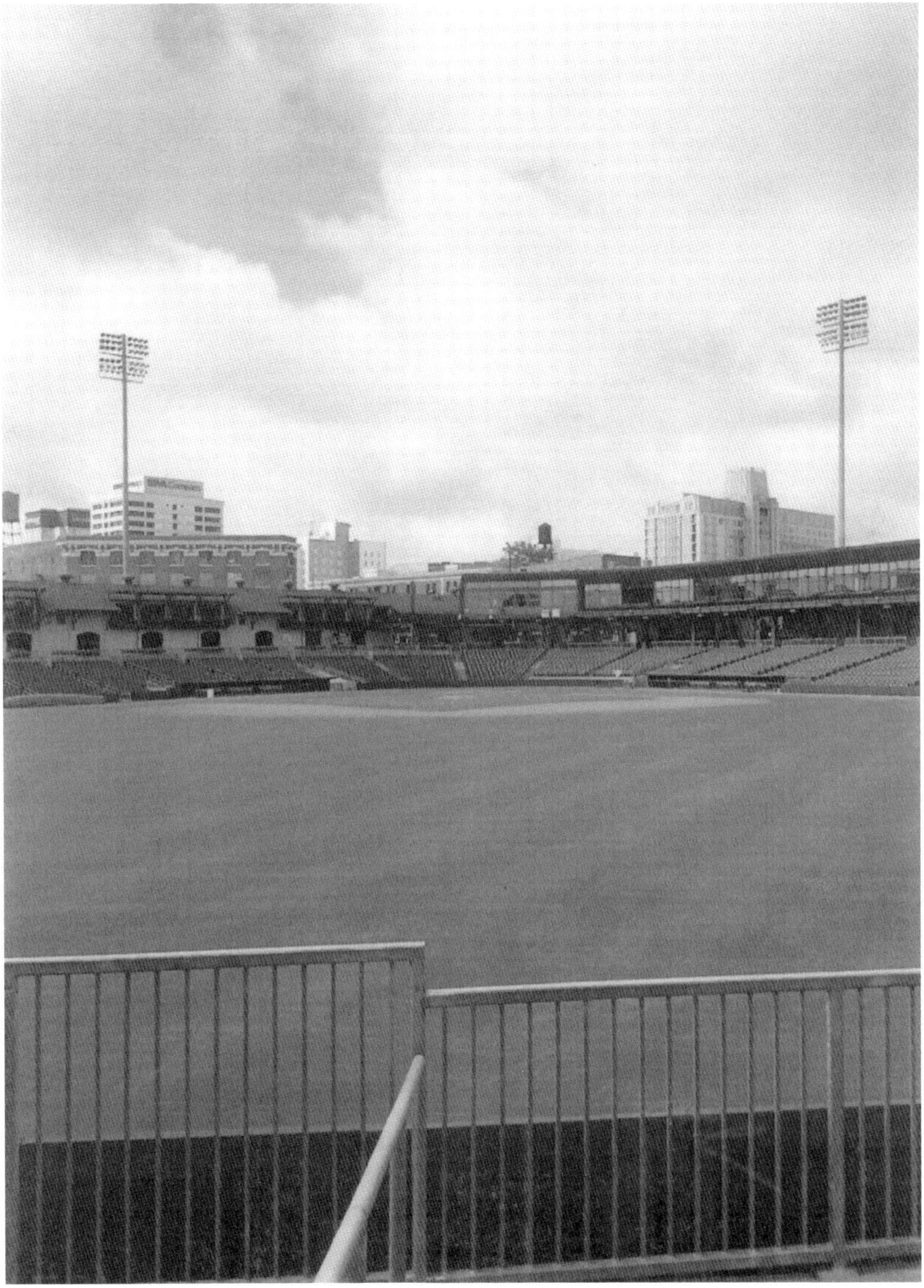

Riverwalk Stadium is more than what is happening in the ballpark. It also provides fantastic views of the cityscape of Montgomery. No matter where one is in the stadium, the view looking out is impressive. A tall building, a train going by, a riverboat, and a blue sky meeting a green ballfield are all aesthetically pleasing. Also, remember there is not a bad seat in the park. (Author's collection.)

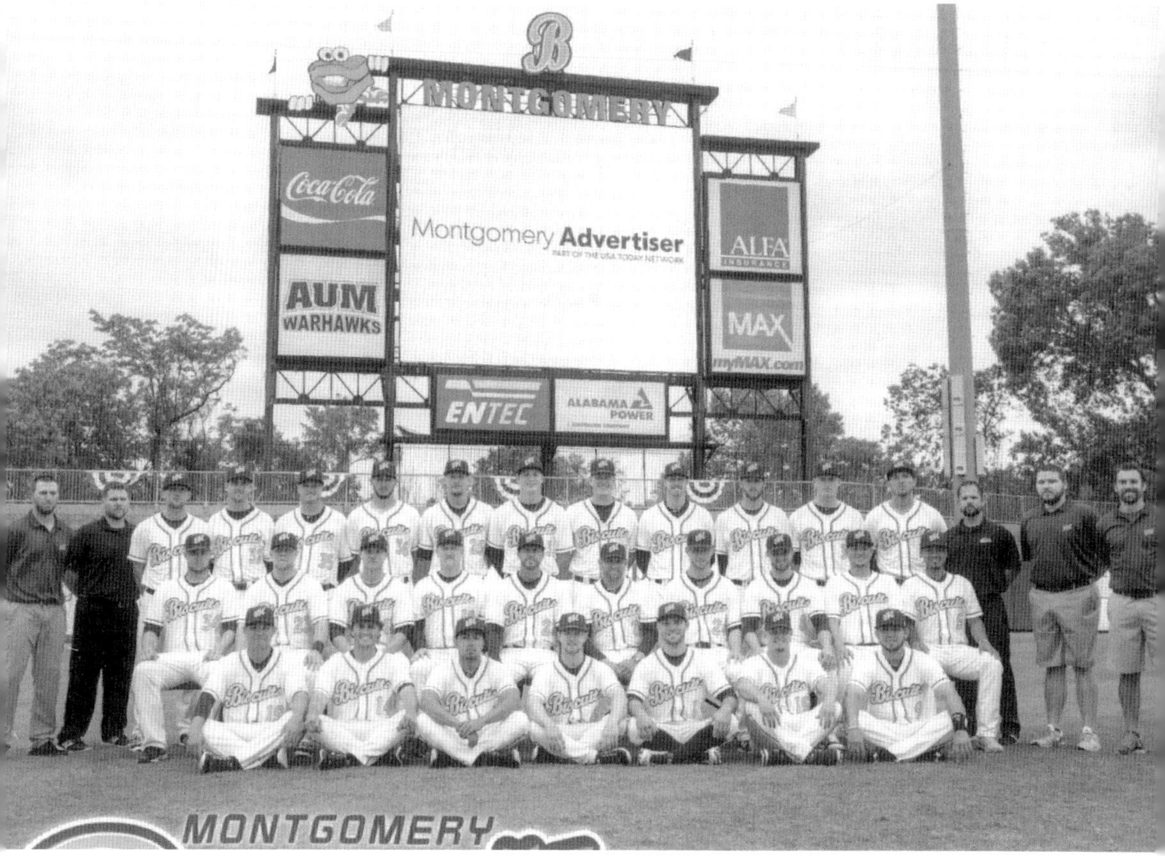

Behind the 2016 Montgomery Biscuits team is the Biscuits Vision HD, a state-of-the-art video board installed before the 2012 season. It gives fans the added bonus of watching replays of exciting events and alerts them to what is happening in the ballpark. The Biscuits ownership realizes that the baseball experience at Riverwalk must be updated and improved to stay relevant to the fans. (Author's collection.)

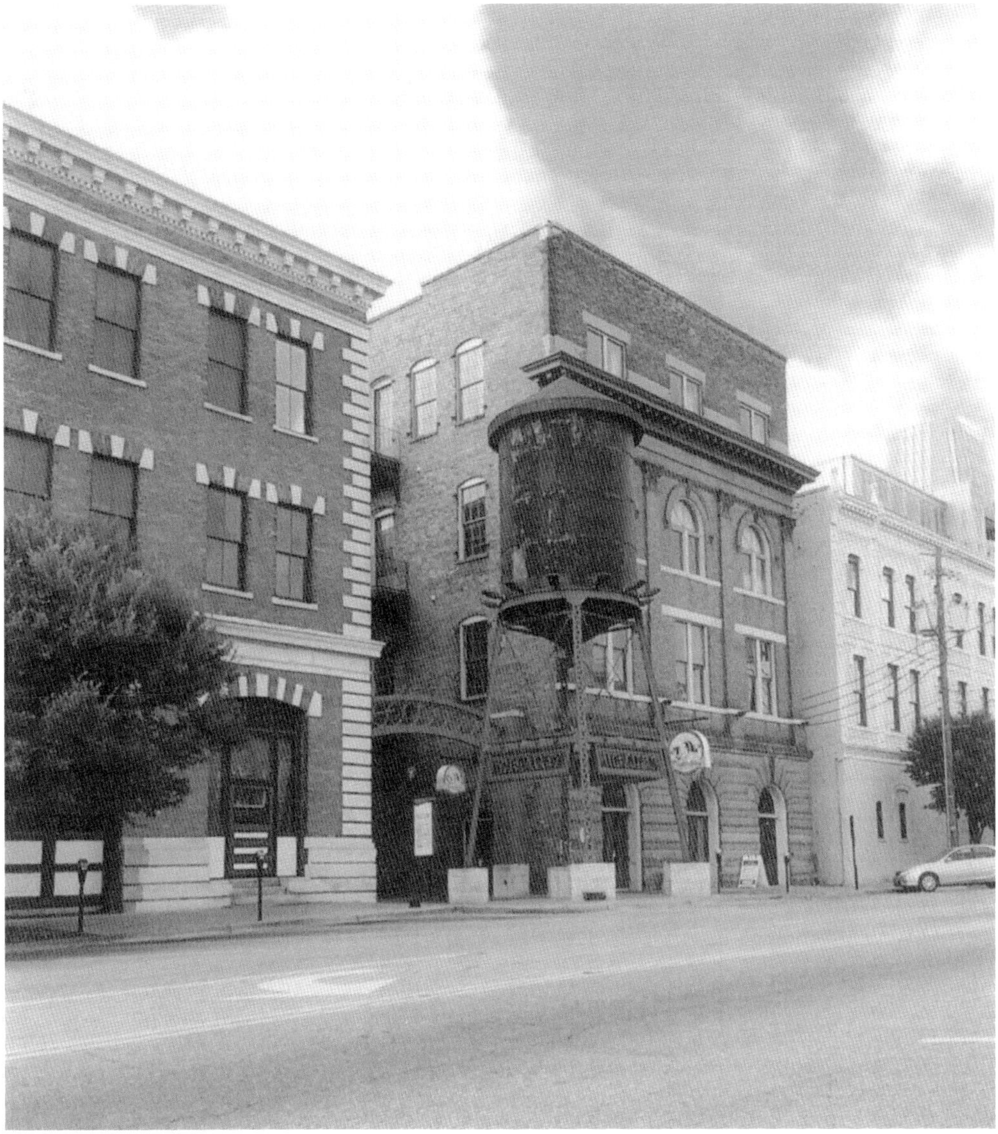

Riverwalk Stadium was just the first in a series of improvements in the downtown area. Just a short block from the stadium, a restaurant and entertainment center opened to be enjoyed before or after a game. An old water tower marks the area and invites fans to walk down to enjoy the atmosphere of the Ally Entertainment District, including food, a microbrewery, and fellowship all in redeveloped historic buildings. The great thing about the Alley Entertainment District is that it is open year-round. (Author's collection.)

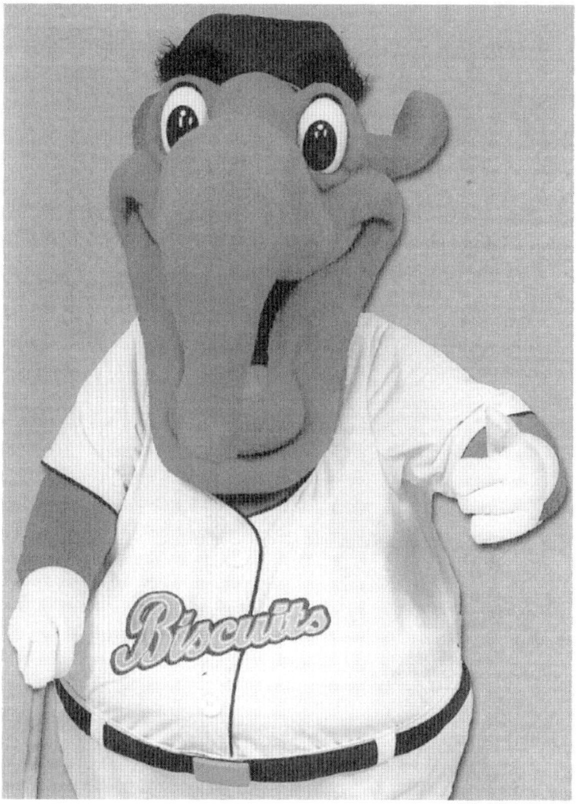

Riverwalk Stadium, Biscuit baseball, and Big Mo and Monty are all part of a package that makes baseball in Montgomery fun for the whole family. It is an exciting time for both the serious baseball geeks and the casual sports fan. Come for the game and leave with the history. (Both, author's collection.)

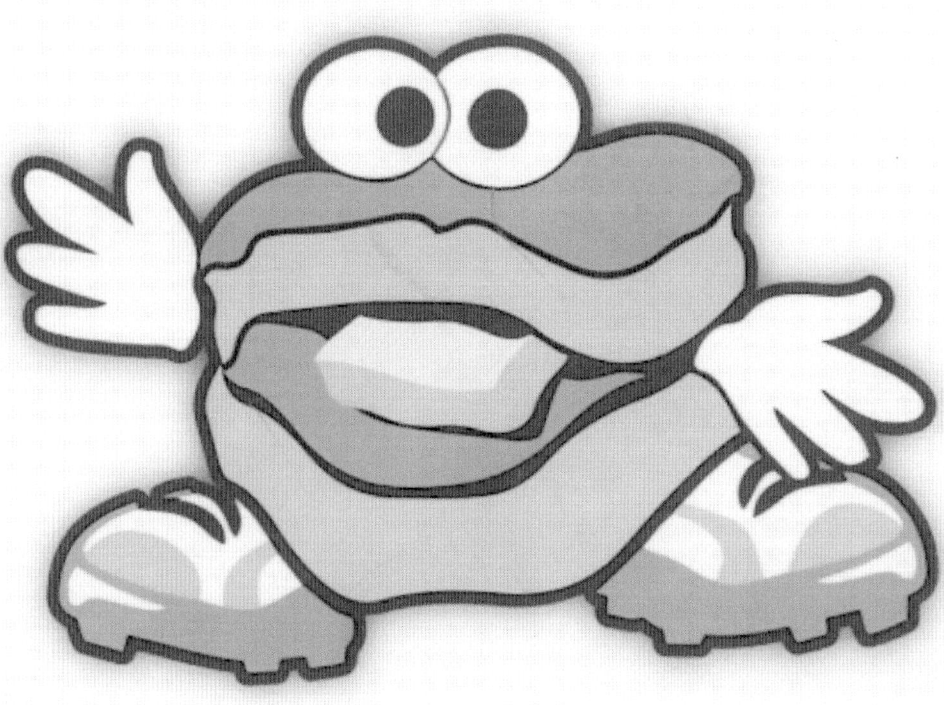

10

Favorite Sons

Every city has its local baseball hero, local players who make it to the "show" in Major League Baseball. Townsfolk follow their careers as they first learn about them in newspaper accounts of their high school successes. Then, their signing with a professional team makes the local news at 6:00. When they finally make the major leagues, people are so proud of them, it is as if they are part of their family. Fans check box scores to keep up with their achievements. This chapter shares the stories of favorite Alabama sons of baseball.

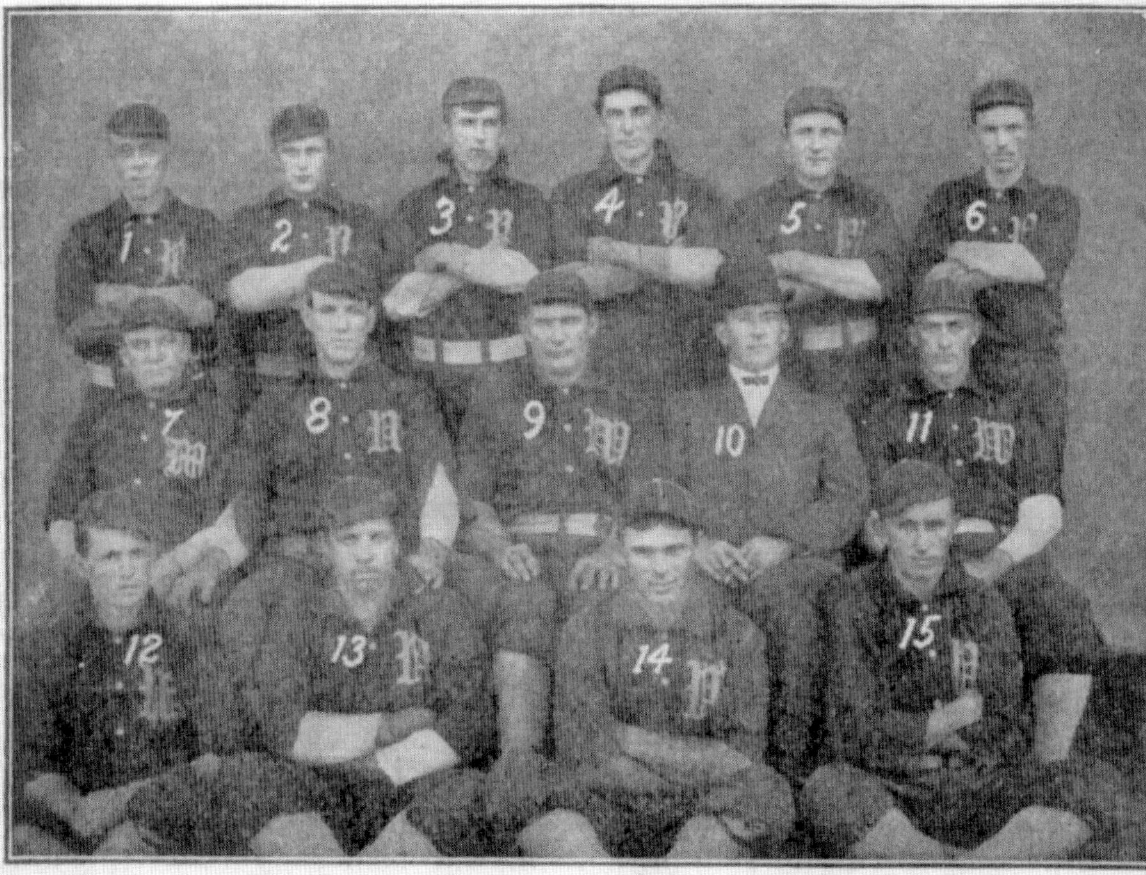

1, Lee; 2, Oldring; 3, Starkell; 4, McCoy; 5, Millerick; 6, McMakin; 7, Yeager; 8, Mullaney; 9, Durrett, Mgr.; 10, Hale; 11, Brouthers; 12, Busch; 13, Molesworth; 14, Schwartz, Capt.; 15, Thornton.

MONTGOMERY TEAM—SOUTHERN ASSOCIATION.

Arthur Brouthers was one of the first baseball players from Montgomery, Alabama, to play professional baseball. His career began in 1902 with Charlotte. In 1905, Brouthers played for his hometown team, the Senators. Images of players can be difficult to locate, especially when a player never made it to the majors. For Brouthers, this team picture of the 1905 Montgomery Senators is the only photograph available. Brouthers is No. 11. (Author's collection.)

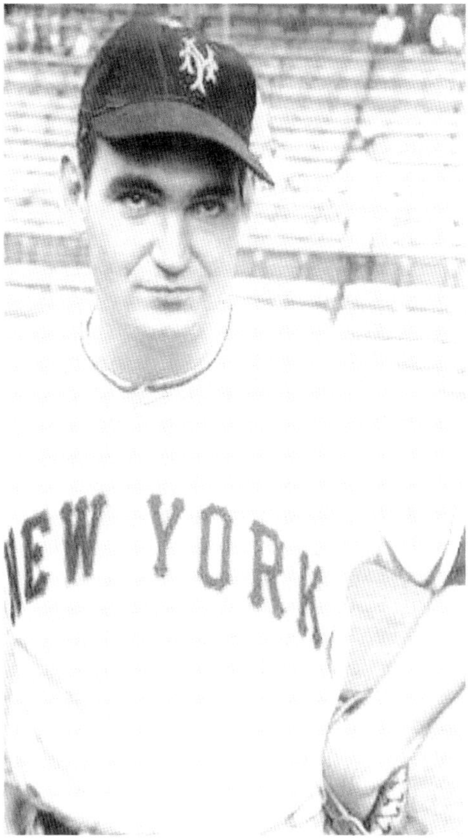

James Lamar "Dusty" Rhodes was born in Montgomery County, Alabama. Rhodes's major league career of six years with the New York Giants would be largely forgotten except for his Most Valuable Player performance in the 1954 World Series. The New York Giants entered the World Series against the Cleveland Indians. It was Rhodes's clutch hits that won the series for New York. In game one, he hit a pinch-hit home run for the win. In game two, he hit a game-tying single, followed by a home run later in the game. In game three, a two-run, pinch-hit single enabled New York to sweep Cleveland. For his efforts, Rhodes was named MVP of the series. Later that year, Montgomery celebrated Dusty Rhodes Day with a parade, gifts, and a special dinner for this favorite son. (Both, Alabama Department of Archives and History.)

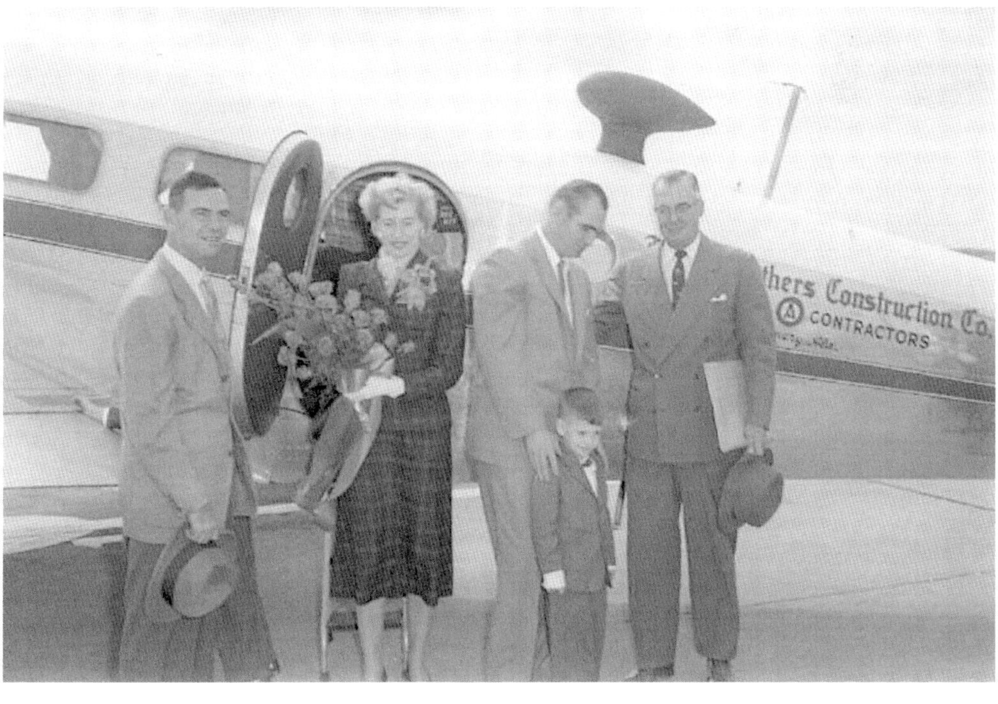

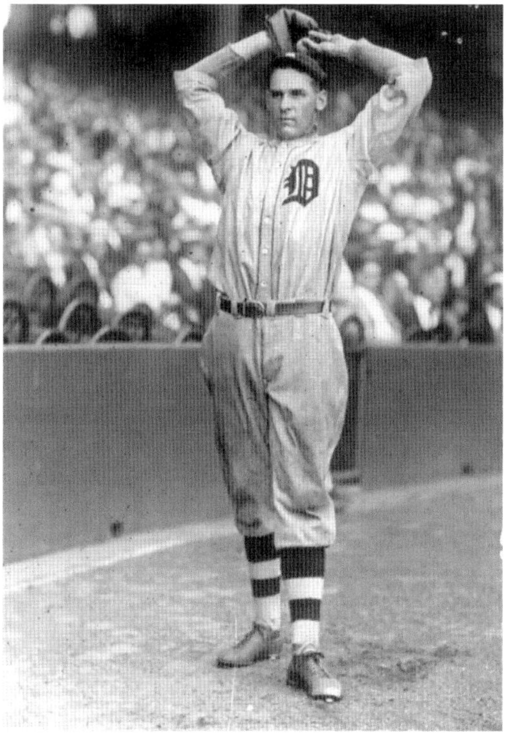

Ed Wells was a long-time resident of Montgomery after his playing career. He spent 14 seasons in the major leagues, primarily with the Detroit Tigers and the New York Yankees. Wells had the distinction of playing on the same teams with Ty Cobb and Babe Ruth. He was living in Montgomery when the Babe came to the city for a banquet in 1948. After the banquet, Ruth spent the evening visiting with Wells, talking about the good old days. Wells is pictured at left during his days with Detroit, and below at Birmingham. (Both, courtesy of the Friends of Rickwood.)

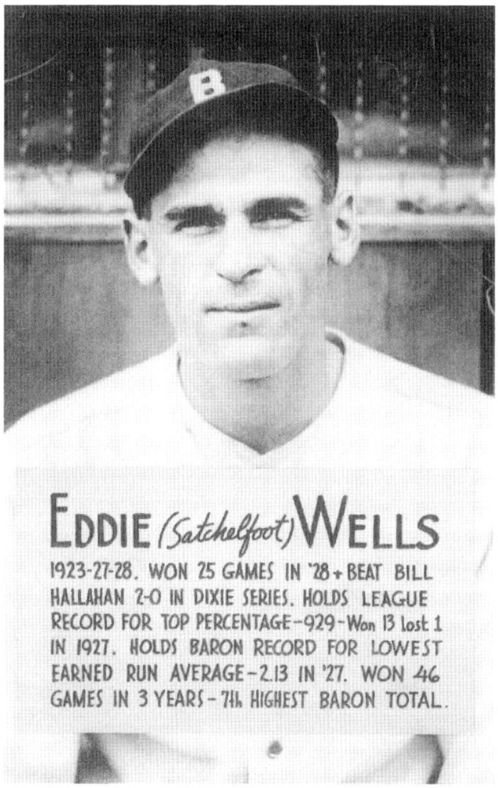

Ernie Wingard was from Prattville, Alabama. He pitched two years for the University of Alabama in 1920 and 1921. After college, Wingard was pitching for a semiprofessional team in Bastrop, Louisiana, where he got to know Joe Jackson. Jackson, banned from Major League Baseball in 1919, was also playing semiprofessional baseball. The next season, Jackson asked Wingard to join him on a team in Americus, Georgia. A mentor-student relationship developed between Jackson and Wingard. When Wingard made the St. Louis Browns team in 1924, Jackson traveled with him as his personal advisor and coach, even though association with Jackson could have been frowned upon by baseball management. After four years with St. Louis, Wingard was back in the minor leagues. In 1940, Wingard pitched for the Montgomery Rebels. For part of the season, he also managed the team. Jackson is pictured at right, and Wingard is below. (Both, author's collection.)

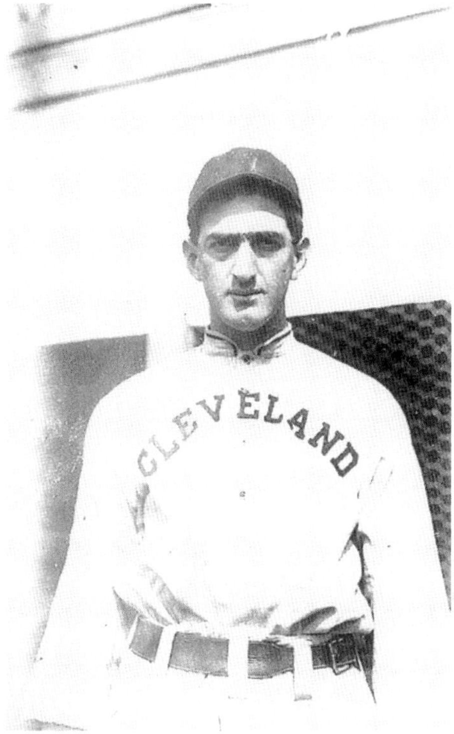

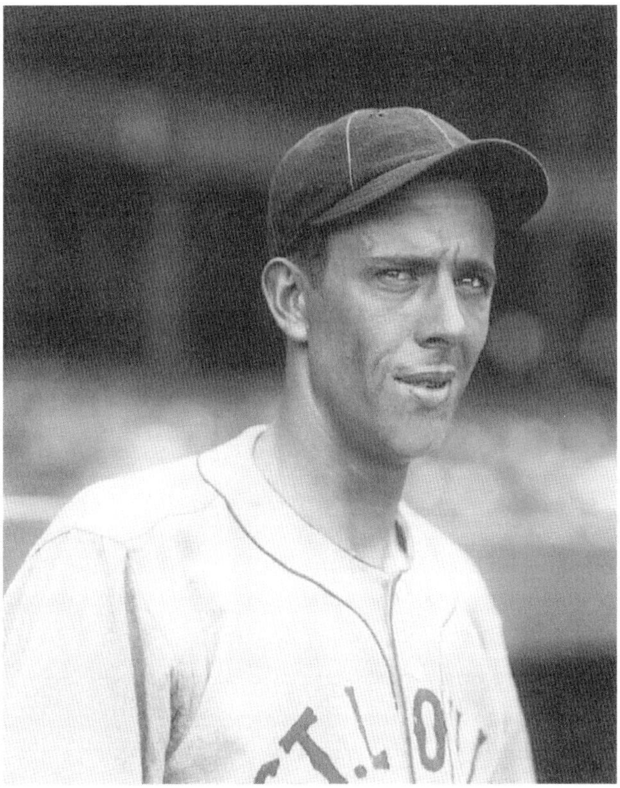

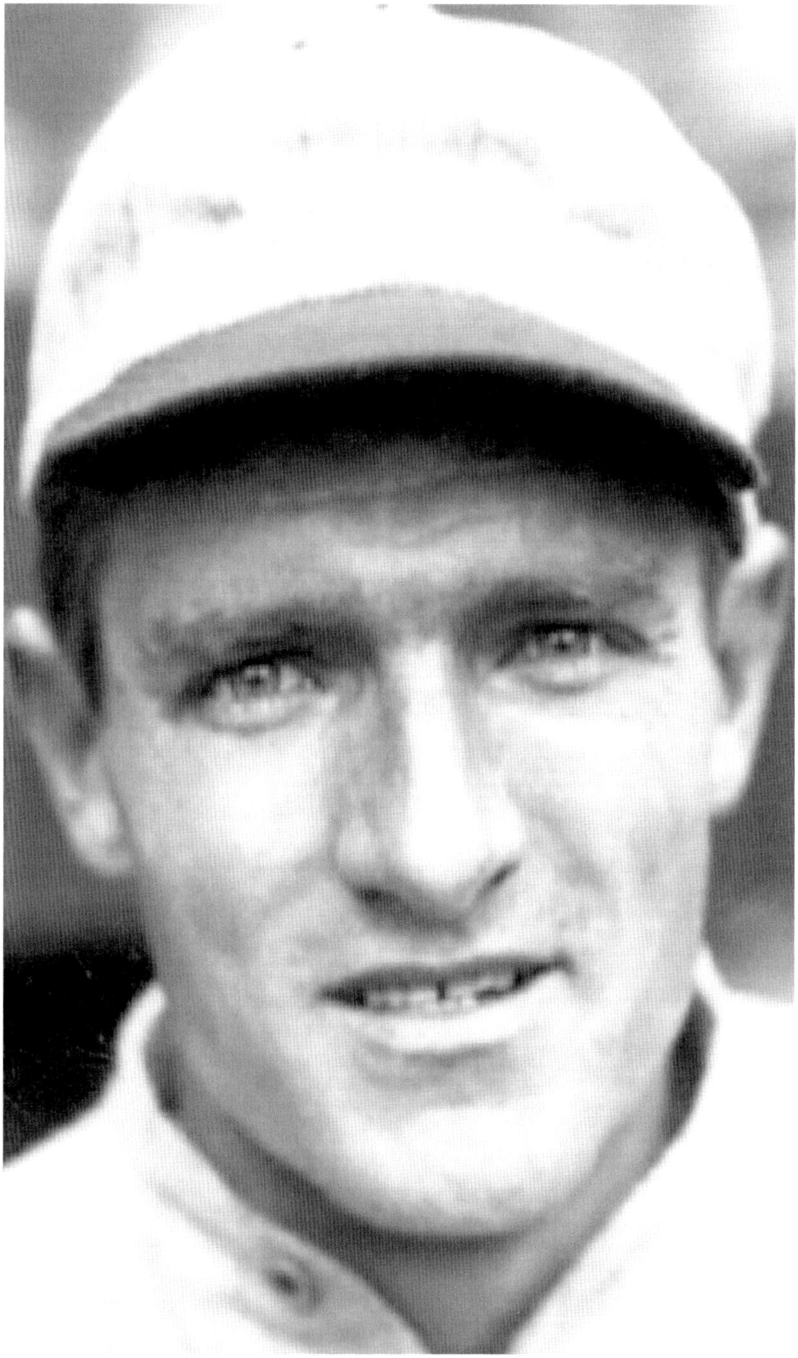

Tom Oliver was born in 1903 in Montgomery. In 1922, he was given a tryout with the New Orleans Pelicans. When he did not make the team, he signed with Laurel in the Cotton State League. Olive would finally make the big leagues in 1930 as an outfielder with the Boston Red Sox. After 1933, he was back to the minor leagues, hoping to make a comeback. After the 1942 season, Oliver joined the Navy and served in the South Pacific on the USS *Grayson*. (Author's collection.)

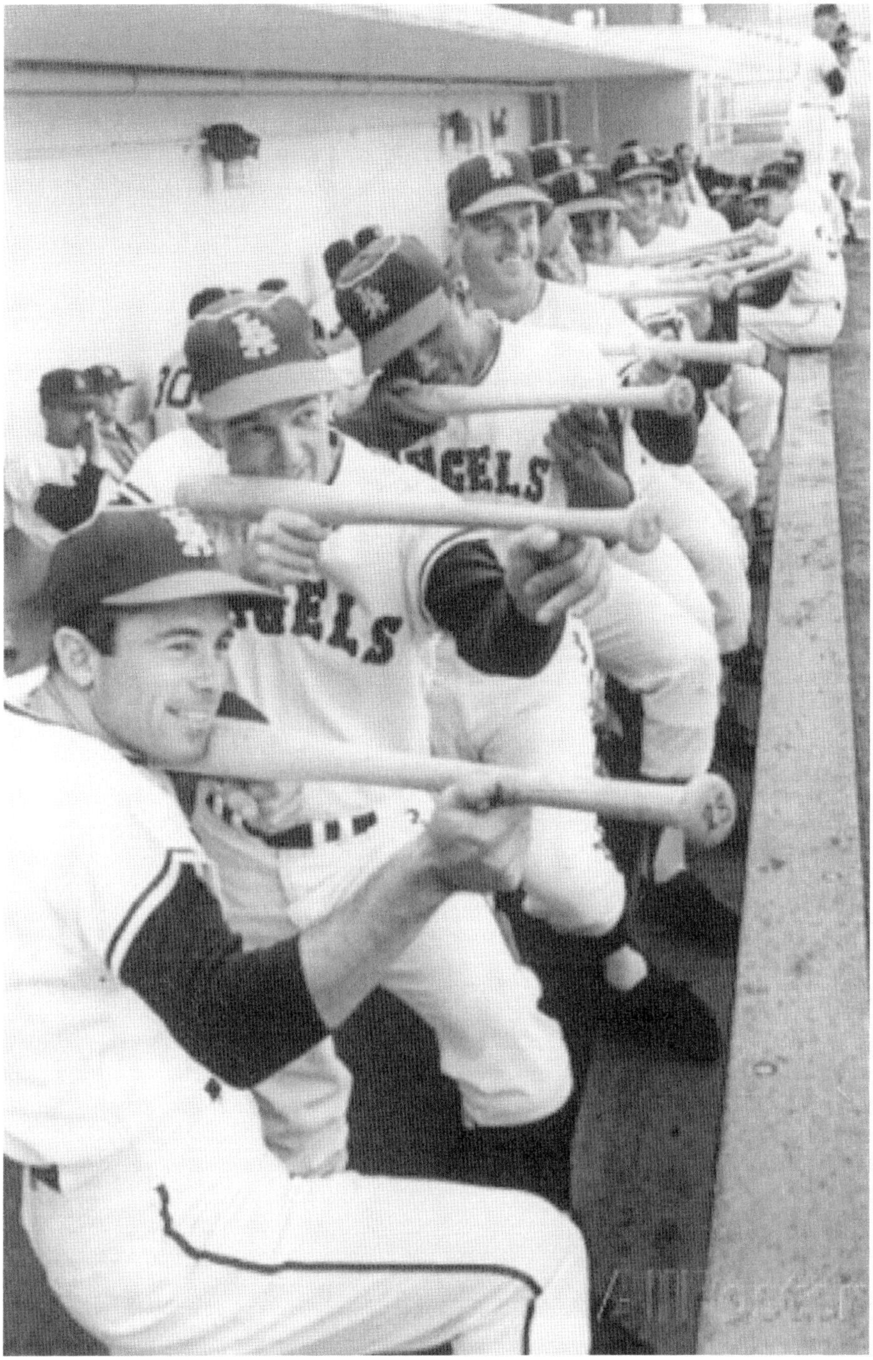

Billy Moran began his major league career with the Cleveland Indians. In 1960, Cleveland sold his contract to a minor league team. It looked as though his career was going down, but during the season, the newly formed Los Angeles Angels acquired Moran's contract. He went on to have several good seasons with the Angels. Moran is second from the left behind former Montgomery Rebel Albie Pearson. (Author's collection.)

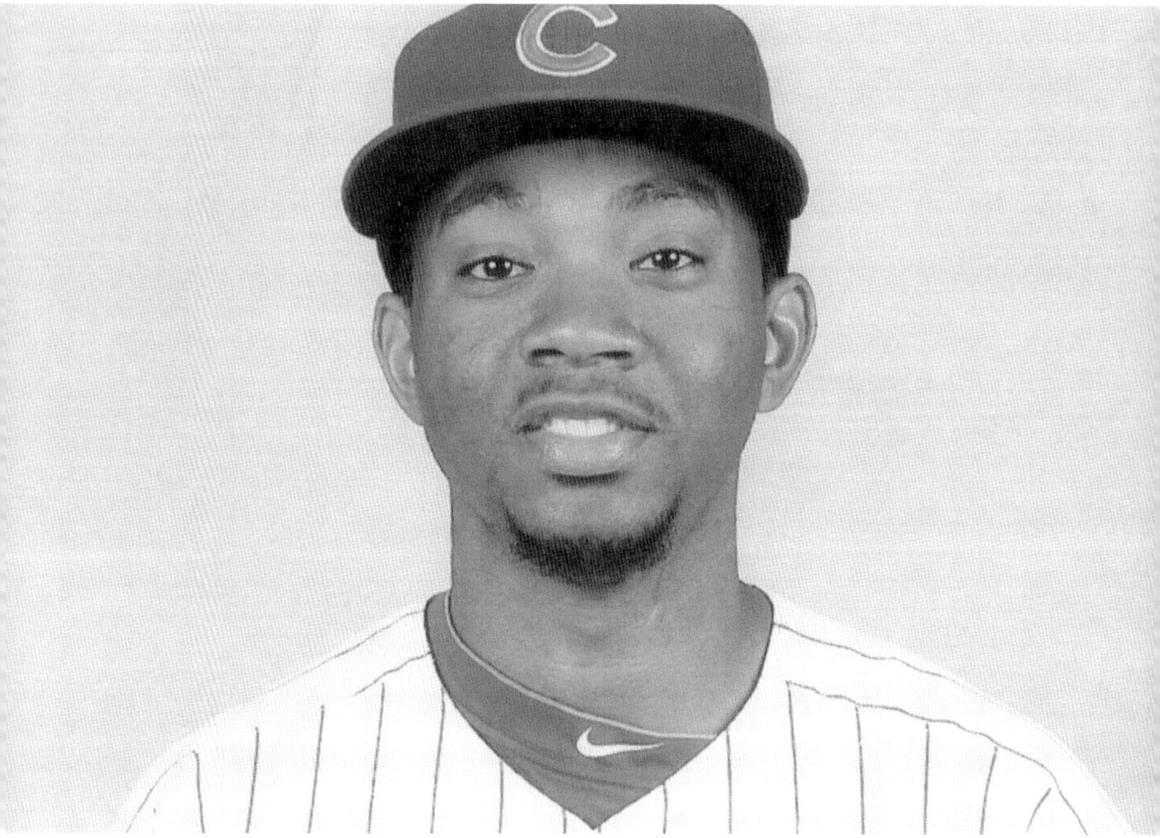

Wesley Wright, who was born in Montgomery, was drafted by the Los Angeles Dodgers in 2003. After four years in the minors, he was selected by the Houston Astros in the rule five draft in 2007. The next year, he was pitching in the major leagues. Wright's career has taken him to five other major league teams. He is presently in Triple-A, trying to work his way back to the major leagues. (Author's collection.)

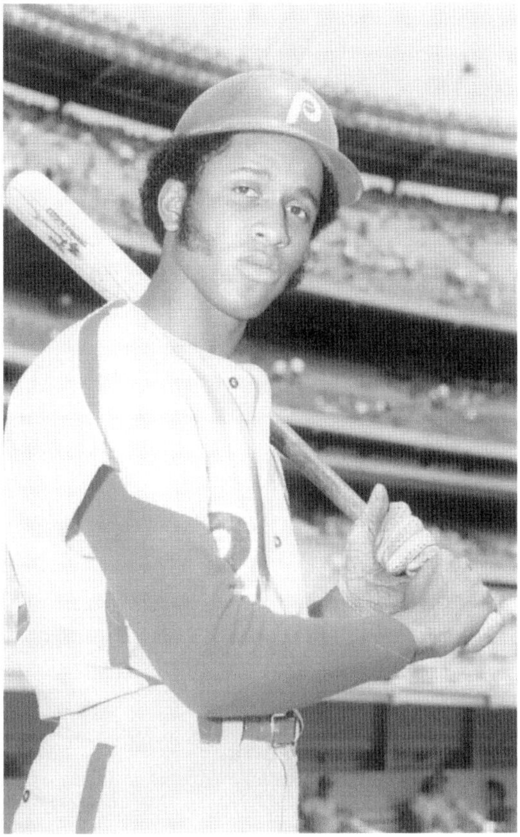

Oscar Gamble was born in Ramer, Alabama. He was discovered playing baseball by Negro League legend Buck O'Neil. He is remembered for a famous quote about the chaos within the New York Yankees clubhouse: "They don't think it be like it is, but it do." Gamble is not only remembered for his hairstyle, but also for hitting 200 home runs that kept him in the major leagues for 16 years. In 2016, Gamble was inducted into the Alabama Sports Hall of Fame, a well-deserved honor from his native state. (Both, author's collection.)

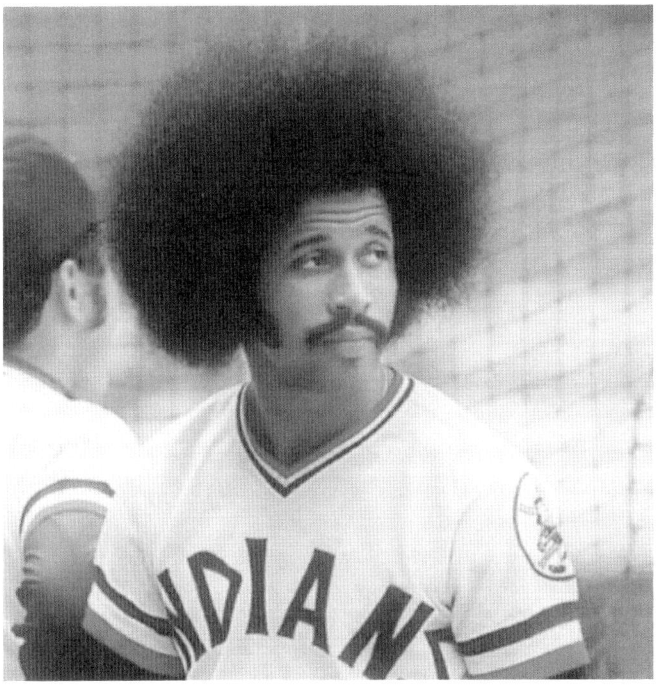

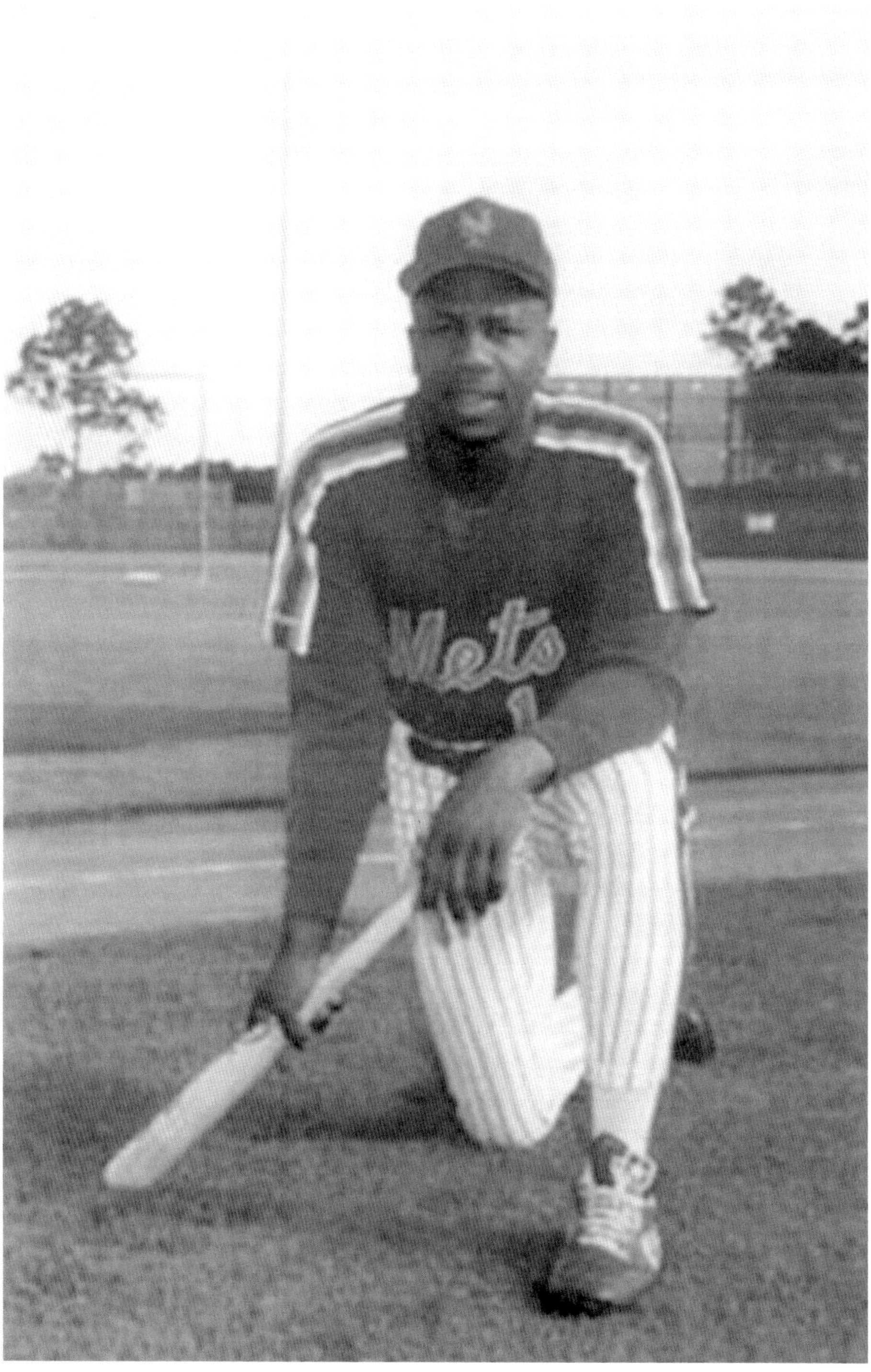

Lou Thornton played five seasons in the major leagues, with the New York Mets and the Toronto Blue Jays. Thornton was the manager for the Montgomery Wings in 2001, a team in the Independent Southeastern League. (Author's collection.)

Joe Caffie was born in Ramer, Alabama, also the birthplace of Oscar Gamble. In 1950, Caffie played in the Negro League with the Cleveland Buckeyes. The next year, he signed with the Cleveland Indians. He spent parts of the 1956 and 1957 seasons with the Indians. His nickname was "Rabbit" because of his speed. After 1961, he retired from baseball, never having received a chance in the major leagues. (Author's collection.)

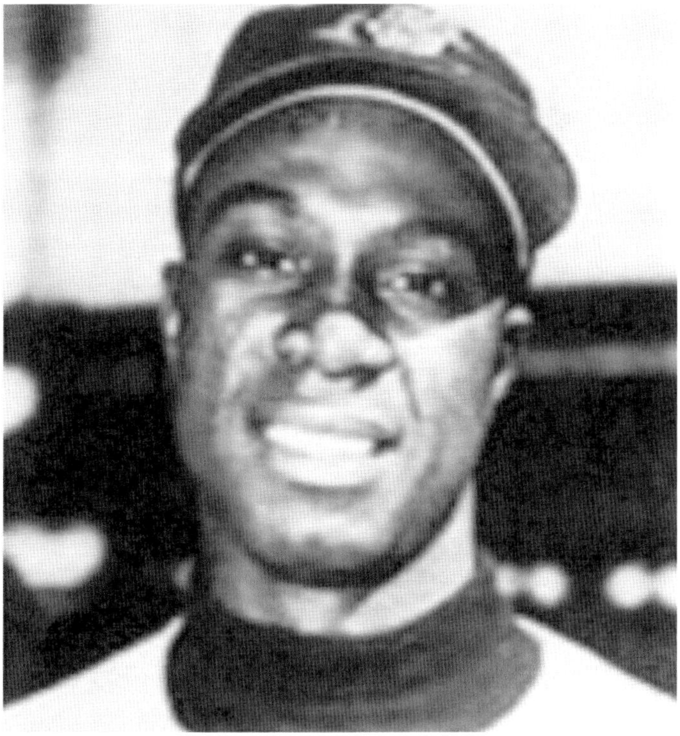

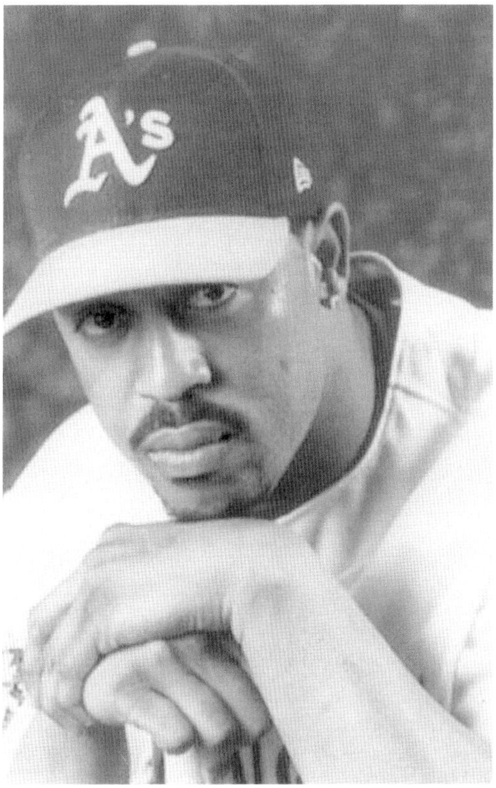

Terrence Long from Montgomery was drafted in 1994 by the New York Mets, but a 1999 trade to the Oakland Athletics is where Long made his mark on the game. His 1999 season with Oakland included a 288 hitting average, 18 home runs, and 8 RBIs. His impressive performance earned him second place in the voting for Rookie of the Year in the American League. Long continued to play Major League Baseball until 2006. (Author's collection.)

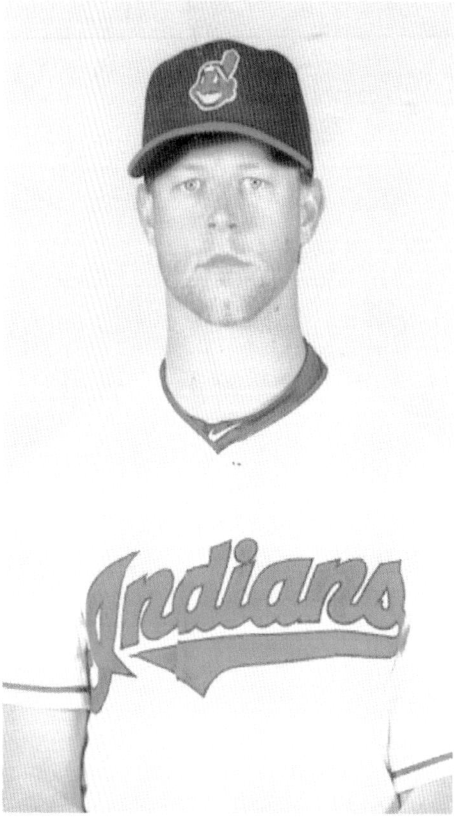

Austin Adams is from Millbrook, Alabama. He signed with the Cleveland Indians in 2009 and has played with the Indians for parts of three seasons. He is currently playing for the Columbus Clippers, the Triple-A team in the Cleveland Indians minor league system. (Author's collection.)

Marlon Anderson was born in Montgomery, but grew up in Prattville. At Prattville High School, he was coached by legendary Alabama baseball coach Roger Lambert. Anderson played college baseball at the University of South Alabama, where he was conference player of the year. Anderson's 11-year major league career took him to six different teams, including to the Mets twice. His movement from team to team seemed to always place him in the middle of a pennant race with an opportunity to excel. (Author's collection.)

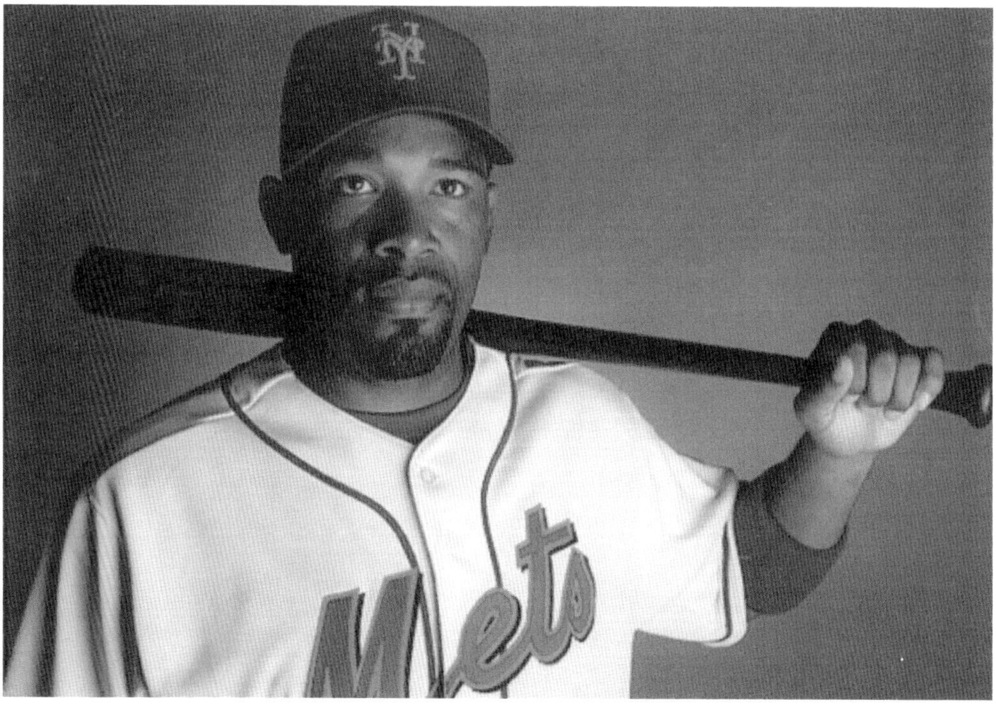

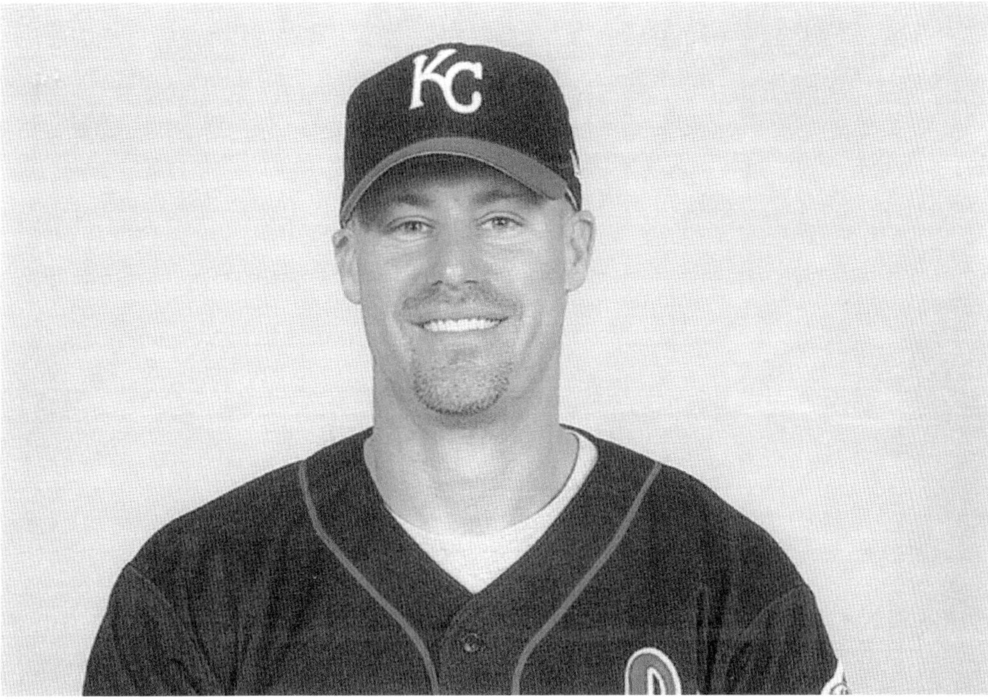

Jarrod Patterson was born in Montgomery in 1973. He played high school baseball in Clanton, Alabama, and was drafted by the New York Mets in 1993. He made his major league debut with the Detroit Tigers in 2001. In 2003, he played for the Kansas City Royals. After 2006, Patterson retired as a player. (Author's collection.)

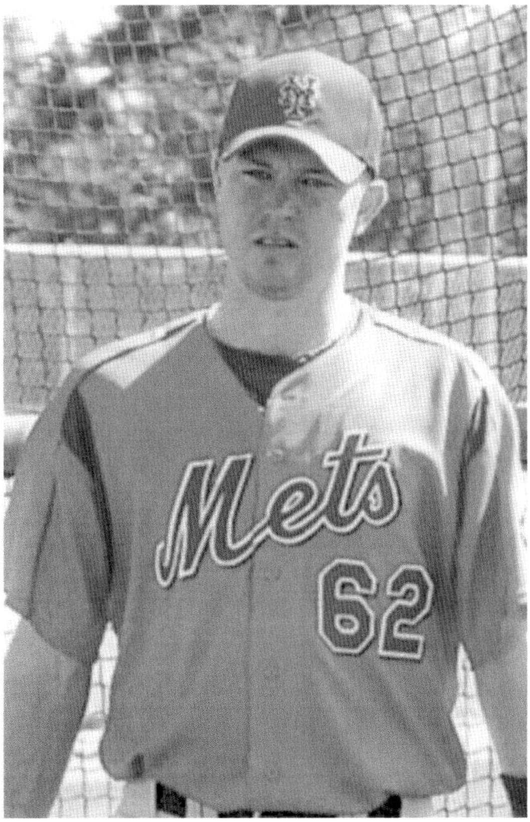

Craig Brazell was born and raised in Montgomery. He is the son of former Montgomery Rebel Ted Brazell. Craig knows and understands baseball in Montgomery, and chose baseball as his career. In 1998 he was drafted by the New York Mets, making his major league debut in 2004. His walk-off home run in a late-season game against the Chicago Cubs that year ended the Cubs' chances of returning to the playoffs. By 2007, Brazell was with the Kansas City Royals. From 2008 to 2014, Brazell played baseball in Japan. (Author's collection.)